Stop Making Me Cry

A Journey Through Emotional Pain

Madison R. Carter

Paperback: 978-1-64085-527-4
Hardback: 978-1-64085-528-1
Ebook: 978-1-64085-529-8
Library of Congress Control Number (LCCN): 2018968459

BIO022000 Biography Women
BIO026000 Personal Memior

This book is dedicated to
all those who have walked through a difficult time.
Nobody gets to go through life with no pain.
Everybody has a story.

TABLE OF CONTENTS

INTRODUCTION

The idea for this book started in 2015. My life turned out much differently than I had envisioned it. I never thought someone would treat me so horribly. I never thought I would get divorced. I never expected I would write a book. I finally realized that there was a need for someone to talk about the abuse, the neglect, the isolation, and emotional pain so many people go through every day. When I was in the midst of a difficult situation, it was hard to find a purpose to my life. But I began to wonder if I were able to help somebody who was in my situation, it would be worth it.

As you read this book, you might find yourself asking, "Why didn't she stand up for herself?" But remember people often have trouble setting boundaries for themselves as they go through life. It's hard to remember you are not weak and hopeless. Those who have been abused for a long time forget the strength within themselves because their spirit has been broken.

It's important to remember that anyone who goes through intense trauma or abuse over an extended period of time can be formed into a brilliant diamond which is only formed through heavy, extended pressure. Survivors are stronger, more resilient, and deeper.

This book is intended to help you understand the pain, difficulty and confusion abuse victims may go through. The events in this story are actual events. Please do not take what happened in this story to think that is what should happen in your story. Nobody will have a story quite like you. The important thing to do is choose what is right for you. You will have to make the decision that's right for your life. This book is not intended to tell you what you should do for your life. I pray that if you are confused, you will gain clarity. If you are hurting, I pray you will find healing, and if you are empty, I pray you will find fulfillment.

1

RUNNING AWAY

The sun had not yet peeked over the horizon, but the sky held just enough milky white light that it was safe to drive without tail lights. Grace bolted out of bed as soon as the sky lightened. There was no time to waste. She dressed quickly and jammed her feet into her sandals. Grace squeezed around the bed and tiptoed to the front of the RV. Her children were still sleeping. It didn't matter. They needed to move.

Grace climbed into the driver's seat and removed the large reflective windshield covers that kept them safe from prying eyes. She started the engine and put the folded covers behind the driver's seat, then pulled out of her parking spot on the small residential street. The tiny houses were packed onto postage-stamp-sized lots.

When Grace had pulled into this spot last night, it was dark, and she barely looked at the neighborhood. She had just shut off the engine and put up the windshield covers before going into the back to hug and comfort her children.

"How do you feel that I took you away from Dad?" she had asked.

"I feel safe," Emily announced, snuggling into Grace's arms.

"What about you, Ben?" Grace asked.

"I feel relieved," Ben said. Grace could see it in his eyes.

"You made the right decision, Mom," Jimmy offered, a smile spreading across his face.

Now they were only facing the fear of Perry finding them and forcing them to return to him. She hoped he wouldn't think to look for them in this area. Grace had moved the RV to the poor neighborhood and parked on the street in front of some houses. With all the other vehicles parked on the side of the road, she hoped the huge RV would blend in.

Grace knew she needed to make a stop before getting onto Highway 40, so she found a small gas station and withdrew five hundred dollars from the ATM because that's all it would give her at one time. She also bought an atlas because she did not have her phone. Perry had her phone, so without the map, she would have no help with directions.

The attendant said, "We don't sell too many atlases anymore."

Grace replied, "I'm running away, and I don't have my phone."

The attendant laughed. "That would be nice, to get away without my phone for a while."

Grace smiled at the attendant and went back out to the RV; then she drove onto Highway 40.

The RV, beat up after Perry's careless accident, didn't have a driver's side mirror or a left turn signal in the back, which made merging onto the highway tricky, but she had learned from Perry how to merge carefully. Grace tried to match the speed of traffic. She cautiously brought her left wheels onto the line and hung out there for a few seconds before looking over her shoulder to see if anybody was beside her. She could not see the road at all behind the expanse of the RV. Only after she'd peeked over her shoulder would she slowly move over to the next lane. She'd done it lots of times and never had an accident.

She headed east. She didn't have a plan. She was making decisions as she went. The deserts of the Southwest had a beauty of their own: the rock formations, the hills and plateaus, the arid landscape, the trees short and few. The road stretched out forever. It looked completely different than Ohio, which was lush and green.

Grace talked to herself as she drove. *Should I head straight to Ohio? What if Perry suspects I'm going to Ohio and follows me? He would try to stop me. Maybe I should go to Arlington first. He probably wouldn't expect me to go there to get the boxes we left at Scott's house. Perhaps I should go there and pick up the boxes, then go to Ohio. I don't know if we're getting divorced or just separating for a while, but if we are splitting up, I want those boxes. They have our pictures and things the kids made— sentimental items. That way if he shows up at my mom's house, I won't be there.*

It was a good thing she didn't have her phone, so Perry couldn't call or text her. She knew if he called she would feel compelled to answer the phone. Grace thought she should head to Ohio as fast as she could, but knew it would take her a while to get there since she was stuck driving in the right-hand lane without a driver's side mirror.

Grace wondered how she had gotten to this place in her life. She had never intended to leave Perry. She always planned to work things out and to make their marriage thrive. It didn't help that the kids kept throwing rapid-fire questions at her.

Her baby, Emily, asked, "Are you getting divorced? Will we ever see Daddy again?"

Her middle child, Jimmy, had always been closest to Perry. "Can we stay at Grandma's? How long will we stay? Will Daddy come to Ohio?"

From Ben, her eldest and most troubled child came the pressing questions. "What if he finds us?"

Grace knew they were happy and excited to go to their grandmother's house. They hadn't seen her for more than four years. Grace knew she would have plenty of time to think back over her life and her marriage as she drove across the country with her children.

While Grace's children were peppering her with questions, Grace's family in Ohio heard from Perry that Grace and the kids were missing; they did not trust Perry. What if his report of them being missing was a ruse to divert suspicion from something he had done to Grace or the kids?

Grace's relatives talked about calling places Grace worked. They asked Perry to call the police, but he wouldn't. Perry also told his brother Paul that Grace and the kids were missing. Paul, in turn, contacted Grace's family because he wanted them to know that he supported Grace and that he knew all about Perry's treatment of her. Grace's family was upset, and they prayed for her and the kids.

Grace drove through New Mexico on Thursday. She stayed on highway 40 until she entered Texas. That night they found a rest stop called "Safety Rest Stop." *How appropriate,* Grace thought. She felt like they were a safe enough distance from Perry that she could relax. They came out of the RV, and the kids played for a while. She did some cleaning and cooked supper. Again, they stayed up late because they were excited and nervous.

Grace tried not to dwell too much on her situation so she could get some sleep, but she couldn't help reflecting on how they got here. Perry's behavior had steadily worsened, and now she was running home, just like he always said she would someday. Why had she tried to convince him she would stay?

The only childhood home she had ever known was her parents' farm, where they lived for forty-seven years, as long as they were married. She knew the farm was a safe place. It seemed all her memories were of growing up there.

2

A HAPPY CHILDHOOD

Grace Chupp was born and raised in an Amish family on a pig farm in Ohio, along with two brothers and three sisters. There were ten acres on which to run, work and play. For the most part, she had a pretty happy childhood. Her father, Adam Chupp, was a pig farmer. He had built a farrowing house for mother pigs to go in with their newborn babies; then he had constructed a long building that held eleven pens in a row, where he raised pigs until they were ready to be sold to market. All the adult pigs were free to roam in the fields and sleep in the barn and little side sheds.

Adam had also built a shop where they parked their Amish buggies, and where he kept his tools and machinery. An Amish crew had made their house when Grace was just a baby. Grace's earliest memory was standing at the front door looking out, her head barely high enough to peek out the screen door.

Grace was the Chupps' fourth child and only a year younger than her oldest brother, Willie. She was often so soft-spoken and quiet that people would bend down to listen to her. She was timid and never tried to draw attention to herself, feeling almost invisible at times.

When Grace's mother, Emma, wanted her and Willie to bring in a load of wood for the stove, they would go out to an old run down shed that was used only for storage. They would fill their red wagon with firewood as slowly as possible, all the while talking and telling stories and making up songs.

Willie knew how to make Grace laugh. He made up silly songs. Grace remembered one in particular: *If you see a donkey, if you see a cow, that's all right, that's all right.* They would sing it over and over, laughing at one another and themselves.

If Willie and Grace had any spare time, they went out in the barn, which was their favorite place to play. It was far from the house and provided them with almost unlimited fun. There was a hayloft on one side and a straw loft on the other. In the middle was where the tractor and the manure spreader were parked.

A long rope hung from the highest roof beam down to the floor. Willie and Grace swung from one loft to the other, over the tractor and manure spreader. They took hay and straw bales and made tunnels out of them. When they were in the bale tunnels, it felt like their secret hideout. There they couldn't hear Emma calling them telling them they had to come in. They could easily spend hours playing in the barn.

However, they also had daily chores—the cow required milking every morning and night. When she came into the barn to eat, Willie milked one side, and Grace took the other since each was too small to milk the cow alone. They carried the bucket of milk between them back to the house. Willie and Grace took turns cleaning the pens in the long pig house every night.

Eventually, Grace convinced her father to pay her ten cents each time she scraped the pens. Every year after that, Adam gave her a ten cent raise until she was making sixty or seventy cents a day. Grace enjoyed having a little money. She usually saved it, since she didn't need to buy herself anything; her parents provided everything for her. She never had any idea their family was any better or worse off financially than anybody else.

Adam and Emma had two large gardens, and they butchered their pigs and cows. Emma made bread, butter, cereal, noodles, cottage cheese, and ice-cream. She canned applesauce, corn, peaches, tomatoes and green beans, peas and all sorts of other vegetables. There were bushels of potatoes from the garden, along with lettuce, onions, and strawberries. Emma was a skilled seamstress, and she sewed all the family's clothes. She made blankets and even coats. Emma was resourceful; as she grew older, Grace was thankful for her mother's lessons.

Grace always thought she was Adam's favorite child, even though neither he nor anyone else ever expressed that. She adored her father and thought he was the most handsome man in the world.

When Grace was a small girl, too young to go to school, Adam had been an Amish school teacher. She remembered him coming home from school in the buggy. She would tear out of the house and remind him to give her a candy heart. He kept a whole bag of candy hearts in his closet with cute little sayings on them: "*Be Mine,*" "*My Dear,*" "*You're Sweet.*" Grace assumed those were her father's secret messages to her.

Adam built Grace a playhouse. While he never said it was her playhouse, she assumed it was for her because when he finished, her dolls and their bed, and her mini play kitchen with its little table and chairs, were all moved into it. She didn't mind that her siblings and the neighborhood kids played there. She would never have dreamed of keeping such a fantastic prize to herself.

Many evenings, after supper, Willie and Grace would sit on their father's lap or hang out with him while their mother and older sisters cleaned up in the kitchen. He would tell them vivid stories from the Bible, all in Dutch. Adam talked about Noah and the ark, or Jonah and the whale. He made the adventures sound so exciting and dramatic that it made the children laugh. Their dad was a wonderful storyteller.

Adam was skilled at many things. He was musical, artistic, and a builder. Most importantly to his children, he spent time with them. He played ball with them and table games too. He did magic tricks and told jokes. He sang with his family and community. Grace never saw Adam raise his voice to Emma. She never heard him raise his voice to anyone. She saw that her father got along well with everybody.

Being Amish, Grace's family was pious. They prayed before and after every meal, and they also knelt in the living room to pray before bed each night. Adam and Emma were strict disciplinarians. They made sure that all of their children were well behaved, especially in church, where children had to sit quietly. The kids got spanked for many reasons, including talking when they were supposed to be quiet, working too slowly, and any other inappropriate behaviors. The Chupp children learned to respect their parents, but they also lived in fear of disappointing them. That fear was common among the Amish.

The children learned to work quickly and work hard, instilled with the fear of the church and their parents. They didn't dare to defy or question their parents or the church. Parents raised their children the way their parents had reared them. In the Amish community, all parents and even teachers would spank disobedient or defiant children.

Grace remembered being called aside into the storage room by her teacher, who proceeded to accuse Grace of cheating on a test. Grace didn't deny it; she justified her actions by telling her teacher she had seen someone else also do it. Grace got spanked by her teacher that day, and she never cheated again.

As Adam and Emma grew older, they became gentler and more patient, which changed some of their parenting methods. They learned how to discipline more graciously. They learned to lean on the Holy Spirit to guide them.

Grace started going to the Amish school in their district when she was seven years old. It was an old-fashioned schoolhouse with a bell on top that rang to notify the children it was time to go inside. There were about forty students in the school, and they only had grades one through eight. Grace did not learn to speak English until she went to school, where the students were required to speak English instead of Dutch. When she first learned to speak English, the older kids sometimes laughed at her attempts. The children also had to learn proper German since Pennsylvania Dutch is different from German, although the two languages have some similarities. The Amish Bible was written in German, and the preacher spoke the language at Sunday services, so the children were required to learn it.

Grace had a lot of bittersweet memories of school. At recess, the students played softball; she was always afraid to hit the ball. When they played dodgeball, she was afraid the ball would strike her. In the winter, it was bitterly cold. Grace was allowed to wear boots, warm tights, a dress, a coat, a scarf, and a bonnet, but her legs were always painfully cold because Amish girls were not permitted to wear pants. The children were allowed to trek into the woods beside the school where there was a small frozen pond on which they would ice skate and slide.

Once, Grace was so cold that when she got back to the schoolhouse, her legs were bright red. She took off her coat and stood with her back toward the wood-burning stove in the middle of the building, so close that the back of her apron melted onto the side of the stove, where it stayed for many years.

Five buggies arrived at the school every day. The students would unhitch the horses and put them in the shed where they had hay and protection from the weather. The other kids walked to school. Grace and her siblings, Esther, Susanna, and Willie, drove to school in a buggy on cold, snowy mornings. They cuddled together under a warm blanket and sang on the way. Sometimes, Esther and Susanna yodeled. The girls were shy about their singing, so they stopped before they got to school. When it rained, the children would play games inside during recess; there were some table games and a ping pong table.

One day, the two teachers planned a surprise for all the students. They divided the students into two teams, and each group received a scavenger hunt list that led them on a wild chase all over the school property. Finally, both sides ended up in the storage room where there were bowls of popcorn and Kool-Aid to drink. The students gorged themselves, and then they cleaned up, sweeping the floors and emptying the trash as they did every day.

There were four girls in Grace's grade. They were best friends and classmates and often spent the night at one another's houses. They spent every day together and played together at recess. Grace brought a doll to school, and at the break, the girls went out to the trees at the edge of the schoolyard and played house and church. They not only played with their dolls out there, but they also ate lunch together under the trees. It was their little clubhouse. The four girls loved to play together and sometimes would even share their meals.

Life was not all roses though. There was a bully who picked on Grace a lot. Once he purposely stood on her foot. He pushed kids and played unfairly. All the kids knew he was different. He was an only child who was adopted. His biological mother had not been Amish. It was almost unheard of to have only one child in an Amish family, and adoption was also very rare.

Grace's school experience was mostly good. The students played games and made memories. Once, Adam bought a box full of Snickers candy bars. He decided each child at school should have one, so every student got a bar. There were leftovers, so on the way home from school, Esther, Susanna, Willie, and Grace threw them to the kids walking beside the road as they passed them in the buggy.

After school each day, they immediately changed out of their school clothes and into their everyday clothes. They were to start on their chores right away. The children helped in the garden or the yard and cleaned out the barn. There was so much work to be done. Supper was usually at five o'clock, and they always sat in the same seats at the table.

After they finished their work in the evening, Grace often read a book, played with toys, or played outside. Willie and Grace used their imagination to pretend they were English or doing something exciting. One time, Willie taped a piece of paper to his shirt right where a breast pocket would be, so he could pretend he had a breast pocket on his shirt, so he could pretend to be English. The Amish don't have breast pockets on their shirts, just like they don't have zippers on their pants. Grace sometimes pretended she was English by wrapping her Amish dress around her body, so it would look like she was wearing something sleeveless. The Amish always wore long sleeves.

Winters in Ohio were brutally cold. Grace and her siblings had to bundle up with coats, scarves, bonnets, and shawls because they still had to go outside every day at school for recess. It was rare for their school to be canceled due to snow or weather, but Grace remembered once it was because the temperature was twenty-nine degrees below zero. Even in the winter, the children still had to do their chores, despite the freezing temperatures.

The children loved to play in the snow. Willie and Grace were always ready to go sledding or play games, or even make tunnels in the five-foot-high drifts. Sometimes the snow got thick enough to keep the door from opening, but they fought their way out so they could take care of the animals. Many winter days they played indoor games like Monopoly and Candy Land.

One winter day, Adam went out to do the chores. In the farrowing house, there was a litter of piglets that was very cold, so Adam put them in a cardboard box and placed it on top of the cold stove. He lit the fire and went out to do some other chores; while he was gone the stove heated up and the box caught fire. The inside of the farrowing house burned, killing all the pigs and about fifteen cats. The neighbors noticed the smoke and called the fire department. They put out the fire, but it was a sad day.

Grace's family did not put up a Christmas tree or Christmas lights, but they still celebrated the holiday in their humble way. On Christmas morning, the children came down into the kitchen and at each of their places at the table was a bowlful of candy! Emma once gave Grace a homemade robe that buttoned down the front and was blue and had lace. Grace felt so very special wearing that warm robe. Although the Amish sometimes gave one another small gifts, the holiday was not as big a deal for them as for the English. Nevertheless, it felt like a big deal to Grace and her siblings.

Every other Sunday the family went to church. Each Amish family hosted church services in their home once or twice a year. Amish communities split into districts, so families only went to church with other Amish families in the same area. Each district had a bishop who was the highest Amish authority of that church. The bishop got to decide what rules the church would follow. In the Chupps' district, they were not allowed to wear brightly colored clothes; they could only wear dull dark or pastel colors. Nobody was allowed to have bicycles. The Chupps wanted to be obedient because they felt it was respectful to God to be as good as they could be. They obeyed all the rules and followed the leaders of the church.

Typically, neighbors and friends came several days before and moved furniture, cleaned all the walls and ceilings and washed the windows in the home where the next service was scheduled. People prepared lots of food. Then on Sunday, some families would arrive thirty minutes in advance.

Each district had several ministers who took turns speaking. They each had a different message, always expressed in German or Dutch. Grace could not understand what was said. The church service was three hours long. At some point, there was slow, drawn-out singing from the German songbook; one song could take ten to twenty minutes because each word was dragged out. Someone would call out the song number so everyone could turn to it in the hymnals, then one man would lead the first syllable of each line, and the rest of the congregation would join in. There was a time of prayer when everyone would kneel and bow down over their benches.

Church services bored Grace. She sat beside her mom, and when she got tired, she put her head down on mom's lap and took a nap. The highlight of the three-hour service was when a pan was passed through the rows so that each child could have a selection of snacks: saltine crackers, graham crackers, soft sugar cookies called church cookies, and straight pretzels. Each child had a handkerchief. Grace would use hers to hold her snacks. She took her time and used them as a way to entertain herself through the long and tedious service. She would play with her food for a while, stacking it different ways, then she would slowly nibble at the snacks, trying to make them last as long as possible, trying to endure until the end of the service.

After the service, the benches transformed into tables for lunch, which often consisted of red beets, dill pickles, white store-bought bread, homemade Amish peanut butter, and coffee or tea. Grace was always jealous that the babies got to eat egg noodles. People sat around and talked until mid-afternoon.

Once children reached age eighteen, they were considered old enough to decide if they wanted to become a member of the church. If there was interest, several young people would be baptized at a special service and would thereby join the church. During the months leading up to baptism, the young people would receive specialized instruction and training to become members of the Amish church. Each young person who wished to become a member would kneel before the congregation while the ministers poured water from a pitcher over his or her head.

The initiates would recite vows and prayers which would mark them official members of the Amish church. If any church member decided that they wanted either to leave the church or not follow some of the rules, all remaining members of the church had to ban and shun them. The shunned could not eat with or have fellowship with church members. They could not engage in business or exchange money with church members. Shunning was the Amish attempt at tough love. The shunned people would be cut off from family and church events and would be told not to come to visit unless they dressed in Amish garb.

The Amish firmly believed if someone was not Amish, that person was bound for Hell. They thought they were the only ones who were right. Despite that belief, they nevertheless taught that there was no certainty about whether anyone was going to Heaven. The Amish doctrine was that a person could only live their life as piously as possible, and hope that if they did enough good works, God would let them enter his Heaven.

A common Amish saying was "Once you die, you have to walk the narrow path, which is only a foot-width wide, and on one side is fire and brimstone and on the other side is ice and water. If you make it across that path, then you can get to Heaven."

That idea is not in the Bible, and Grace wondered if the person who said it knew that it suggested no matter how you lived your life, you just had to make it across the narrow path to get to God's Heaven.

The Amish planted a fear of Hell into the minds of church members from the time they were small children. The Amish were afraid to die; they were afraid of seeing the devil. They were fearful of doing something wrong, so they tried to do things as correctly as possible, and especially obey all the rules of the church. The Amish were also afraid of the devil possessing them. They were taught to do things in such a way that the devil could not gain a foothold in their lives.

For the Amish, there was a powerful sense of things being either right or wrong. There was no middle-ground. It was up to the bishop and ministers to decide what the rules were, and what behavior was right or wrong. If anyone had questions, he or she needed to talk with the ministers.

Church members were not encouraged to read the Bible for themselves, nor were they expected to question any of the ministers' decisions. They were supposed to accept the way things were and go along with it. The Amish encouraged unity and community. If anyone suffered a loss or experienced difficulties, their neighbors and friends—and church—were there to step in and help and rebuild and assist in any way they could. The community was there to support its members and do anything it could to help them.

3

WORLD TRAVELER

Adam and Emma were the type of people who opened up their home to visitors. The Amish expect that people will come and spend the night if they traveled from a distant place. The Chupps always had a guest room that was reserved only for guests. Amish people would come and spend the night, and English people came, too.

According to the Amish, there are two kinds of people in this world: Amish and English. It does not matter if an individual is black, Mexican, Japanese, or European. If they were not Amish, they were English because they only ever heard them speaking the English language.

Once, a Christian couple from India came and spent the night with the Chupps. The couple had converted from Islam. The couple was showing American churches a film about what life is like in other countries for Christians persecuted for their faith.

This couple invited the Chupp family to an English church to see the film they were showing. The Amish believe that their community members should not visit any church that is not an Amish church, but the Chupps went regardless and decided not to tell anyone about their visit to an English church. The church was small, about the size of a small house, and fewer than twenty-five people were there. Their new friends shared their story and showed a film about Christians in India.

After the film, a family named Perkins got up and sang a song called "The Church of God Is Moving." The family had five children. The Chupp family was intrigued and excited to see a family who sang together because the Chupp family often sang in Amish people's homes when they visited the sick or the elderly or went to gatherings.

After the evening service, the Chupp family made the acquaintance of the Perkins family. The Chupps invited the Perkinses to their home. Adam and Emma had always had questions about God and the Bible; they were searching for the truth and wondered how they could achieve salvation. They were hungry for God.

Mr. and Mrs. Perkins were happy to answer questions. The couples sat around the table, opened their Bibles and looked up the answers. Adam and Emma were so excited to meet new friends and perhaps, find some answers to their questions. It was close to midnight when the Perkinses finally left.

For the next two years, the Perkinses came over to the Chupps' house on a regular basis for Bible studies. Other English people joined in the Bible study group.

While the adults studied the Bible for answers, the children played together either in the barn, swinging from loft to loft, or in the basement playing ping pong, or upstairs in the bedrooms playing hide and seek. There was almost no limit to the things that the kids could do on the farm.

The Chupps found a Christian church to attend. It was a new church and very small. An older couple came and picked up the Chupps in their van and took them to church every other Sunday, while on the alternate Sundays they attended their Amish church.

The Chupps loved the new church. The members greeted them with hugs and warm handshakes. People smiled and encouraged one another. It was a unique experience for the

Chupps to see people standing and singing excitedly, clapping their hands, raising their hands, dancing, and praying out loud. It was a marked contrast to the Amish church, where hardly anyone smiled, and services were solemn.

In the Christian church, the Chupps could hear and understand the word of God as the preacher spoke. They learned all about the truths in the Bible and felt it was setting them free. In the Amish church, the ministers spoke only German, and the children could not understand the scripture or the messages. The ministers did not preach the Word of God; instead, Scripture was used solely to defend the Amish-made rules and to manipulate people into living in fear and obeying their laws.

The Chupps continued to alternate churches until the Amish ministers confronted them. They gently reminded Adam and Emma that it was against the rules of the Amish church for them to visit a non-Amish church and that it was not permitted to have Bible studies in their own home. Adam and Emma explained that the Scripture was teaching them to gather together with other believers, in one another's homes. The Chupps explained they were seekers of the truth and wanted answers to their questions, but that the Amish ministers could not answer their questions.

Adam and Emma backed up their choices with Scripture so the ministers could not argue with them. The ministers made sure Adam and Emma knew that what they were doing was wrong, Adam and Emma believed they did a thorough job in explaining that they were not doing anything wrong, as they were not rebellious or known to be strong-willed.

Although Adam and Emma Chupp did not believe they were doing anything wrong, they weren't exactly open with their Amish community. The Chupps had a big secret; they were going to an English church and making new friends. Some of their new friends had even given them English clothes, and a few were so generous they gave the Chupps two cars—one was a green Lincoln Continental, and the other was a Chrysler New Yorker.

With all the charity coming their way, to the Chupps it seemed they were being guided by God to leave the Amish church. While the English were welcoming them and giving them things, the Amish were pushing against them and criticizing their choice.

Adam bought a banjo at a flea market and decided to teach himself how to play it. He played it upstairs in the back bedroom. One day, one of the neighbors, an old minister, came over to talk to Adam. Willie started to tell the minister Adam was playing the banjo but quickly realized he couldn't say that, so instead, he scampered up the stairs to get Adam. He was embarrassed that he'd almost told on his father, but Willie decided to laugh it off.

The Chupps hid the cars, which they didn't know how to drive, in the shop. One day, the same neighbor came over looking for Adam. He walked into the shop and saw the cars there. The ministers confronted Adam and Emma and warned them they were headed down the road to Hell if they did not stick to the Amish rules. Adam and Emma confidently responded that the Bible supported their actions. They quoted the scripture and specific verses and said they did not feel guilty.

Not too long after, they skipped the Amish service and went to the English church. During the Amish church service, the ministers announced that the Chupp family was excommunicated and banned. They were to be shunned, and they were no longer members of the Amish church. They would no longer be permitted to eat with the Amish, to exchange money with them, or go to the Amish church services. Shunning was a last-ditch effort by the Amish ministers to bring the family back to the church. The family did not discover they had been excommunicated until the next day when their children went to school.

Emma told her daughter Susanna that when she was at school on Monday, she should inform all the students that they needn't bring their lunches on Tuesday because Emma was going to provide a hot meal for them. Susanna did her job. However, that night, when the students went home and told their parents that Emma Chupp was bringing a hot lunch the next day, the parents had to explain that they were not allowed to accept food from her because she had been excommunicated and shunned. Several Amish men had to drive their buggies from house to house to explain to the students they needed to bring their lunches. One of the ministers came to the Chupps' house and told them the news that they were banned.

Adam and Emma were a bit shocked at first, but they quickly realized they were happy to receive that news. They felt free from the Amish rules and their bondage. They were free to drive cars and wear whatever clothes they wanted. They could dance and listen to music. Since none of their children had become members of the Amish church, they could not be banned; it was only Adam and Emma. Since they were the ones paying the school, the school could no longer accept payment from them, so the Chupp kids continued going to the Amish school for free for the rest of the school year.

Esther bought a guitar and started learning how to play it. Willie found an old fiddle and took lessons. He loved playing the instrument so much; he played it every day. His family grew tired of hearing the loud squeaks on the fiddle, but eventually, he got better. The Chupp family sang and played their instruments wherever Adam could find a place for them to sing. They played bluegrass gospel music and sang in three-part harmony. They played at the nursing home in their small town, and also at churches and other meeting places; this continued for a few years until Esther got married and started her own family.

When Grace was ten, Emma talked to her about Heaven and Hell and living for God. Grace decided she wanted to accept Jesus into her heart. Although this was an exciting time in their lives, Grace was not happy. At the age of eleven, Grace started to feel rejected by her older sisters who had their friends, while Grace didn't feel like she had any. Her older sisters didn't want Grace hanging around with them and their friends, so they pushed her away.

"You can't be in here, Gracie. Go play with the younger kids," her sisters insisted.

Grace struggled with feeling rejected, worthless and unloved. She cried and felt left out and lonely. She didn't think her parents loved her because they never told her they did, nor were they in the habit of giving hugs.

Grace was the quietest of the Chupp children. She felt insignificant, small and unattractive, and often felt ignored, undeserving of love or attention. Grace had been taught to be humble and not be prideful, so never learned how to give or receive love in a healthy way. She struggled with feelings of loneliness and unworthiness.

She did not feel close to her parents or her siblings. Throughout her childhood, it seemed she was closer to her friends and could tell them things that she couldn't say to her family. She often felt her friendships impacted her more than her family, so when she began to feel like she had no friends, it made her sad and depressed. She felt as if she was under a dark cloud for a few years, feeling unloved, unwanted and unattractive.

Grace wrote a note to her mother detailing all of her feeling of insignificance and insecurity, and how she felt unloved. She believed that if she died or ran away, nobody would miss her. She thought she could be easily replaced. Grace left the note on Emma's pillow. That night, when Grace was going to bed, Emma came to her room and told Grace she did love her. Then she hugged Grace. That was the first time Grace remembered her mother hugging her.

Grace continued to struggle with feelings of depression, loneliness, low self-esteem, and suicidal thoughts until she was fourteen.

It also did not help that her family would occasionally leave her behind at home or church. Sometimes when it happened, nobody noticed she was missing for several hours.

During this challenging time, a sweet girl named Becky encouraged Grace and told her, "God will be your friend, and God is always with you. God has a purpose for your life."

Grace wanted real friends, not just an invisible deity. Becky talked to her so much about God, however, that eventually Grace started to believe and began talking to God as if He were her friend. Grace told God whatever was in her heart as if He was a friend sitting in the room with her. She turned to Him when she was feeling low.

Over time, Grace learned to deal with feelings from her childhood, so they did not impact her. She learned forgiveness for those who may have hurt her as she came to understand they did not do it intentionally. Her feelings of rejection and hatred melted away, and she was able to find peace with her family and resolve the feelings of hatred and bitterness.

When Grace was fourteen, she joined the church youth group. They met at church every Wednesday night. At meetings, the kids would sing songs about worshipping God and then hear about His message from the leaders. At youth group, Grace saw God speaking through kids her age. Kids lifted their hands in surrender, bowing or laying down in worship or reception to God's voice. Grace saw God moving through the youth group, and she got excited. She had never prayed so much before. Grace was willing to surrender everything to God. Serious about being as dedicated to God as she could, Grace did not listen to anything but Christian music and tried to live as righteously as possible. She joined the worship team when she grew older, and she was involved in a prayer group.

Every Labor Day weekend, the youth group took a trip that they paid for with fundraisers, such as car washes. They rented a bus to take the youth on a trip. They rode to Minnesota, Iowa, Pennsylvania, Indiana, Michigan, Ohio, and Kentucky. The group visited churches or homes where they could help out or minister in some way. When they finished their work, they had a day of fun on the Labor Day holiday and go to either a beach or an amusement park.

When Grace was fifteen, she became a nanny and assistant to a family with three children. She helped prepare the meals, do the laundry, and with general housekeeping. Each night Grace would fall into bed, exhausted, her back aching. She stayed with the family for six nights a week, and she only went home two times a week.

When Grace was sixteen, she was invited to go to Costa Rica to stay with a family who had two small boys. She helped out with general housekeeping. Grace stayed there for three months and became involved with two churches. She learned some Spanish from a book and made many friends. She visited an inactive volcano and saw some beautiful places. She also joined a water class and learned how to swim on that trip.

When Grace was seventeen, her church took a team of people to the Dominican Republic for two weeks. The group sang songs and did musical skits and puppet shows, all in Spanish. They learned enough Spanish to talk to people and pray with them. They visited Rio San Juan. Grace was shocked to see mud huts with dirt floors. Children were running around naked because they were poverty-stricken. She saw houses held up by sticks to keep them out of the water. A lot of those people had nothing. The experience and the contrast between the village and the church members' lodging in a nice hotel affected Grace deeply. Each day they went out and did their program in a different location. The group led many people to Jesus.

When Grace was eighteen, she decided to visit Costa Rica on her own to visit the friends that she had made two years before. This time she stayed with a church member who did not speak any English. Grace stayed with her for one month and learned more Spanish. There she met a nice young man who was excited about coming to the Lord. They fell in love. They shared their first kiss one night while they were standing together under an umbrella in the rain. He seemed like a wonderful guy.

Her relationship with her boyfriend didn't last long. She went back home and had to say goodbye to him. She wrote him and called him, but within a few months, he stopped responding. Finally, she wrote him a letter telling him if he cared for her at all, he would write or call. He didn't, so she never communicated with him again.

That autumn in late September, Grace accepted a post as a nanny for a family in Connecticut. The family lived in West Hartford, and they had two adorable girls. She stayed in their cozy little attic in their century-old house for two months.

When Grace turned twenty, she traveled to the Dominican Republic again, with a team of thirty people from her church. As before, they took to the streets and reached out to the public. They learned Spanish songs, danced, did puppet shows and skits, shared their testimonies, and passed out tracts or pamphlets. They traveled to Santiago, where they stayed at a huge house called Casa Grande, which was owned by the Johnson family. They went to Rio San Juan where they stayed at a beautiful hotel. They interacted with the impoverished people of the Dominican Republic, and it made Grace realize how blessed she was merely to live in the United States.

After returning from the Dominican Republic, Grace visited Toronto, Canada, with a small group from her church. A church was having a revival, and there were services every day. Grace stayed for a few days with her group, then spent a few extra days in Canada visiting Niagara Falls.

The following year, Grace was invited to go back to the Dominican Republic to stay with the Johnson family for nine months. The Johnsons were an American family who had been on the mission field for at least ten years. They had three young boys they were homeschooling. Grace's duties included making meals and reading to the boys. She also made a new friend. Wendy lived about forty-five minutes from Grace's family in Ohio, and she came to spend a month with the Johnsons while Grace was there. They were roommates. She taught Grace to dance, and they had a lot of fun together.

Grace spent the second month of the Johnson family's absence with a native family who was pastoring a small church in the city of Salcedo. They had one small child. They wanted Grace to pay them five American dollars a day for the privilege of staying with them. They also wanted her to write letters to her friends and family to ask for more money. Grace had been using the money she had saved from working in restaurants before her travels, but she didn't have much extra.

One day, the mother told Grace a cyclone was coming. She wanted Grace to call her family and say goodbye, as she was afraid the storm, Hurricane Georges, would kill them. The Dominican Republic is a small island in the Caribbean Sea often hit by hurricanes. Grace called her family to tell them she loved them.

When Hurricane Georges hit as a category four hurricane, everything blew sideways. It was loud; it sounded like a speeding freight train for twelve hours. They lost power. They prayed and went to bed with the wind still howling.

The next morning, after the wind slowed down and it was quiet again, they looked at the destruction and devastation left by the storm. The storm caused one billion dollars in damages in the Dominican Republic, and of the three hundred eighty people who died during the storm, many died as a result of mudslides triggered by the torrential rain from the storm. It was a sobering experience for Grace.

Grace's money was disappearing quickly. Nobody had sent her money, and it was time for her to go home. She had built friendships with the people in the church, but she had to leave.

She traveled back to Santiago and the Johnsons. She did not stay the remainder of the nine months, as the Johnsons decided they did not need her help anymore, so they told her she could decide if she wanted to return home. She missed her family, so after only six months she returned to the United States. She asked her friend Wendy for help surprising her family. She had stayed in the Dominican Republic for just six months, so they weren't expecting her home.

When Grace landed in Ohio, it was late at night, so she slept at Wendy's house. The next morning Wendy and her mother took Grace home. When Emma saw somebody had arrived, she came outside. Wendy first carried out Grace's suitcase and said they had brought something from Grace; then Grace jumped out of the car. Grace hugged her mom, her sister Diane, and her brother Kevin. They were so excited that Grace was home, they headed to visit their neighbor Emily, an elderly lady. Grace walked into Emily's house and surprised her.

After the initial shock wore off, Emily exclaimed,

"I prayed for you while you were in that horrible hurricane. We heard about it, and we were worried."

That warmed Grace's heart. Emily was the closest thing she had to a grandmother. Grace never had relationships with her grandmothers, so it was a blessing to have a substitute grandma to pray for her.

Then they all went to Grace's sister Susanna's house. Susanna and her husband had four small children. They were all happy to see one another and Susanna was surprised. They all talked at once and their words cascaded as they tried to catch up on everything they needed to say. Grace loved holding her nieces and nephews.

Later that evening, after Adam came home from work, dinner was prepared, and Grace sat at the table with everyone else. No one had told Adam that she'd come back. When he saw Grace, he loudly exclaimed, "What! What!"

Everyone laughed at his surprise. Grace thought that was the best day ever, coming home and surprising her whole family. The six months Grace was gone was the longest she'd ever been away from home.

For the next two years, Grace worked and saved up enough money to do more traveling. When she was twenty-three, she decided to attend a five-month school at Youth With a Mission (YWAM). Emma dropped her off at the bus station, and Grace rode the bus to a part of town where there was a lot of crime. Grace had a six-hour wait until the coach for the next part of her journey came at four o'clock the following morning. She had several large pieces of luggage, and she was the only one sitting in the bus station.

A dark-skinned older gentleman, who was probably in his late 50s, began talking to her. When he found out she would be sitting in this bus station by herself all night, he became concerned.

"This is a bad part of town. It's not safe here. You should not be sitting here by yourself for that long."

Grace began to think he was right. She was a defenseless girl in a crime-filled part of town. She thought perhaps she should listen to his advice.

The man continued speaking.

"You should come with me because it's not safe for you to stay here in the bus station all alone."

Grace did not know what she should do. Should she trust a stranger in a dangerous part of town who says she should not stay here alone, or should she stay at the station? She decided to trust him and put her luggage into his car.

He seemed friendly and non-threatening and offered to get them something to eat. He stopped at a small restaurant and bought them some shrimp. Grace presumed they would eat the food in the car and then go right back to the bus station.

Suddenly, he said, "Oh I know where we should go."

He took her to a house that he said belonged to a friend of his. Nobody else was there. It was a dingy little place with no frills, but it wasn't messy. They sat at a small table in the corner of the living room and ate their food. Grace had an uneasy feeling he had ulterior motives, so she told him how she came to know the Lord and how her family came out of the Amish. The man asked her questions, and they had a pleasant conversation. When they finished eating, he indicated he wanted something more.

Grace stood up. "I want you to take me back to the bus station right now."

She opened the door and waited for him to leave.

"Aw man, I thought you was a big girl."

To her great relief, they got back in his car and headed back to the bus station. She was grateful to be safely back at the bus station, and she hauled all her luggage up to the second floor where there were two security guards.

Grace sat down and eventually fell asleep. Around two-thirty in the morning, Grace heard a bus leaving and realized she had missed her bus. She called Emma once someone came into the office. Emma was horrified to learn Grace was still at the bus station.

She said, "There is another bus coming at eight o'clock tomorrow morning. You have to get on that bus."

When that bus came, it was full, but Grace insisted she had to be on that bus. There were no seats left, so Grace sat in the front, on the steps, right next to the driver. She finally made it to Cincinnati, and eventually to Orlando.

There were twenty students enrolled at the YWAM school. They spent three months in the lecture phase, where she learned to see God as her father and how to strengthen her relationship with Him. Immediately after the lecture phase,

Grace and a team went to Thailand. She saw God providing for her friends and answering prayers. In preparation for traveling to Thailand, the school taught them how to deal with the culture and what to expect.

Thailand was hot. It was the hottest place she had ever been. The people were friendly and very proper. The first week there, the group went to a small remote island for a week to rest from doing three months of classroom lectures and traveling. They had a devotional time each morning and evening, but the rest of the time they spent playing volleyball with the locals or snorkeling or canoeing or laying on the beach watching hermit crabs. On the way to Bangkok, they traveled by boats back to the mainland, then took an eighteen-hour train ride.

It was a miserable night of travel. The team sat on seats that had no cushioning. There were no headrests, and the backs were too low. There were too many people allowed to ride on the train, and there were not enough seats. People stood in the aisles. At night, those people laid down on the floor. The people sitting couldn't sleep because there was nowhere to lay their heads unless they were willing to rest it on the shoulder next to them.

There was a bathroom on the train. Grace weaved her way through the people strewn in the aisles. The restroom was a small closet with a hole in the floor. There was no toilet. She assumed the splattering on the walls was urine, possibly worse, so she didn't want to touch anything, but she had to reach out to steady herself as the train swayed back and forth.

One of the things the group did was teach English. They joined with a small church but did not openly profess that they were a Christian Church. Instead, they presented their church as a place for people to learn English. There were five levels of English. Grace taught level one, which is the beginner level. All schools taught English, but the students were not encouraged to practice speaking it. Grace worked with one of her teammates, Patti.

Once they finished their teaching assignment, they arranged a "Congraduation" party where the students did skits in English for the teachers. It was a way for the teachers to say "congratulations, you've graduated" to the students. It was a lot of fun for the teachers to hear the students practice their English. They all laughed so much.

The summer Grace turned twenty-five, Grace went to England and Ireland with a close girlfriend named Jessica. They spent a week in each country. In England, they stayed with a family who went to the church where the pastor was affiliated with Grace's church. The family had a small two-story house. There was a tiny circular grass backyard. The houses were equally small and squeezed together. The cars were small, the streets were shorter and narrower, and the towns and villages were small.

Grace and Jessica visited the town of Sheffield and visited the church. They also visited Sherwood forest, where Robin Hood lived. They saw a tree, so old that beams of wood supported its branches. The young women also visited old castles and cathedrals. They went to London and took a tour, and they saw the Crown jewels, the London Bridge, the Houses of Parliament, St. Paul's Cathedral, Big Ben, the palaces, the Thames River, and more. It was a wonderful week.

They also visited Ireland, which was beautiful, green, and lush. They met up with a young couple from Grace's church who were missionaries in Dublin.

After she and Jessica returned home, Grace found out about an opportunity to take Bibles into China. She and her brother Willie joined a small team of ten people who went to China for three weeks. They went to Hong Kong and joined up with a missionary, and then they took a train into the middle of China; it was a twenty-five-hour trip. They distributed Bibles and books to the missionaries so they could distribute them to the natives. They saw the vast landscape and the beautiful mountains, terraced with rice fields. Grace fell in love with China.

The missionaries visited an orphanage, which was strange and sad. The precious children had no one to love them. The babies did not cry because there was nobody to hold them, so they went in and held the babies and stayed for several hours.

The group also visited a remote Hani village where the natives lived in thatched three-story houses. The ground floor was where the animals stayed, the second level was where the families lived, and the top floor was for drying crops. The Hani people wore homemade clothes, heavily embroidered and beaded with bright colors over black fabric. The team walked out among the rice fields, and the villagers came and stood around them and watched them. They handed out candy and balloon animals. It was a wonderful trip.

Grace didn't know that China would be her last trip out of the United States. She did not yet know that this chapter of her life was closing and that God had more plans for her.

4

THE SINS OF THE FATHER...

P erry was from Texas. His mother and father were also from Texas. Perry's father Scott grew up in a Bible-believing, violent home where he witnessed his father beating his mother. Scott was also abused, yet his mother stayed with his father. Scott was exposed to pornography as a teen and used it to escape mentally from the abuse and horrific things he witnessed. He also suffered sexual abuse at the hands of relatives. He never talked about abuse because it was too shameful.

Perry's mother, Carolyn, grew up in a Southern Baptist home. When she was a child, an older man molested her, and later she had a sexually inappropriate relationship with her brother. Carolyn told her mother, and her mother put a stop to it, but she never talked to Carolyn about it, so Carolyn grew up living in shame, never really understanding what happened to her.

When Scott started a relationship with Carolyn, he was in the seminary, training to become a Baptist music minister. He neglected to tell Carolyn about his violent father. He was starting to display early warning signs of obsessive-compulsive and bipolar disorders, but Carolyn was too inexperienced to know the warning signs. Neither of them knew that the other was not a virgin when their relationship began.

The couple was advised to wait until Scott finished seminary before getting married to take the pressure off of Scott, but for her to feel okay in God's eyes, Carolyn decided they needed to get married as soon as possible since they were already having a sexual relationship.

Carolyn was eighteen when they got married, too young to make an entirely logical decision, especially given that the sexual attraction between the couple was powerful and they felt ashamed about having an intimate relationship before marriage.

The pair quickly produced three children in three years, Patty, Perry, and finally Paul. Carolyn was not able to nurse Perry, even though she tried. She was advised by her mother-in-law to give him the bottle, so he did not properly bond to his mother.

Scott's secret addiction to porn led to several extramarital affairs. The Lord revealed to Carolyn that he was with another woman. She caught him cheating on her when the Lord told her where he was and she went there and saw him with another woman. She was devastated and confronted him. She told him she knew he was secretly meeting with other women. The resulting argument turned violent, and Scott beat and raped Carolyn in front of their three small children, who were all younger than five.

Scott constantly criticized Carolyn and belittled her.

"If you weren't fat, I'd want to have sex with you. You haven't lost the baby weight, so you're just going to be fat forever. If you were thinner and more attractive, I wouldn't have to have sex with other women."

He made her feel it was all her fault. Carolyn felt like she was going to have a mental breakdown. When she was feeling at her worst, she took the children over to her husband's parents' house and left the kids there while she tried to get herself together. She committed herself to a psychiatric hospital to try to get well.

Meanwhile, the kids were at their grandparents' house. Perry cried inconsolably. Nobody could comfort him. Eventually, Carolyn came back, but the damage had been done, and Perry could not trust his mother again. In his mind, his grandmother and other relatives were untrustworthy and were all going to hurt him. He could feel his grandmother's hatred toward him. She loved Patty, who was the apple of her eye. Because his grandmother never had girls, she claimed Patty as her own. She did not care for Perry or Paul and even blamed Carolyn for getting pregnant and having boys.

Eventually, Scott and Carolyn divorced, and the three kids lived with Carolyn, who felt very broken and abused. She had to become the financial provider. She worked so much that she wasn't able to give the kids the attention they needed. They played with other kids and ended up doing inappropriate things because nobody was watching them. Perry felt his mother neglected him when he needed her most.

Carolyn hated her life. Life had not turned out the way she hoped for, and she was caught up in the throes of being a single mom and feeling devastated that she did not have a connection with any of her children. She did not supervise them very well. As a result, the children were molested by neighborhood kids, as well as by relatives when they were quite small.

Scott was caught up in his addiction and did not care to be involved in his children's lives. He went from one girlfriend to another. The children lived with Carolyn for a while. Then they would choose to stay with Scott for a while, even though he did not have an emotional connection with them. None of the children received counseling or had anyone talk to them about what happened. The cycle of abuse and sexual addiction was successfully passed on to the next generation.

The divorce tore Perry apart. He was a sensitive little boy who loved his mom and dad. He felt as if his heart ripped in half because half was with his mother, half was with his father. Perry started mistreating his little brother Paul. He was operating out of the hurt in his heart and didn't know how to deal with it. He became disrespectful and rebellious to teachers and other authority figures in his life. Perry felt Scott was never emotionally available to talk to when he needed him.

Carolyn began dating the first man that came along that was far from a Southern Baptist. Her former mother-in-law constantly praised her son, Scott, for being a great father, and said how proud she was of him, but she continuously criticized Carolyn and called her a slut. The children learned that a Christian man who beat and abused his wife and children and committed adultery got rewarded with praise, but that a hurting, abused woman who recognized her sexuality and dared to build a life for herself gets called a slut and an adulterer.

Every summer, the children went to Arkansas and spent the summer with relatives. They played outside all day, riding their bikes and four wheelers, fishing and climbing trees, and swimming. Along with play, Perry also learned how to work.

During one summer, Carolyn committed herself to a psychiatric ward for six weeks. She was trying to get help for herself. It was the longest the children had been without their mother. It was hardest on Paul.

One hot summer day, Perry's grandfather told him to pick potatoes out of a big field. Perry went out into the field and picked up potatoes until he was hot and tired. He went into the garage and opened the refrigerator there. The only thing in it was beer, so he cracked open a beer and drank it. That was his first taste of beer. He didn't like it, but to a thirsty boy, it was refreshing.

After a full day of work and play, they would have cornbread, okra, black-eyed peas, squash, beans, and deep fat fried chicken. His mother and aunts knew how to cook delicious southern foods.

Patty and Perry developed binge eating disorders and started gaining weight. Food was their way of disassociating from the fights, the abuse and whatever else was causing them stress. Food provided an escape from the pain in their lives. The two children were attending Weight Watchers' meetings with their mother before they were teens.

Perry's grandfather also trained him to take a shower. Afterward, Perry was not to get out of the shower until he had dried himself off and wiped down the walls of the shower with a squeegee and then dried the squeegee. Only then could he get out. If he disobeyed, the consequences were harsh. Perry promised himself he would never do that to his kids.

His grandfather was a force with which to be reckoned. Sometimes he beat not only the kids but also his wife. He treated her terribly, yet she stayed with him. In his old age, he mellowed out and became a loving, gentle old man. Perry told himself that it was never okay to hit a woman and that he would never hit his wife.

Eventually, Carolyn started dating Joe Rodgers, who was in the singles group from church. They got married when Perry was still young. Perry chose to live with his father while his siblings decided to live with their mother. Perry would eventually miss his mother, and then he would go live with her. The family moved a lot, so Perry went to a different school every year. Changing homes every year was hard on Perry; he was always the new kid in school. He was bullied and picked on, and had to work extra hard at making friends. He felt like he never had a stable home. "Home" became wherever they lived. As a result, he became an unstable person.

Perry's dad had a perfect house. Everything was in place. Everything stayed neat. The kids found out quickly that if things got messed up or moved, they would get to see their father's rage. They'd get yelled at or spanked.

One of the children spilled grape juice on the carpet in the living room. Despite their efforts at cleaning it up, the stain remained. They knew they were going to be in deep trouble when their father found out, so they moved the chair over the spot on the carpet. The distraction worked for a while, but eventually, Scott found out, and they did get in trouble.

Perry grew up in an environment where things had to stay in perfect condition. His dad and grandfather both believed that people are here to serve and take care of their belongings, not the other way around, so they had to take care of their cars and keep them waxed and shining and cover them with a tarp. They kept their house perfect and specific rooms were not for kids to play in, and they were punished for breaking their grandfather's rules.

There were times when Perry was supposed to be in school, and he would skip his classes and instead go to the library and read. He was not held accountable, and so he did whatever he wanted. He was rebellious and disrespectful to his mother and Joe. As a teenager, he became more rebellious and disrespectful to Carolyn. Joe did his best to correct Perry's behavior and help him learn to respect his mother, but giving him a beating at sixteen years old was not appropriate. Perry grew to resent Joe.

Joe and Carolyn moved to Florida to be involved with a church in Fort Myers. Perry chose to go with them for a while. He said goodbye to his high school girlfriend and promised to write to her. After a while, he moved back to stay with his dad Scott. When he went back to see his girlfriend, she told him that his cousin had come over to her house after Perry had left and pressured her to have sex with him. Perry was heartbroken. It ended their relationship.

Perry tried to have friendships with girls. He found it easier to have relationships with girls than with boys. Sometimes the relationships had sexual tension, but that caused awkwardness, and he wanted girls to feel comfortable with him. He did not want girls to feel pressure from him. He was a gentleman, but it seemed each relationship he had with a girl, she always ended up walking away from Perry and breaking his heart. He learned that girls would always stab him in the back.

When Perry was older and out of high school, he decided to go to Atlanta, Georgia. His cousin was married and had a family there. Perry became a taxi driver there, but he couldn't make enough money. He lived in his taxi for a while; then he lived with his cousin for a while. His cousin cheated on his wife and left her for a new girlfriend, then the cousin and his girlfriend moved back to Texas and had another child.

Perry also moved back to Texas and stayed with his dad. He did eventually find a girlfriend and was sexually active with her. She became pregnant. On her own, she decided to have an abortion. Perry was devastated, feeling as if she did not value him and her relationship with him enough to keep their baby. Perry hoped someday to find a woman who wanted to have his child.

After staying with Scott for a while, Perry decided to move to Indiana to live with Joe and Carolyn. Joe was a pastor of a church which had gone through a church split. They had only moved to Indiana a year before Perry came to live with them.

Perry had used drugs. He struggled to stay focused and had used marijuana to help him calm down and focus his mind. When he had gone through a hard time, he would do a mind exercise during which he would picture the cross and Jesus on the cross. He would imagine himself under the cross with the blood of Jesus covering him. He said doing that mind exercise helped him to center his mind on Jesus and think clearly and feel peaceful. Perry began doing this mind exercise when he was feeling desperate, and he cried out to God that God needed to help him or he was going to turn to marijuana again. God helped him find that mind exercise so that he wouldn't turn to drugs.

Perry was attending Joe Rodger's church. Joe told him he could work his way up into a position of leadership, and that's what his intentions were. After he and Grace had been together for a few months, however, he stopped going to church. He grew tired of the hypocrisy and all the backbiting and gossiping. Perry believed every time he met with God, he was attending church, as he thought himself the church.

No doctor ever diagnosed Perry with bipolar disorder, narcissistic personality disorder, or borderline personality disorder. He refused any counseling. He slowly became narcissistic and controlling. He refused to get premarital counseling. He declined to be mentored or to be accountable to anyone but God and himself. He rebelled against any authority.

Perry became hard-hearted over time and he continued to struggle with his relationship with Carolyn. He despised and hated women. He often claimed women were backstabbers and would always break his heart eventually. He blamed his mother for their broken relationship. He blamed her for not nursing him as a baby. He called her terrible names and suggested that she should be a lesbian. He claimed she neglected him and wasn't available to him as a child when he needed her.

Even as Perry entered adulthood, he had a strained relationship with Carolyn. He was disrespectful to her and continued to blame her for their fractious relationship. There were times they would be cordial and have pleasant conversations, but many times he brushed her off and did not value her or see her as an important person in his life.

5

COUPLEHOOD

After her trip to China, the summer she turned twenty-six, Grace told Emma she was ready to meet her husband. Emma and Grace began to pray for God to prepare the man who would be "the one." Grace felt she had waited a long time. Her sisters had gotten married at nineteen and twenty-two years of age and Emma had married Adam at twenty-four. Grace wondered when it would be her turn. She felt the urge and desire to get married and settle down. She wanted to fall in love and be married for fifty years, and grow old with somebody, and become comfortable with them, the same way she saw her parents doing.

She believed the reason she'd had to wait an extra-long time was that God was finding someone extra special. Grace often cried but trusted that God was preparing a special man for her.

Grace was kind of new to the internet and wondered what it would be like to meet somebody on the internet. She found a matching service and created a profile, saying in her background that she grew up on a farm, she enjoyed singing and playing guitar. She also mentioned her passion for God.

The matching service sent her profiles of men, but she was not interested in any of them. She did not respond to any of them and just deleted their message, because she was looking for a potential life mate.

After several months, when she had almost given up hope, she received the profile of a man named Bob, who also had a passion for God. He said he loved God, twice. She became very excited and immediately sent off a message that she was interested, then went to bed with a smile on her face.

She received a message back from him, and he also expressed that he was interested in her. They exchanged email addresses and sent each other notes. She asked him to tell about himself and what God is doing in his life. He sent her this letter:

Greetings,

I am exceedingly joyful that you returned my message. God is transforming me into an incredible man of faith. He is imparting me with wisdom because I am beginning to be quiet before the Lord. I find myself becoming less and less talkative in prayer. That is good because I'm not afraid to speak. I am an excellent public speaker, but what I have to say is not as important as what God wants to say through me.

God is preparing me for great work. I feel called to be a head pastor of a large church. God is preparing me for great responsibility. I have a heart for missions. I was raised under a Reach, Teach and Send mentality. I went on my first mission trip to Paraguay, South America at 13 years old.

I am forging a path to accomplish God's work. I have been asked to start as a part-time janitor at my step-father's church. I love it. It is teaching me to be a silent servant. After a year I will begin an internship that will turn into a full-time position within the staff. I am becoming wiser every day.

I play guitar and piano and sing. I enjoy writing songs. It's where I enjoy being creative. I am very curious to meet you. I am a leader, not a follower.

The woman God is preparing for me must be kind, not be afraid to travel, be patient, detail oriented, love life. She must be satisfied with a modest lifestyle, be diligent and affectionate.

Get back to me and share what God is doing in you.

Perry Lawrence

Grace was so excited because they seemed to be similar in their walk with God and they both played guitar and piano. With each message they exchanged, the feeling he was "the one" became stronger, but she also found out his name was not Bob.

The following month, Grace went to the Bahamas with her friend, Cindy. The trip had been planned months in advance. The women drove to Florida, stopping to visit Grace's brother, Willie, and some friends at the YWAM base in Nashville. They then visited her sister Diane during her stay at the YWAM base in Orlando.

Grace and Cindy drove to Fort Lauderdale and got on a small cruise ship. They sailed to the Bahamas, but they didn't do much while they were there, as Cindy became ill and slept a lot. They still had a great time. Grace wished she could take a cruise with a man she loved, however.

Not long after their trip, Grace continued her communications with Perry. They exchanged some more emails, then spoke on the phone. Grace thought Perry had a lovely voice and he told her the same. He told her he wrote songs and sang one for her.

"The reflection of the magnet, the reflection of the madness, telling a tale of sadness, and bringing itself down to the lower bowels of the human soul."

Grace was impressed that he could also sing, as singing was meaningful to her, too.

She asked, "What are your goals are for the future?"

"I want to get married and have kids someday," Perry replied.

"How would you want them educated?"

"Homeschooling has been on my heart. I was not home-schooled, but I think it would be better than public school."

His response floored Grace. "I want to homeschool, too! It's imperative to me because I was homeschooled. I never went to public school."

Their first conversation lasted almost an hour. It seemed they had so much to discuss.

The next morning, Grace went into the kitchen and said. "Mom, I have something to tell you. You'd better sit down. I met a man, on the internet. We had a conversation on the phone, and he's a nice guy. He loves the Lord and lives only an hour away. We want to meet face to face."

Emma's face was troubled. She warned Grace to be safe and to meet the man in a public place. She even offered to host their meeting at Grace's family's house.

Perry and Grace exchanged photos so they'd know whom to look for at their first meeting. He sent her a picture in an email. She sent one through the mail.

They planned for Perry to come to Millersburg and meet Grace at Taco Bell. From there they could choose to go somewhere to eat. Grace was very nervous and excited. She knew this was it; she was going to meet her husband.

It was a cold December evening. She slipped on her gloves and noticed that her gloves were so worn and old, her fingers stuck out through the tips of the gloves. She quickly ran back inside and exchanged them for a better pair. She didn't want him to realize just yet, how homely and country and unfashionable she was. She didn't care about fashion. She often dressed casually and wore plaid, but she did want to make a good first impression.

Once Grace arrived at the Taco Bell, her mouth was dry, and she worried she would not be able to speak, so she decided to get a water bottle at the drive-through. As she went through the line, she saw Perry walking inside. She gulped down some water and then she went inside and saw him sitting at a table. He looked tall. She went over and introduced herself.

"I'm Grace. Are you Perry?" They smiled at each other.

"You have holes in your gloves."

She looked down, and to her horror, her fingers were sticking out of her gloves. She shoved them in her pockets. She was embarrassed to have grabbed another pair with holes in them. Perry, however, was impressed to see Grace was not perfect, that she was real and down to earth. He liked that about her.

They laughed and talked about where they should go for dinner. The couple decided to go to a small local café where they ate dinner and talked about music and churches and families, asking one another questions incessantly.

When the conversation slowed down and came to a stop, they found themselves staring into each other's eyes. Grace felt spellbound and averted her gaze because it seemed to be getting intense. The waitress started vacuuming the room, and they could hardly hear each other. They laughed about it, even though it was annoying.

Later, Perry wrote her a letter about their first meeting.

> When we were eating at the cafe, halfway through dinner, I was looking into your eyes. Suddenly I could see into your eyes. At first, it startled me because I've never experienced that before. I could see into your eye. Your spirit and emotions were there for me to see. God opened the door between us. I could see that it startled you, too.

They didn't want their enchanted evening to end, so Grace invited him to her house. By that time, there were several inches of snow on the ground, and the snow was falling thickly. Perry followed Grace to her parents' house. Adam and Emma were sitting in the living room, and there was a warm fire in the stove. Perry and Grace stood by the stove, Perry's six-foot frame towering over Grace.

Perry said, "Someday I want to have a stove like this in my house."

Grace smiled, thinking, *You mean our house.*

They sat down and started talking to Adam and Emma. Perry told them he loved bluegrass music, which was the kind of music they played. Soon they were talking about bluegrass festivals. Grace watched Perry. He was handsome and gentle, yet muscular and stocky.

Grace sat across from her parents and Perry, thinking, *I like him. What if he doesn't want me the same way? I think he could potentially be my husband, but what if he only thinks of me as a friend? Maybe he likes the fact that we play bluegrass music and that's all that interests him.*

After a while, she invited him to her room, and they talked about and listened to music. She showed him her guitar. He played it and sang. Grace wanted to know what his intentions are. She asked him to tell her what he was feeling.

"I feel like everything in my life has led me up to this moment. I feel like I was supposed to meet you tonight and I feel that you are the one for me."

Grace smiled shyly and said, "I feel like you are the one for me, too."

After they both confessed their feelings, they sat there reveling in the new and exciting emotions. Grace felt like this was the most exciting moment of her life, yet also the scariest. It felt like they were going to spend the rest of their lives together.

Grace tentatively asked him, "What's our status? Are we friends? Are we dating? Are you my boyfriend?"

Perry said, "Sure, I'm your boyfriend."

Then they smiled and sat together and talked some more. At eleven o'clock, Perry finally got up to go. He could hardly leave because he just wanted to stay with her. Grace walked him to the door. He asked if he could kiss her.

"Not on the lips." Perry kissed her forehead.

He had an hour to drive home to his mother's house. She was on the couch waiting for him, eagerly waiting to hear about his evening.

She said, "Well, tell me about your evening."

"Mom, I've just been with my wife."

The next week, they planned for Grace to come and meet his family. He planned to drive an hour to pick her up and drive an hour to take her home so they could have more time to talk. When Perry arrived at her house, Grace was so excited that her boyfriend thought it was worth driving two hours to be with her. Emma snapped their picture before they left.

They had an hour to talk. Perry shared his vision for the future. He planned on working and saving toward their future home. Perry spoke of working at his step-father's church. He said he had a pastor's heart and would like to be a pastor someday. As Perry talked, Grace felt such admiration for him. He seemed so mature, speaking so openly about the future, setting goals and planning how to accomplish them. She thought Perry would make such a wonderful husband because he would know how to work and take care of his family. Plus, he had a passion for God. He seemed to be everything she wanted in a husband.

Grace was nervous about meeting Perry's family. Before they went into the house, they prayed together. Perry's large, beautiful mother, Carolyn Rodgers, hugged Grace and made her feel so wanted and welcomed. Then Grace met his sister, Tiffany, and his stepfather, Joe.

Their house looked like something you might find in a home and garden magazine. It was perfect. They had a huge Christmas tree in the living room decorated with wide ribbons and huge golden flowers. The ceiling was vaulted, and garland wound around the railing.

Carolyn had made a meal fit for a queen. Creamy potato soup, Mexican squash, okra with tomatoes, black-eyed peas, fried chicken. It was way more food than the five of them should eat. Plus, there was a beautiful cake with fruit on top made by Tiffany. Grace couldn't believe her eyes. She felt like a queen.

During dinner, Perry was funny, making everyone laugh. Grace was thrilled, thinking herself lucky that Perry also had a sense of humor.

After dinner, Perry took Grace went to his room and they talked and shared some music. He sang her some more songs he wrote. They stayed for another hour, and then he took her home.

The following week, Grace and Perry thought it would be great for their families to meet. Perry's family came to the Chupps' and met her parents and her brothers, Willie and Kevin. They hit it off, and the mothers seemed to bond right away. Their families seemed to love and accept one another instantly. By Christmas, the rest of her family had met Perry. They were thrilled that Grace had found such a great guy. He made everyone laugh. They loved being around him. He seemed to be the life of the party. Susanna secretly thought he was so wonderful that he might soon be her favorite person instead of Grace.

Grace entered the relationship with Perry for the long term. She had every intention of making it last for fifty or more years. She wanted to commit herself to him and grow old with him. They got along so well; they seemed to be a perfect fit. It was hard for her to find things wrong with him. It seemed as if they had known each forever because they were as comfortable around each other as an old couple. However, she still wanted him to propose to her.

One night, after they had been dating for three months, they went to see a musical at the local high school. The auditorium was packed. They were there with some of the people from Grace's small church group. Perry joined them even though he was tired and had come straight from work. Grace was thrilled to be sitting next to him during a play. She had been attending theater productions for years, but this was the first one with Perry.

Afterward, they were sitting in his car. Grace was shivering and said, "I'm cold. My hands are cold; it's your job to keep my hands warm."

Grace wanted Perry to hold her hand. He took her hand and started stroking it. Then he pulled out a ring, the most beautiful ring she'd ever seen, and said, "Marry me?"

Her mouth dropped open, and her eyes grew large. She started laughing. "Yes!"

The ring had heart shapes in the band, and it had a small center diamond surrounded by cubic zirconium rocks. It looked like a flower. She thought it was so beautiful and showed it off to her friends that night. Grace was thrilled to finally be engaged and finally have a beautiful ring and a wonderful guy.

Perry made Grace feel so loved. He made her feel special and told her all the time she was the most beautiful girl in the world. He showered Grace with hugs and kisses, and he held her hand. He was very affectionate and gave her lots of hugs. He gushed about how good she smelled. He made her feel like she was his queen and he told her over and over that he loved her. He also said he loved her more than anybody else could ever love her.

They would sit and talk for hours. It was always hard to say goodbye. Grace was always smiling and happy. She would tell anybody who would listen about her wonderful guy.

Perry had all the qualities Grace wanted in a husband. He was godly and involved in the church. He had leadership qualities. Perry talked about his vision for the future and ways to reach his goals. He was a nice guy and was popular and well liked. Many people thought he was funny. He was smart and knew about a lot of different subjects. They held the same religious views. They had the same goals and wanted to homeschool their future children. He was the special man she had been waiting for.

The couple agreed they should be equal partners and work side by side supporting one another. Neither of them should be more important than the other, and they would make decisions together. They agreed on financial decisions. They set standards for their relationship and how they would deal with conflicts. They had decided they would live somewhere between Millersburg and Westerville. They both sang and played guitar. They seemed to click when they met, and even their families clicked when they met. Perry and Grace both had a passion for God. They were both ready to be in a relationship and felt God brought them together at the right time. Everything seemed wonderful.

Grace started making her wedding dress with Susanna's help. It took months of work. Three months before the wedding, Perry convinced Grace that she should move to Westerville, into his parent's house. She agreed to it because she loved Perry and decided she could get a job there. She quit her other jobs. It was difficult for her because Perry was traveling each week to a different state where he would work with a team, but Grace wasn't sure what they did. He did that for over a year while they lived with his parents. His sister had moved to Florida and Perry was only home on the weekends.

While they were living with Joe and Carolyn, they heard a lot of talk about the church. Because Joe was the pastor of a church that had recently gone through a church split, they often heard news the rest of the church people wouldn't learn. There had been allegations of sexual abuse within the church. As a result, there was a scandal, and the church was divided. The pastor left, taking half of the congregation with him. Joe became the pastor of the remaining half.

Perry soon grew tired of all the behind-the-scenes talk and wanted to stop going to church. People were fired. The church was getting ready to move into another building. They were spending their weekends together, and they stopped going to church. Grace would still have enjoyed going to church, but she enjoyed spending time with Perry so much, she gave up going to church.

Grace also stopped going to the other two churches she had been attending before she met Perry. She stopped going to the small group because she moved away from her hometown. Grace did not feel like the small group was helping her grow anymore and she had become discouraged. She was getting ready to commit her life to Perry and to leave her family to settle down with Perry.

Perry did not want to take premarital counseling because he said they would work things out as they went along. "There's nothing that we can't talk about and work through if we keep the lines of communication open. We do not want someone else to get in our business and tell us what to do."

The decided if they faced conflicts, they should talk it out, pray it through, and work it out themselves.

Grace and Perry were crazy in love with each other. They were so happy when they were together. They laughed and couldn't keep their hands off each other. They were always holding hands and hugging and kissing. Grace loved all the affection Perry loaded on her because her family hadn't been affectionate while she was growing up. She wanted to be able to give and receive affection from the person she loved. It seemed all her dreams were finally coming true.

They planned to get married eleven months after they met. Perry wanted a small wedding, but Grace wanted a large wedding with all her closest friends as bridesmaids. She wanted her dad to walk her down the aisle. Perry wanted to elope and have a small reception of about twenty people afterward. Grace was ready to agree to that because she loved him so much, but his parents convinced him that he needed to do what Grace wanted. Although they planned to have a large wedding, Grace compromised by only having one bridesmaid, her sister, Diane, and one groomsman, Perry's brother, Paul.

The day before the wedding, Perry took part in decorating the church and getting it ready. He thought he was in charge and started an argument with Grace in front of everyone who had come to help. Grace didn't like that.

The day of the wedding, as Grace was getting ready, Esther popped into where Grace was getting ready. She looked panicked. "Perry is taking all the cards off the gifts."

Grace said, "Well, tell him to stop doing that."

It didn't do any good. Perry continued to take all the cards off the gifts because he wouldn't let anyone tell him what to do. It caused them to have the first fight of their marriage.

It was a beautiful wedding. It was finally Grace's big moment. She felt like she had waited her whole life for the moment it would be her turn to walk down the aisle with her father and marry her very best friend and lover. She saw many wonderful friends and relatives all looking at her walking down the aisle of her home church. She and Perry made their vows to stay together during hard times and easy times, through the joy and pain, no matter what.

Grace did include her closest girlfriends in the wedding, even though Perry didn't allow them to be her bridesmaids. One was a server; one played music, and one helped Grace get ready.

They had a great reception afterward. While everybody ate the delicious food, Adam's family and a few others got up and sang songs. Even Perry and Grace got up and sang. Perry made everybody laugh. People came and blessed them, and then they headed off on their honeymoon.

They spent their honeymoon at a bed and breakfast. It was a remote, quiet place out in the country. It was peaceful, and they saw hardly anyone besides the owner. Perry was very sick and thought he was going to die if he didn't get up and take a walk. They just rested for five days, not doing much except watching movies and taking walks. When they returned from their honeymoon to open their gifts, they had no idea who gave them what because Perry had removed all the cards searching for money. That's how they began their married life.

The world Perry grew up in was opposite that in which Grace grew up. Perry grew up in a city, moving from one large metropolis to another throughout his life. Grace had always lived in a small town, in the country, or on a farm. Perry moved nearly every year and went to a different school every year, which contributed to his unstable life. He did not seem to have a firm foundation. In the deep South, he was taught to address people as sir and ma'am and to say please and thank you. Perry believed as long as he called someone sir or ma'am, he was respectful, even if he was not.

Perry's family taught him it was disrespectful to go to someone's house without being invited. In Grace's community, visitors were expected to drop in any time, and no one was offended. All visitors were welcome.

Perry expected that once he was married, Grace would leave her family. He expected her to break the bond with her family. Grace was willing to move away because she loved Perry. She was adventurous and thought she could handle living far from her family, but in Grace's world, when a couple got married, they often lived close to relatives. Family bonds remained close, and everyone expected that the wife would spend considerable time with her family.

Perry and Grace never realized how much cultural background would make a difference in their relationship. The small differences would later become a vast canyon in their relationship. Perry and Grace thought they had so much in common, but because they came from different cultures, they later wondered what they ever thought they had in common.

6

THE HONEYMOON IS OVER

Perry and Grace continued living with Joe and Carolyn. Grace continued to work and be a caregiver. Perry continued to travel every week to a different location and work with a team. One day, while Grace was at one of her client's house, Perry called and said he was in Minnesota. He wanted to go to Canada since it was close and he'd never been there. Grace assumed he would enter Canada and return the same day.

When he called three days later, he said he had gone into treacherous territory where very few vehicles were traveling and he was still traveling. It was very dangerous and mountainous. Perry told Grace about his adventures, telling her he loved the thrill of it. Grace was shocked, wondering why he would do that. He said it was his last trip since he was now married, so he wasn't free to do impulsive things like that anymore. Grace wondered if he regretted marrying her or felt as if she was going to drag him down now that they were married.

Not long after that, Perry said he wanted to get a house. He was ready to move out of his parents' house and start a family. They had been married six months, and they found a small house on the south end of town. It was a two-story, two-bedroom house that they could rent-to-own. It wasn't precisely between Westerville and Millersburg like they had agreed, but Grace figured since they had cars, they could still see their families. She was still working for an agency as a caregiver. Perry decided to find a local job delivering pizza. He also looked for other jobs, but each job he got lasted only a few months.

Grace became pregnant after they had been married for seven months. When she told Perry, he didn't react with excitement as she had been anticipating. He was shocked, and he acted as if her pregnancy was interrupting everything. He began staying home a lot after that, excluding himself from family events. He seemed to prefer being alone, almost as if the Perry Grace knew was disappearing forever.

They had planned to take a trip to Wisconsin with Grace's family. Grace went without Perry. When Grace went to see her family, and announced they were expecting, Perry stayed home. He suddenly preferred not to see her family or his family. Grace thought he would get over it, and once he accepted that she was pregnant, he would return to his fun-loving and happy self. That didn't happen, however. He isolated himself and spent a lot of time alone.

Grace's cousin Andy got married about a month after Grace found out she was pregnant. Grace was asked to be the matron of honor since she and the bride were very close. The night before the wedding, Grace went to the rehearsal, Perry said he would come the next day, to the wedding.

The morning of the wedding he called to say he wasn't coming because he was going to work at home. Grace started crying. She probably should have just let it go, but it upset her. Emma saw how upset Grace was and decided to talk with Perry.

"You should be here to support Grace. You told her you would be here. We are planning to take family pictures, and we want you in the pictures. You're part of our family."

"I'm sorry, I wish I could be there, but I'm sick as a dog. I have diarrhea, and I'm throwing up," Perry said. "I should stay home and get some work done now that we're going to have a family and I need to support her financially."

Although he claimed to be sick and working, he nevertheless had time to talk on the phone for hours, dominating their time and manipulating her whole family. Grace felt embarrassed that they were taking family pictures and everybody was there except him. They wanted him to be a part of their family, but he was excluding himself.

That afternoon, Esther told Grace she was upset that Perry hadn't come and that he'd made Grace cry.

"Grace, he's not good enough for you. He makes me so mad and I just want to punch him in the nose."

Grace's whole family was mad at Perry for lying and making excuses and not being a part of the family. He had upset Grace, which in turn disturbed the rest of the family.

When Grace got home that night, Perry asked if anyone said anything about him not being there.

"Yes."

"Who was it? What did they say?"

"I don't want to tell you; you don't need to know," she said.

"Gracie," he prodded, "tell me. You have to tell me these things. If you don't tell me, you're keeping things secret from me, and I won't be able to trust you anymore."

"It won't do any good to tell you."

He continued to prod her until she felt forced to tell him what her sister had said. That was the beginning of a wall between him and her family. There was a cycle of Perry not coming to see her family, her family feeling as if he was rejecting them, and then her family saying something that would hurt his feelings, which would cause him to reject them even further.

When some of Grace's close friends got married, Perry and Grace fought about going to the wedding. They were on their way to the event when a fight erupted. Perry told her she was being a b**ch and said he didn't want to be with her and threatened to turn around and take her home. At that point, Grace gave in and submitted to him. They went to the wedding, but they were very late.

The next morning, the fight continued while Grace was in the kitchen fixing her breakfast. Perry told her that he had gone to the wedding for her but that he hadn't wanted to go. Once he went upstairs, Grace grabbed her purse, her breakfast, and the Bible, and went out to her car, which was parked on the street. Just as she reached her car, Perry came out the door, naked.

"GRACE, COME BACK!"

"NO, Perry," she shouted back. She got into her car and drove away.

She intended to have some alone time for a few hours, then return, but he called her cell phone over and over until she answered. He begged her to return, as if he was going to be sick unless she returned. He made her promise to come back, so she drove around three blocks and returned home. She was gone fewer than ten minutes.

When she came back, he was sobbing on the bed. He cried and pouted and gave her a guilt trip for leaving, even though she hadn't been going permanently, only for a few hours. They made up, and she apologized for upsetting him. He was afraid that she would leave him, like all the other girlfriends he ever had. He thought girls were cruel and would break his heart. She assured him that she would stay and not reject him like the other girls. She tried to prove how much she loved him and hoped that would help him heal from his past. She wanted to help him have a healthy relationship with her.

Perry was a permanent clinger. He was emotionally needy. He blamed his father for not being emotionally available; he blamed his mother for neglecting him. He blamed all his past girlfriends for leaving him and stabbing him in the heart. Grace was the perfect person to mend his broken heart. Perry took advantage of Grace's caring nature. She was a giver, and he was a taker. He roped her in, and Grace cared for him and promised to stay with him always because she was loyal and faithful. She was sure she could help him heal his heart by listening, caring and sympathizing with him and counseling him.

It didn't matter how much Grace gave to him or tried to help him. Perry would still, always, permanently, be a clinger. It was his nature, and he could not change it if he tried. Perry clung to Grace so that she would see how needed she was and would willingly stay. Perry convinced her that she needed to take care of him like a mother if she wanted to prove her love to him or prove that he could trust her.

Perry had his ideas about pregnancy and birth. He did not want Grace to take birthing classes. She took them anyway, but he did not attend and did not seem supportive of what she wanted. She got mad at him and punched him in the arm. She wanted to do a home birth, but Perry wanted a hospital birth. He knew nothing about home births, and he wouldn't have been a good birth coach, so they planned to have a hospital birth. Perry did not want any of her family to come to the hospital when she had the baby. He wanted the only people in the room to be the doctor, the nurses, and him and Grace.

Once Grace decided to quit her job so she could be a stay at home mother, Perry decided to leave his job too. That frustrated Grace to no end, as he thought they would live off her savings.

Instead of working, he began smoking, and for the first time, Grace seriously considered leaving him. When she told him that, he was incredulous. Grace had never lived with a smoker and never wanted to. She began to question whether

her standards were too high and she should put up with him because, after all, she had committed herself to him.

Perry asked if he could grow marijuana. Of course, Grace wouldn't approve, but he went ahead anyway. Whenever she smelled the stench of cigars or marijuana or whatever else Perry was smoking, it infuriated her. She retreated into the bedroom more and more, and he escaped into the garage more and more.

Their baby was born on a cold night. At eleven o'clock, she told Perry she was having contractions. He said it was time to go to bed, so he slept. She couldn't sleep as she was having contractions every five minutes. She waited until they were coming only three minutes apart, then at two in the morning she told Perry they needed to go to the hospital. She sat out in the car and waited for thirty minutes, which seemed like forever. She couldn't go back into the house; she was in agony.

Meanwhile, he was inside, leisurely taking a shower. By the time they reached the hospital her cervix was dilated to nine centimeters, and the baby was coming out. They barely made it. Her labor lasted only five hours.

Perry was so proud to have a son, whom he nicknamed Ben. When it was time to go home, Perry wouldn't let the nurse buckle Ben into the car seat; he said he wanted to do it. When they arrived home, Grace lifted Ben out of his seat and realized the baby had not even been buckled. Grace was angry, but she soon learned not to express her anger towards Perry; it just angered him more.

They adored their new baby and loved to watch him instead of television. They loved to watch him hold his first toy and waited to see him smile at them. Ben brought joy to their hearts. Grace was seeing a side of Perry she never saw before, his father heart. He was soft and gentle. He enjoyed holding Ben and snuggling him.

Perry said he would get a job, but he didn't. He spent several hours every day out in the garage, playing and recording

music. He would write music and come up with some inter-
esting songs. Grace did not like his music. They were harsh
and loud, rough and bordered on vulgar. Perry was often
angry, and so his songs sounded angry. He also smoked out
in the garage. She couldn't believe he was smoking. Perry also
had long phone conversations with old friends from Texas
or her little sister Diane. He was changing into a completely
different person from the man she'd married. Her heart was
breaking, but she tried not to let it get her down. She had
every intention of staying with him and proving to him how
faithful she could be.

Perry was lazy and did not want to be an employee or
get a real job. He tried to make money by buying and selling
used cars. He looked for vehicles on eBay or craigslist and
then try to sell them for more than he paid. That lasted only
a few months because Perry wasn't very good at fixing them
and selling them again, nor did he have the time or put in
the effort to work on them.

Perry decided to start his own business. He wanted Grace
to help him by sending out emails every day. She also helped
put packages together and get them ready to send in the mail.
He posted ads so that people would seek him out. Then he
sent them applications. Perry would accept them unless he
perceived them to be troublemakers. Then he sent them the
program he wrote, but it was not complete.

Perry got frustrated with Grace and yelled at her, daily.
He started calling her vulgar and demeaning names. He called
her b**ch, whore, moron, idiot, retard, a**hole, stupid, and
lazy. He also started calling himself foolish and an idiot for
marrying her. It was a challenge to do the work Perry wanted
her to do with a baby in her arms. The business fell apart in
less than a year because it was not complete.

Grace's sister, Susanna, called Perry to ask him a
business-related question. The call turned into an awful ordeal
because Susanna couldn't get off the phone with him. Perry

talked on and on, insulting her. He was mean and twisted and hurtful. She had called him while driving, and after arriving at her destination, she sat in the vehicle and talked to him for a while longer. Perry rambled on and on and on, causing her to cry.

Susanna finally went inside the house, still on the phone, still crying. Perry was torturing her, and she couldn't hang up on him because she was too polite. Susanna knew Perry would have been offended and said she was rude and disrespectful. Finally, she got off the phone and cried and cried. Susanna was angry that he had turned a business phone call into an unprofessional tirade. She soon learned phone conversations with Perry were always negative.

Perry didn't help with dishes or laundry or any cleaning, nor did he help take care of the baby. Grace had a lot on her plate. Perry pressured her to do more housework. He expected the house to be neater and cleaner, and he also expected her to make food for him. He wanted her to stop talking to him about things in his world, such as what he's doing, and finances and his business, his music and his duties. He only wanted her to talk about things in her world, housecleaning, the baby, grocery shopping, her family, and her duties.

Once, Perry came up to the nursery where Grace was sitting in the rocking chair, holding baby Ben. Perry wanted her to do something for him. She got up and put the baby down, and as she was walking toward the door, Perry grabbed her and pushed her, causing her to fall. He blamed her for not moving fast enough.

Perry often yelled at her and Grace cried easily. She was utterly frazzled and tired. Perry did not help her; he expected her to help him, yet he did not want to explain things to her. He expected her to follow him blindly without asking questions or challenging him. She was learning that questioning or challenging him would enrage him.

He accused her of not following him. She tried to be more submissive and often apologized for what she did that offended him. She cried nearly every day. She tried to bend herself around Perry to be what he wanted her to be. She tried to be and do everything he said he needed because she thought if she could, he would stop being so angry. That never happened, however. Nothing she did ever changed him, he just got worse and worse.

While they were dating, Grace said she wanted their relationship to be a partnership, in which they could work side by side, no one being more important or over the other, but after they were married, Perry announced he was going to be the leader, and he was going to make the final decision about everything. He wanted Grace to follow his leadership because God had set the man to be the leader of the wife and God would give him the direction. All Grace needed to do was submit to him.

Perry repeatedly asked her if she had extra money. She did have a secret stash he did not know about, but she meekly gave it to him. He spent that money. He spent it all. Before they married, she had three thousand dollars, plus a retirement account. Perry spent all that money. He got credit cards in Grace's name and maxed all those cards out. He spent money impulsively. Perry felt he did not have to pay back his debts because he said the companies were rich and didn't need his and Grace's money. It didn't bother him if they had bad credit, because he said in seven years the debt would fall off the credit reports and they could start over. Perry ruined their credit.

Perry even dictated how the family slept. Sometimes he wanted Ben to sleep with them just so he could cuddle with him, but that would not help them all get enough sleep. Grace wanted Ben to sleep in his own bed. She had to get up during the night to nurse Ben back to sleep. She was Ben's world. He was with her most of the time. She hardly ever saw Perry spend any time with Ben. Perry was in the garage it seemed more than anywhere else. He missed out on a lot of time with Ben, and that was his choice.

Every few weeks, Perry and Grace planned to visit her family, but each time they planned to see her family, Perry found an excuse not to go. He hadn't seen her family for nearly six months since he'd started excluding himself from family events after Grace announced she was pregnant. Perry didn't want to be around her family or his family. He had a problem with several people in her family. He perceived that Grace's family would reject him and as a result, he excused himself from joining them.

On Father's Day, Perry said she should go and see her dad. He said he would go too, for lunch. When it was almost time to leave, she let him know when they needed to go.

"Well, that's not going to happen." He continued to watch TV until it was past the time they needed to leave, then he went out to the garage for thirty minutes. She was sitting in the house, fuming. Finally, he came into the house to get ready to go.

Grace got herself and Ben into the car. When she was in the car waiting for him, he said he couldn't find his phone, so she called it several times. A woman's voice answered it.

"Who is this?" Grace asked.

"Maryann."

Grace didn't know any Maryann. Perry became enraged when he found out Grace had called his phone. She didn't know she wasn't allowed to call it. He just blew up at her. Finally, they left the house an hour and a half later than originally intended. Grace was angry.

They were on the road headed to her parents' house when Perry said he hated her attitude and didn't want to be with her if she was going to be a b**ch. He turned the car around and they headed home. She was crying. Her family was expecting to see them. Grace apologized for being a b**ch. She promised herself never to sabotage their trip again if they were on the road headed to her family.

Her family wondered who had offended him, with whom he claimed to have a problem. Grace often cried because of the rift between her husband and her family. She couldn't mend the hurt he felt, nor could she mend the pain they felt from his rejection of them. She felt like it was her duty as his wife to be the mediator between him and her family and try to help both sides understand each other, and forgive each other and get along.

When their car was having trouble, Perry took the opportunity to let Grace know it was her duty to get a message to her family that they would not be coming to Millersburg for six months to a year. Her cousin Jenny wanted to come to see her and Grace explained that she couldn't see her for six months to a year. Jenny couldn't understand why, if Grace couldn't come to Millersburg, Jenny couldn't travel to Grace. They were both crying. Perry was busy working on his business and didn't want to see any of Grace's relatives.

Each day Perry would be in the garage for several hours. Grace wasn't allowed to enter his world. She tried to talk to him about going to see her cousin.

He exploded at Grace. "You were supposed to get the message across to all your relatives! They must understand we cannot see them!"

"I don't understand why I must be at home with you when you spend so little time with me. Why can't I go out and see people? I could meet her somewhere. She doesn't have to come here," she replied through tears.

Perry wasn't spending much time day or night with her. He barely even slept with her because many nights, he wasn't coming to bed until four or five or even six in the morning. She fought with him, and he finally agreed that she could go to meet Jenny in town.

They met at a restaurant, and another couple came along too. It was like old times again. It was so fun and refreshing to be with her old friends. The times she got to see family and friends were few and far between. Perry was slowly trying to isolate her from her family and friends.

Grace wasn't taking care of herself and was very tired as a result. Some nights she was up until one or one-thirty in the morning sending out emails for Perry. One day, Grace felt like she was going to faint. She told Perry that she was going to pass out.

"No, you're not.

Grace slumped in a chair with everything going black.

"You just need to eat protein. Go in the kitchen and make yourself some eggs."

Grace went to a doctor. She was pregnant again. When she came home from the doctor, Perry blamed her for her pregnancy.

"You must have slept with somebody else."

Before they could get into the house, he flew into a rage. He kicked the door hard and broke his toe, then he banged his head on the wall and crumpled to the floor sobbing and yelling.

"IDIOT. I'M SUCH AN IDIOT. I'm stupid for marrying her. Why did I marry her?"

Grace was sitting in a chair sobbing. She didn't know what to do. She couldn't comfort him; he had scared her. How could she console him when he was directing his anger at her? Of course, she hadn't cheated on him. She was confused. What was wrong with her that made him think he was stupid for marrying her? Their relationship had become strained.

Her doctor sent her to a counselor. The counselor asked Grace questions about her home life and their financial situation. When Grace revealed how Perry was behaving, the counselor grew concerned. She told Grace she should get more counseling. Grace talked to Perry about it, but he refused to see a counselor or let her see a counselor.

"Why do they need to know our business? There is nothing they can say or do that we don't already know. We know our situation better than anybody else. We don't need to tell them about our private business. They don't need to know the personal details of our marriage. If we have problems, we need to talk to each other to figure things out. There's nothing we can't talk through. We love each other enough to work through our problems."

Ben was five months old, and Grace was beyond exhausted. The way Perry was treating her, belittling her, demeaning her, making her feel worthless, was slowly killing her inside. Her days were often filled with terror and fear and rage. She cried every day. The man she married had turned into a monster.

Perry was concerned that Grace would potentially neglect Ben. He wanted her to keep Ben with her all the time. She was okay with that because she did not think Perry was good at taking care of Ben. Perry did not seem to be very interested in Ben. If Ben made a peep when they were out at a restaurant, Perry made her take Ben out of the room, into the bathroom. He would not let her nurse at the table, so she had to nurse in the bathroom. Sometimes she nursed Ben while sitting on a closed toilet, sometimes she stood. Ben nursed every hour and a half, sometimes for up to thirty minutes.

Susanna and her family came to visit Grace. Susanna was also pregnant. Perry did not wish to see her, so he left while she was at their house. When he came home, he sat in the car until Grace came out to see if he was all right.

"I blame you for this. You know I did not want anyone to come over. I have a lot of work to do, and I do not want to see anybody in your family. They are invading my space. This is my home."

Embarrassed, Grace told Susanna that Perry wanted them to leave. One of Grace's nephews saw his Uncle Perry and excitedly asked if he could hug him. Susanna said he could. The child ran up to Perry, but Perry stood behind the car door and kept the car door between him and the boy, preventing a hug. It was awkward and embarrassing for the nephew who stood there for a while until he realized Perry did not want to hug him or welcome him. Grace left with Susanna's family and went downtown to a park and spent more time together, while Perry stayed home alone. Perry was rude and selfish.

Once, when Perry and Grace were in a Mexican restaurant, Ben cried and Perry told her to take Ben out. Grace came right back when Ben was done crying. During their meal, the lady at the next table asked if she could hold Ben. As the woman was holding him, Grace was horrified to realize poop was overflowing out of Ben's diaper.

Grace quickly took him and laid him down in her chair and took off his diaper and clothes. Perry took the dirty diaper and dirty clothes and wrapped them all in Ben's blanket, leaving Ben with nothing to wear except a diaper and a burp rag. Grace was mad at Perry for wrapping the clothes and dirty diaper all together in Ben's blanket. Perry was angry at Grace for the way she did everything. He seemed to be mad at her all the time.

On the ride home, Perry commented that the woman who held Ben was not with a man and was probably divorced and that's because she was such a b**ch. He thought she was inserting herself into their marriage. Grace did not see any such thing. She merely saw an adoring mother who missed holding her own tiny babies.

A pattern developed in which Perry got angry about something Grace did. He criticized her and told her how he wanted things done. She cried and apologized. If she spoke up about what she wanted, he said she was rude and selfish. He, on the other hand, was the most ignorant person she had ever known. He commented on a woman he saw on TV or in a restaurant being dominating. Grace commented how judgmental he was. Then he got mad at her for her comment and said she was starting a fight. She apologized again and started crying.

Grace was under pressure to meet Perry's expectations of how she should be keeping the house clean and neat, while also satisfying his needs and fulfilling her wifely duties. She was also trying to figure out how to take care of Ben's needs when he was sick, crying too much, or not sleeping enough.

Grace did not know about the things Perry did in the garage. She was under strict orders not to go into the garage. He told Grace she was not meeting his emotional needs, that she wasn't emotionally available. She thought about leaving him many times, but she did not make decisions rashly.

She thought *I love Perry. I made a commitment to him. I want to make our marriage work. I want to show him that I'm submissive to him and following his lead. I want to talk out our problems.*

Perry criticized her so often that she just shut down. She felt put down and made to feel like she was his servant and there to serve his needs. Perry reminded her that is what a godly wife does—she puts the needs of her husband above her own. She wanted to be the wife described in Proverbs 31.

She thought maybe their expectations of one other were too high. She certainly wanted Perry to lower his expectations of her. He was very demanding. Grace wanted him to treat her as a friend instead of a wife because he had all these expectations that his wife should fulfill him emotionally, spiritually and physically as his wife. She wanted him to be kind and gentle, to do nice things for her. Grace told him she wanted flowers and gifts, but Perry blamed her for that, too.

"If you treated me better, I would treat you better. If you respected me, I would respect you."

The ball was always in her court. It was all her fault. No matter what she did or said, she couldn't please him.

Grace should have suspected that Perry was cheating on her. He spent countless hours out in the garage. She didn't know if he went somewhere in the middle of the night while she was asleep. He left his phone with a woman named Maryann. His story was that Maryann was someone he worked with and she had some illness, so he reached out to her in kindness. Grace trusted that he remained faithful to her. She was devoted to him, so she thought they had a tight bond and they were close, but he did not feel the same way.

Perry was lying to her. Sex with her was no longer fun for him. They were still sexually active, but sometimes their sex was angry, sometimes it was boring. Very often, Grace was not aroused. Sex was all about pleasing Perry. It was almost never about him trying to please her. She felt sexually neglected, but she never talked about it to him. She was afraid of starting another fight.

Grace believed she should always be willing and say yes to sex whenever Perry wanted it. He reminded her that if she didn't give him sex when he wanted, he would be tempted to find somebody else. She didn't want him to be tempted, so she tried to meet his needs and be everything he needed her to be, because she was his wife and that was what he expected of her. Grace felt she was obligated to fulfill his needs. She began to see that if she dared to say no to sex, she ran the risk of angering Perry and that would start a big fight. He'd yell at her, and threaten to leave her and guilt her for not meeting his needs. She did not want to cause conflict, so she just did what he wanted, even though much of the time, her heart was not in it.

Perry went out to dinner with Grace's younger sister, Diane. He did not want Grace to go along. He said he thought of Diane as his little sister. Perry said he felt he could not talk to Grace and connect emotionally with Grace, so he reached out to Diane to ask if she could give any advice. He said that Diane was easier to talk to than Grace was. He also wanted to advise her to watch out for one of her friends she had been hanging out with because he thought she might have lesbian tendencies. Diane wasn't a lesbian.

At the end of their meal, Perry said, "Well that was fun. We should do it again sometime."

Diane's smile didn't quite reach her eyes. "It was fun, but probably not."

The next day Emma called Grace. "Why did Perry have dinner with Diane? Did you know about this?"

"Yes, I was fine with it."

"Your sisters and I do not think it was appropriate. They would never let their husbands go have dinner with their sisters without them."

After the phone call, Perry became very angry that Emma had stuck her nose into their business. Even Diane had no idea why Perry wanted to have dinner with her. Perry became very upset and fell into a depression for several months afterward. He said he felt rejected and ostracized by Grace's whole family. He was angry and mistreated Grace. Often, she cried and apologized for angering him. She felt guilty for not being able to meet his emotional needs.

Because Perry felt rejected by Grace's whole family, he justified his behavior of being rude to them and avoiding them and keeping her away from them. He was slowly isolating Grace from her family, but she did not see it as isolation. She felt it was her job to mediate and try to mend the relationships between him and her family.

One night, Grace was in the nursery holding Ben, and he was cooing softly. She was waiting for him to fall asleep. Perry came and asked who turned the air conditioner down.

"I did. I was cold."

He blew up and yelled at her. She was having such a peaceful moment; now her peace was gone.

A little while later they were laying on the bed. Perry asked Grace what was wrong. She felt uneasy.

He asked, "Do you want to talk?"

"Yes."

"Do you have a problem with me?"

"Yes."

He rose up aggressively and screamed, "WELL, WHY DON'T YOU GO HOME AND LIVE WITH YOUR MOTHER? I'LL HELP YOU PACK!"

Perry stood up and wrenched Grace's suitcase out of the closet. His face grew red. Grace covered Ben's ears, but he was already screaming in terror. Perry raised the suitcase over his head and threw it on the floor, leaving a small hole in the ceiling. He took Ben out of her arms and hugged him and kissed him. Perry was crying, too.

"If you leave, you will never be allowed to come back."

"I don't want to come back to this."

Perry hugged Ben and cried some more. Grace sat in the chair crying. She didn't want to leave Perry. She wanted to prove to him that she was different from other women and that she was going to stay with him. Perry thought Grace was going to leave him eventually, so she tried to prove how much she loved him and prove how committed she was. She decided to stay to show him how submissive she could be.

Early one morning while she was nursing Ben, Perry came to the nursery door and said he wanted to talk to her. He told her he had an idea and that he needed her to consider it.

"I want to have multiple wives. I want to have many children. God gave me the green light to do it. I don't think there's anything wrong with it. It's Biblical. Think of King Solomon who had many, many wives. Having multiple wives was something that used to be a common practice."

Grace thought he was crazy. God didn't tell her it was okay. Perry thought of himself as a king. He believed he should have multiple wives and Grace could be the head wife. She could be over the other wives, and they would be her sister wives.

"I don't like the idea, and I'm not okay with it. If you did have other wives, I would leave you." He weighed if he wanted to keep pressing the issue or drop it.

Grace finally talked to Emma on the phone one day when Perry wasn't home.

"I feel like I'm an empty shell of the woman I used to be. I cry every day." It was the first time she told her mother of how Perry had yelled at her and called her names, and that she was dying inside. "He treats me worse than anyone has ever treated me. How did I end up with the worst person I know? Why is he doing this?"

Grace was waiting for Emma to tell her to leave Perry, but she didn't say it. Instead, Emma encouraged her to talk to Perry about how she felt. Emma suggested that perhaps if Perry knew how she felt when he mistreated her, he would stop. Grace promised her mother she would talk to Perry.

That evening, Perry and Grace went out to a restaurant, which they did almost daily. As they were sitting down, Perry said, "I just had a strange conversation with your mother. She called and asked me how I was doing. I said everything was fine. Then she said she just wanted me to know she was praying for me. Why would your mother be saying that? Is there something you're not telling me? What have you told her?"

Grace didn't want to confess that she had talked to her mother because he had made it very clear that he did not want Emma to know their business and the personal details of their marriage.

"Well, Perry, there is something I want to talk about with you."

He stood and interrupted her. "What did you tell your mother?"

"Calm down. Sit down and let's talk," Grace whispered.

"Tell me what your mother said or we're leaving."

"Perry, I want to talk to you."

"WE HAVE TO LEAVE NOW," he huffed, his face growing red. Grace didn't want to leave. She wanted to have a quiet conversation at a table, but Perry wasn't going to let that happen. He took seven-month-old Ben and went out to their SUV.

Grace kept repeating she had something to talk about, but Perry kept insisting that they were leaving. Grace didn't want to get in the car. She knew the yelling would continue. The restaurant employees were watching, and Grace hoped somebody would call the police. She did not want to go home with Perry. She would rather be on the street than at home with him, but he physically pushed her into the car and they drove away.

They rode in silence for several blocks, then Perry pulled over in a residential street and got into the back seat and sobbed. He said she was the crazy one for not getting in the car with him. He reminded her that the police could come after him because she made him look crazy. Grace felt numb inside. She secretly wished the cops would go after him. She sat there, stone-faced.

The next morning, Grace called Emma and asked her why she had called Perry. Grace felt that was the worst thing Emma could have done. Because of that Perry had said he couldn't trust Grace anymore, but at least now Emma knew what had been going on. Perry knew she had talked to her mother about him and that went against his rule that she wasn't allowed to speak to anyone about him. Emma admitted she was scared for Grace and didn't know what to do. She didn't know what the right thing would be, so she prayed, and she had told Perry that she was praying.

When Grace was in the third trimester of her second pregnancy, Perry announced that he wanted to go back to church. Grace was excited, yet it felt strange doing it again after such a long time. They started going back to Joe Rodgers' church, but often they did not go to church because Grace had to be in the nursery with Ben. Perry did not want anyone except Grace, including himself, to take care of Ben, so Grace took

Ben into the nursery during most of the service. Perry did not want to hear Ben crying during the service. If there was one cry, he made her take Ben out of the service.

One Sunday morning, Perry told Grace he was tired of waiting for her to get ready. He thought she should be able to get herself and Ben ready and he shouldn't have to wait on her. She was incredulous because she had to wait for him more often than he waited for her. She got herself and Ben ready to go to church. They sat by the door for thirty minutes waiting for Perry to be ready.

When he finally came down, he walked right past her without saying a word, and went out and sat in the car. She quickly grabbed Ben and the diaper bag, locked the door, and put Ben in the car seat and got into her seat.

Perry started yelling. "Why did I have to wait for you?"

"I've been waiting on you for 30 minutes."

"I thought I told you to be ready. You can't get your sh*t together?"

By the time they had driven one block, she was crying. All the way to church, he blasted her.

"Why can't you be more like your mother? She gets up early. She has a happy attitude." Perry criticized her from every angle. He told her what a bad mother and wife she was. She apologized and tried to appease him.

By the time they got to church, Grace was utterly deflated. Her eyes were red from crying, and she was emotionally drained. She felt exhausted from being verbally assaulted all the way to church. They were late and sat in the back. Perry's sister Patty looked at her after the service and commented on how tired she looked. Patty did not know what was going on. Nobody did.

Nobody knew how Perry treated her because once they got to church, he turned on the charm and was friendly and hugging people and showed everybody how much he loved her. They would have dinner with family after church, all while

Perry presented them as a loving family. He acted the part of a loving father and husband, but at home, it was different.

For Christmas, they traveled to Arlington, Texas to visit Perry's father. Grace got to meet more of Perry's extended family, and he spent some time playing music with his cousin. They also went to North Texas to visit Perry's aunt who had a house by a lake, and they met some more cousins. It was a fun and relaxing trip because Perry was on his best behavior.

What Grace didn't realize was that Perry was a narcissist and suffered from a superiority complex that so many tall men have. He was tall and good-looking, which is what attracted her to him, but he grew to believe he was entitled to and deserved special privileges because of his height. Perry thought he was better than others, that he was God's gift, not only to women but to humankind. He enjoyed looking down on people and feeling like he was superior.

Perry wanted Grace to meet his needs, but he was not interested in meeting her needs. He was interested in controlling her and her emotions. He cried and threw tantrums and used anything he could to get his way. Perry was the most important person in their relationship, the only one who mattered. He did not listen when she told him what she wanted. He did not care about her. He cared only about himself. It wasn't easy to see this because he apologized and said all the right things, but he was an excellent liar and manipulator, practiced in getting his way. He believed the rules didn't apply to him.

Perry liked to receive compliments and often if Grace complimented him, he wouldn't return it, but would instead give himself an even bigger compliment. He was very confident and could be socially charming. Perry needed to let people know how smart he was. He argued with anybody, and he didn't feel good unless he felt like he won the argument.

He let Grace know things had to be very high quality to meet his standards. A restaurant had to be high quality to be good enough for him to go there. He wanted his good shirts to be expensive and have a glossy sheen to them. He needed expensive hair products because he was a diva. He needed to spend a lot of time in the bathroom because he was the king. He needed to groom himself for an extra-long time because his appearance and image mattered more than she did.

He also told Grace he needed to eat high-quality foods. Ground hamburger wasn't good enough for him, he needed steak, but it had to be the right cut and it had to be cooked to perfection. He wanted name brand foods, not store brands. He claimed store brands tasted worse to him and were not good enough for him. He had lots of digestive and health issues and wanted Grace to cater to him. He couldn't wipe his butt with the same toilet paper everybody else used. He needed the most expensive high-quality, thick, quilted toilet paper that was extra soft. He wiped himself with their washcloths because toilet paper just wasn't good enough.

He needed Grace because she was nice and stroked his ego. He needed her to take care of his child-like needs. He bragged that he was an alpha male and would not follow anyone.

Perry kept Grace bound to him by telling her she was the most beautiful girl in the world. He lavished her with kisses and affection and swept her off her feet. He said she was his queen, implying that he was a king. However, eventually that behavior stopped, and it was all about him again. When Grace was feeling empty and drained emotionally and verbally abused by him, Perry came back and apologized, filling her up with compliments. He said all the right things to make her feel good again. He roped her back into him and she tried to love and trust him again. She couldn't see the pattern.

7

A NEW BABY AND A NEW HOUSE

Perry and Grace had a second baby one year after their first baby. Ben had just learned to walk. Ben stayed with his aunt Esther while Grace was in the hospital. When Grace got to the hospital, she asked for pain medication, but they said the baby would be born before the drug would have a chance to kick in. Perry was sitting beside her, holding her hand, smiling. Grace struggled to relax and breathe. She gave three hard pushes, and the baby was born. They nicknamed him Jimmy.

Grace weaned Ben so she could nurse Jimmy. Life with two babies was a bit difficult at first, but Grace found ways to adjust. Her eleven-year-old niece, Jazzy, came to help her. Getting housework done was a lot harder. Perry bought a blowup mattress and put it in the living room. He didn't want Grace and the babies to disturb his precious sleep, so he slept in his king-sized bed, and Grace slept in the living room with the babies on the blowup mattress.

Perry seemed to be gone even more and was burying himself in his business. He spent a lot of time out in the garage, on the computer, brainstorming, creating, writing, making music, writing songs, and talking on the phone. He eventually moved a table into the living room on which there was a computer, a printer and a few other things. Sometimes he worked in the house.

Sometimes, Grace took the kids outside while Perry was in the house when he wanted to have some quiet time to get some work done. One afternoon they were out for quite a while and were on the porch swing. Jimmy fell asleep while Grace was holding him. Her arms were getting tired, so she thought she would quietly go in the house and quickly take the boys upstairs. Perry was on the phone, so she quickly walked through the door and went upstairs and put Jimmy in his bed. Then Ben and Grace stayed in the bedroom. Ben had made a few small talking sounds when they came inside, but he wasn't loud. They were as quiet as possible. Perry was in the living room talking on the phone.

After a few minutes, Perry finished his phone call. He was furious that she did not stay outside while he made his phone call. Grace heard several loud booms and crashing sounds. She didn't know what that sound was, but she assumed it was Perry making those noises. Then she heard him go out the door. Grace cautiously went downstairs. While she was still on the stairs, she began to see little splinters of wood all over the living room. She couldn't figure out what she was seeing. Perry had broken something. To her horror, she realized he had smashed her Washburn guitar over her rocking chair. They were both shattered in thousands of pieces.

He had broken her heart, too. Perry had destroyed two things that were precious to her. She knew for sure that he did not value her or her feelings. She should have called the police at that moment, but the thought never crossed her mind. Perry blamed her for making him do it. He said he did it because she had disobeyed him and had come inside the house while he was still on the phone. He made her clean up his mess. She had to pick up all the little fragments of wood. She had to cover up his behavior and take the responsibility because it was she who had set him off.

When the boys were quite small, Perry's passion for Grace had begun to fade. He did not enjoy making love to her. He did not care about how he could meet her needs or help her to enjoy lovemaking. When they did have sex, it was all about pleasing him and doing what he wanted. He hardly touched Grace and rarely fondled or caressed her. He stroked himself more than he touched her. Grace felt neglected and ignored many times during their sexual encounters.

Sometimes they fought, and Perry wanted to have sex after the fight. The sex did not solve anything. Sometimes he was angry during sex and caused her a great deal of physical pain. He was rough, and it caused Grace to feel even more broken. Perry told Grace that the sex was a way for them to make up after a fight. Having sex after a fight was a way for him to dominate her, much like a dog marks his territory. Once he had sex with her, Perry felt he had power and control over her, even though she did not realize that's what was happening.

Sex was not satisfying or enjoyable for Grace for the next several years. She felt as if she competed for his affection with porn and strip club girls and prostitutes and girls he was texting on his phone. Almost everyone seemed to be more important to him than she was.

Things were not always bad. They had fun moments when they went to the park. They went on bike rides. She had a small child trailer attached to the back of her bike to set her two little kids in, and she'd go biking around the neighborhood. They also went out to eat quite a lot.

She became involved in the church. Perry stopped attending, but he said she could still go. She spent nearly every Sunday in the nursery because Ben was very securely attached to her. Often, they had lunch with Joe and Carolyn after church.

Perry's business had fallen apart, and he started another, but that also did not last very long. Perry worked for a short time with a company called NIC. It was an office job. Grace did not understand much of what they did. Perry claimed he got fired from that job because he would not tuck in his shirt. Perry would not yield. He was strong-willed and rebellious and wasn't a good employee.

Perry started working as a taxi driver. He didn't make much money doing that, but he planned to start flipping houses.

He found a new house; a brand-new home where nobody had ever lived. It had two floors, four large bedrooms, a large kitchen, and two living rooms. Since Grace had good credit, and Perry had poor credit, he decided that they should get the house. After living in the first house for two years, he asked the next-door neighbors if they wanted to rent from him. It was an upgrade for them. So the neighbors moved into Perry's house, and Perry's family moved into a huge, brand new house. It seemed huge to them.

Grace loved having a big, beautiful house. The boys had a room they shared. Grace usually stayed in the room with them until they fell asleep. Perry complained about Grace disturbing his sleep when she got up during the night to take care of the boys, so they put an air mattress into the guest room, and that's where Grace slept. The fourth bedroom was Perry's office and was where his computer equipment and all his recording equipment was.

When they moved into their new house, they didn't bring their king-sized bed. Instead, Perry bought a new king-sized bed and nightstand tables to go beside the bed. They also bought a brand-new living room set with matching couch, loveseat, chair, and footstool. Even though they were pretty poor, they bought it all on credit. Perry was taxi driving and not making very much money.

Perry wanted Grace to go back to work when Jimmy was six months old. She went back to the company she used to work for before she stopped to be a stay-at-home mother. They scheduled her to work nights. She only worked a couple of nights before Perry called her in a panic.

"Jimmy will not stop crying. I can't comfort him. Please come home. He wants his mommy."

Grace left her job. She apologized to the company and told them she needed to quit working for them. She said she was sorry for the trouble she had caused. Perry was not capable of taking care of the boys. He did not bathe them. He did not want to change their diapers. He was not comforting or nurturing.

Grace continued to be a stay at home mother. One day, she went shopping at Walmart. Soon after she arrived, Perry called her.

"You need to come home. Jimmy has a big load in his diaper."

"Well, you need to change it. Man up. Be the dad. You can do it." She hung up and continued shopping.

Perry called back a few minutes later and said, "I did it. I changed his diaper."

"Good job. I knew you could do it."

"I threw up. The smell was too disgusting for me and caused me to gag. That's why I can't change diapers."

Perry spent a majority of his time out in the garage. He had a computer out there. He was smoking and spitting on the floor of the garage. The garage grew disgusting because he never cleaned it. Grace took care of the children and met all their needs. She put them in the trailer attached to the bike and went on bike rides. She loved being a mother and enjoyed spending time with the boys. Her other responsibilities included cooking, cleaning, shopping and paying the bills.

Perry dictated every area of Grace's life. He told her when she should pay a bill, what method she should use, how much she would pay. He told her how much money she could spend. He determined how much she could see her family. Perry dictated when they had sex and when they slept together. He made many decisions for her.

Grace did not see their problems as detrimental. She thought all marriages had issues and people didn't talk about them. She was sure that other married couples had fights, too, and that she and Perry were only going through the same problems as other couples.

Grace grew to believe Perry regretted marrying her. He often told her to go home to her mom. He was easily angered and annoyed with her. While Perry often told her he loved her, Grace knew he secretly wished he had not married her.

Perry didn't enjoy being a parent, either. He did not spend much time with the kids. He loved them, but he rarely took care of them. He was selfish and only wanted Grace to take care of his needs. He hardly considered her needs or wanted to take care of her.

Grace realized she was pregnant for the third time. Her cycle was running about a week late. She was happy and excited. She loved the idea of having more children. She told Perry excitedly,

"Guess what! I think I'm pregnant."

"Did you take a pregnancy test?"

"I didn't."

"Well, then how can you know if you're pregnant? You must have cheated on me," he accused her.

Perry called her names and made her feel stupid. He insisted they drive to the nearest pharmacy right away and get a pregnancy test. Grace sat in the car crying, deflated. Perry came out with a pregnancy test in a few minutes. They went home again, and he insisted she sit on the toilet and use the test. He stood in the doorway and watched her. She didn't have the urge to pee, and all she could express was a small trickle which was not enough to get a good reading on a pregnancy stick, so when the test was negative, Perry scolded her and mocked her and made her feel stupid. She went up to the master bedroom closet and hid in the closet and cried. She wanted a baby, but she knew Perry did not.

Two days later, she had a miscarriage. She did not tell Perry; he was so angry, she did not feel safe even confiding in him that she had had a miscarriage. Her miscarriage lasted a week. She thought it was just as well because Perry did not want the baby.

One summer day, money was very tight, and it was time to pay a bill. Perry asked Grace to go to the bank and make a deposit. He was very specific about how she had to make the deposit. He wanted it made in the drive through, but she deposited at the ATM. When she came home, Perry questioned her and flew into a terrible rage when she told him. He was shaking and sweating. He yelled and flipped the dining room table on its side, making a hole in the linoleum.

Grace tried to get him to calm down, but nothing worked. Finally she took Jimmy and went upstairs. She laid him on the changing table to change his diaper. Since there was no way to calm Perry down, she just wanted to get away from him. He followed her into the bedroom room and grabbed her arm and bruised her. She screamed and started crying. He continued yelling. He wanted her to leave again and go back to the bank and fix her mistake. She took the boys with her and left again.

Grace called her mother and told her Perry grabbed her arm and left a bruise. Grace asked her mother if she should leave Perry. Emma didn't know what to say. She had never encountered a situation like this before. Nobody in their family had ever been divorced or abused.

Emma said, "I will come and get you if you want me to."

Grace was undecided. She knew she could not leave while Perry was at home. She wanted to go home and get their stuff and then leave. When she got home, her heart fell when she saw Perry's taxi parked in the driveway.

Perry came out and said they should go for a drive to cool down. He apologized for the way he treated her and told her she should hold him accountable for his actions. He knew his behavior was unacceptable. He apologized and said all the right words. Grace wanted to believe his apology and forgive him.

Grace hoped Perry would change. He tried to convince her that he was improving, but she was blind to the pattern that everything would be good for a while, then he would blow up again. Nothing truly changed. She kept holding on, waiting for the day when his behavior was a thing of the past. She believed in Perry. She trusted he would become better and he would be a great man someday. He told her he could be the nice guy that she needed.

While they were out on their drive, Emma called to find out if everything was all right and find out if she needed to come to get Grace. Grace told her everything was better since their fight was over. When Perry found out she had told Emma what happened, he blew up again. He claimed he could no longer trust Grace. He had told her not to talk to anybody about the intimate details of their marriage. Grace did not think she was talking about the intimate details of their marriage. She did not speak to Emma about their sex life. Grace spoke to her mother when she was scared and needed advice. Neither she nor her mother thought that was inappropriate.

Perry tried to convince Grace they should not talk to anybody about what they fought about because that's not something married couples did. He believed that married couples had fights but didn't talk about it to others. He had seen his grandfather beat up his grandmother. They had been married for more than fifty years. He convinced himself, and Grace, that as long as he was not hitting her his behavior was acceptable. He thought it was okay to yell at her. She told him she didn't want him to yell at her, and he apologized and said he would stop, but he never did.

Their fights were terrible. He didn't physically hit her but he was verbally abusive. Perry kicked a cabinet door in the kitchen and bent the wood. He took one of her baking pans and threw it out in the field next to the house. One night, Grace was standing at the top of the stairs, and he was at the bottom. He was angry, and he threw the remote control for the TV up the stairs towards her. She stepped to the side. The remote hit the door behind her, leaving a three-inch hole. Perry became so angry at her, he got in her face and yelled as loudly as he could. Although he didn't hit her, he pushed her backward until she was laying on the bed and he was standing over her, yelling in her face. He was a bully. He spit in her face as he screamed. Grace just wanted him away from her. She seethed with hatred for him. She thought about leaving him many times but didn't dare make a plan.

Grace knew Perry was watching porn. He told her all men did it and that it was normal. He said he was not cheating on her and there was nothing wrong with him watching porn and taking care of his own needs.

One day Grace came home from shopping. Jimmy had fallen asleep, so she quietly carried him upstairs to her bedroom to lay him on the bed. Perry was sitting in her bedroom in front of the computer with his pants down around his ankles. When he saw her standing in the hall, he became angry at her for sneaking up on him. He quickly got up and closed the door. She told him she wasn't trying to sneak up on him; she was trying to be quiet because she was holding a sleeping baby.

Perry was angry at Grace because he thought she was not only not providing what he wanted but also standing in the way of him getting what he wanted. In his mind, he was allowed to be abusive and angry at her if he didn't get that to which he believed himself entitled.

Grace felt like she needed to accept his excuses. She thought that because he was a man and men have a physical need to ejaculate, this must be what men did. She believed she needed to forgive him because that's what a Christian wife should do. She couldn't expect him to be perfect; she needed to accept his flaws. If other women could forgive their husbands for cheating on them, then she could forgive Perry for watching porn. She tried to be everything she thought Perry wanted her to be. She tried to have sex whenever he wanted it so that he would not be tempted to look for someone else. She wondered what the women in the porn videos had or did that she was not doing or didn't have. She felt like she was competing with them for her husband's attention. She tried to fulfill all his needs and to be and do all that he needed from her.

Grace should not have accepted his excuses to watch porn. Nothing good came out of it. It did not help Perry or their marriage in any way. If women have to keep themselves in check and not cheat on their husbands, then men also need to discipline themselves and keep themselves in check. They are not entitled to watch porn to fulfill their needs.

Grace knew she needed to forgive Perry, but, when there was no repentance, no change of heart, and no change in behavior from him, she felt she should at least stand up for herself, if not for her marriage, and not put up with his porn watching. She needed to realize that it was not her fault that he was watching porn. It's not because she wasn't good enough. It's not because her boobs weren't big enough. It's not because she wasn't giving him enough sex. He watched porn because he wanted to see other women. That was his problem. It wasn't her fault.

Perry often did say he was going to find a prostitute because Grace was not giving him the sex he thought he deserved.

Grace didn't realize that was what he wanted because he was selfish. If she dared to stand up for herself, Perry told her she was selfish and wasn't showing him love. He tried to make her feel guilty so that she would give him what he wanted. He was not interested in meeting her needs, only in making sure she met his needs.

Grace put up with a lot of crap from Perry. She endured a lot that was solely inflating his ego. By submitting to him, she was giving him power over her, and he became abusive with that power. He was not a giving, loving, gentle husband as talked about in the Book of Timothy.

One day when Grace was home alone with the boys, Ben threw a temper tantrum. He was entirely out of control screaming and crying and throwing a fit. She put him in the highchair for some time out. Grace finally decided she had to spank him. Ben calmed down after that. He was able to understand that she was not giving in to him. Perry and Grace had agreed that they would not spank their children, but she made a judgment call, not because she was angry, but because she thought it the best way to diffuse the situation.

A few days later, Grace told Perry what happened and how well it worked out. His eyes filled with rage.

"WHAT! HOW COULD YOU? That is not what we agreed on, Grace! You abused our child! I can't trust you anymore! I'm going to call the police! I'm going to have to turn you in!"

He would not calm down. Instead, he recorded Grace confessing that she spanked her son in a moment when he needed it. Perry threatened to turn her in, but he didn't call the police, probably because he had marijuana in the garage.

Perry was driving a taxi at the time. Often, he would come home very late, or in the early hours of the morning. Grace often laid awake at night fearing Perry was with another woman. One night, he came home around midnight. He confessed that he had visited a strip club that night.

"Why would you go there?

"Because I had a customer who wanted to go there. I went into the strip club and watched the ladies. It just made me more thankful for you, because you're more virtuous than those ladies. Those ladies are just trashy whores. I'm thankful for the way you are and that you're not like one of those girls."

The way he said it made Grace feel privileged and special. He made her feel wanted and beautiful. He often told her she was the most beautiful girl in the world. It was his way to justify visiting a strip club. He reasoned he was honest about it, so she should accept his behavior because he wasn't hiding it. Perry claimed the strippers were trashy whores to make Grace feel better about herself, even though he enjoyed watching the strippers.

One day Emma called Grace and said they would be coming through Westerville. They were willing to pick up Grace and the boys on the way to an event if they wanted to go. Of course, Grace wanted to go. Perry became enraged that they wanted to come over without his permission and take away his wife and kids. It was just for the day. Grace tried to explain that they wouldn't bother him and they wouldn't come in the house. She assured him she'd be back later the same day, but he wouldn't have it. He wouldn't let Emma come, and he wouldn't let Grace and the boys go with them.

He even had a problem with Joe and Carolyn coming over. One day, they needed to come over to drop off some diapers and supplies because Perry and Grace were poor enough to need assistance, but Perry yelled at them on the phone and told them they couldn't come in. They waited in the driveway for a while, then they left the packages at the front door and went away. Perry was a total jerk to his family and Grace's family. He was a jerk to people in public. He was a jerk on the road to other drivers. He was rude and disrespectful wherever he went.

Perry had a big problem with Joe. One night, he and Joe went out to talk. Perry recorded the conversation because he wanted Joe to confess something. He asked Joe if he remembered beating him up when he was sixteen. Joe remembered, and they talked about it. Perry claimed Joe threatened to kill him when he was a teen because Perry was so disrespectful to Carolyn. Joe admitted it. Perry wanted Joe to know that he could defend himself now and if Joe became a threat to him, he would have to defend himself, meaning he would be willing to kill Joe. Perry made a point to let Grace know about this conversation. He wanted Grace to realize he was capable of killing someone.

Carolyn talked to Grace several times about leaving Perry.

"Grace, I don't know why you don't just leave Perry."

Grace was still trying to prove how committed and submissive she was. Grace asked Joe and Carolyn if she could stay with them if she did decide to leave Perry. They said that would be fine.

Grace didn't know how to leave. Sometimes she hated Perry and other times she felt like she still loved him. She thought she wanted him to be in their boys' lives, but at times he acted as though they were not important to him. He spent hours in the garage. It was rare that he engaged with the boys. He never fed them or bathed them, and he rarely changed a diaper. He barely played with them, but he told Grace he was a good father because he was there. Grace knew Perry would be devastated if she left. She did not want to hurt him. She didn't know how she would be able to get herself and the boys and their clothes away from him. The police would have had to be involved, and she knew he would be so hurt if she involved the police. She knew he would come after her and that it could end badly if she attempted to leave.

The economy was on its way down. Their monthly mortgage payment went up by several hundred dollars. They weren't making enough money to be flexible with anything. Suddenly, they couldn't make the payments on their new house. They had only been there one year. They received an eviction notice for non-payment. Perry decided they should sell as much as they could and move to Texas to live with his father, so they had a garage sale and then packed up what was left. Grace left some things at her parents' house. They put a lot of boxes into Joe and Carolyn's garage. Perry and Grace packed up their SUV and drove to Texas.

The renters at their first house stopped making payments because the husband cheated on his wife and she he left him. They abandoned the house. Roaches and mice moved into the house. Food and clothes were left, and the lights were left burning. That house also went into foreclosure.

There were many times as they talked about moving to Texas that Grace thought about leaving Perry. She had grown discouraged and hardened. Her heart had been broken so many times, and she hated Perry. As he yelled at her, Grace thought about how much she hated him. So many times she swore that, once they got to Texas, she would turn around and head back to Ohio without Perry.

As they were packing their stuff into Carolyn's garage, Perry asked Grace, "Are you moving to Texas with me?"

"I'm thinking of not."

"What? Why?"

"It's because you smoke and I told you I hated it and you continue to do it."

"I'll quit."

Grace thought it would be great if he did quit, so she decided to give him another chance. But time proved he never quit.

The night before they left for Texas, they met Grace's whole family at a restaurant to say goodbye. Grace dearly loved her family and secretly dreaded moving away from them. She had a lot of anxiety, but she tried to present a cool facade. However, inside she knew things were falling apart. She was afraid to tell her family what was really going on. If Perry found out that she told her family the truth about their marriage, he'd say she ruined everything and that he could no longer trust her. It would be her fault if her family did not like Perry and he would try to keep her away from her family. She wanted her family to like him so she could continue to have some communication with them. She was blind to the fact that he was already trying to separate her from her family by moving them to Texas. She was afraid of Perry but couldn't seem to accept what he was doing.

Grace tried to present to her family that while they were in a financial crisis, their marriage was good. She didn't want them to worry about her because then they might confront Perry. If they confronted Perry, that would be bad for her, so she told her family that she loved Perry and that they were happy.

Despite an uneasy feeling, Emma said, "If you're happy, then I'm happy for you and happy to let you go."

Emma tried to let go of Perry and Grace and give it to God. She knew many of Perry's relatives lived in Texas, and that Grace looked forward to getting to spend time with them and making new connections.

Grace knew Perry did not have warm feelings for her family. She knew he hated Ohio. He was depressed, and he knew it. Ohio was going through an economic recession, and he couldn't make enough money. Many people lost their homes. They weren't the only ones.

Their last night in Ohio, they spent the night at Carolyn's house. The next morning, after breakfast, they said their good-byes and started for Texas. Grace tried to ignore her uneasy feelings. She was determined to make the best of the situation and stay committed to Perry. She tried to make him happy and do what he wanted.

A root of bitterness had grown in her heart because of how awful Perry had been to her. Sometimes she hated him. There was hardly any love in her heart for him.

Perry was a psychopath. He manipulated Grace by doing anything he could to get his way. He lied to get her to feel sorry for him so she would do things for him. He lied about what he was doing to get her to do what he wanted. He did anything to control her.

Grace felt she was always walking on eggshells around him. She was afraid to tell him she wanted to see friends or family, or that they wanted to see her. She was scared to make him angry. He made her feel guilty for wanting to spend time with anyone besides him. He knew her weaknesses and where she was vulnerable. He used what he knew about her to hurt her and cut her down. He knew just the right words to say that would hurt her the most. He made her feel confused, scared, embarrassed, and alone. He was rude to her and said horrible things about her friends and family. He slowly cut people out of her life to isolate her more and more. He said it was because they were a family and he loved her so much, but it was about control and isolation. He did not want her to have anyone or any support telling her what he was doing was wrong.

When Perry made her cry, Grace confronted him; he always apologized and said he knew what he did was wrong, but then, he would somehow blame her or her friends and family for what he did, saying somebody triggered him. Somebody always did something he did not like that made him angry, and he took his anger out on Grace. He made her feel bad for confronting him or saying anything at all. He promised he was going to change and make it sound like he was sorry. However, he did not seem to have remorse, and he did not respect her feelings or address her needs at all.

Perry always managed to tell Grace how much hurt he felt, and how broken his childhood was in ways that made her feel sorry for him. He begged her to promise she would never leave him.

When Perry did something nice for Grace, he did it solely to receive recognition and praise. He wanted to appear as a wonderful person. He would bring it up to her multiple times to remind her of the nice things he did, to prove he wasn't a bad guy. He wanted to control how she felt about him.

Before they were married, Perry was so funny and seemed to be the life of the party. He was charming and friendly and nice, but it had been a façade, and after they were married the mask came off. He trapped Grace into staying with him by being wonderful at times. He wanted to hear her say how lucky she was to be with him.

Perry always wanted to know what she was doing. He called her multiple times during the day, and if she didn't answer his calls, he would continuously call until she answered. Then he would be furious and accuse her of cheating and keeping secrets from him. However, he was allowed to do whatever he wanted. Grace wasn't allowed to question him. He had control over her and everything she did.

Grace couldn't see that she was being abused. She knew she did not like the way he yelled at her, but she thought she could change her attitude and it would help him calm down. She thought that if only she could help him heal from his issues, he'd be the soft man she knew he was. When he told her she needed to be grateful for what she had, she agreed with him. When he told her she was selfish, she agreed that she needed to die to herself, just as the Bible says. Grace needed to humble herself and give up her rights and do whatever was in her power to get along with him. She needed to see him as more important than herself.

Grace made sure she did things that spoke his love language, which just happened to be acts of service. He often reminded her that if she made a sandwich for him or did other favors for him, he knew that she loved him and that's how she could best show him that she loved him. She wanted to show him her love. She wanted him to feel her love, so she did her best to make sure she was filling his love tank by fulfilling her obligations and doing what a good wife is supposed to do. It never occurred to her to demand that he should meet her needs.

Perry loved to quote Proverbs 27:15. "A nagging wife is like a dripping faucet."

Grace did not want to be a nagging wife, so she shut up. Whenever she reminded Perry about anything, he believed that she was nagging. She did not know how not to be annoying and nagging. After a while, she shut down and tried not to say anything which did not help her feel heard or improve their relationship.

The abuse happened slowly, gradually, over time. Grace could not see it beginning to form into abuse. When Perry told her to hurry up or told her how stressed he was from working so hard, she excused his impatience because she felt it was her duty to make things comfortable and easier for him. He constantly reminded her it was her job, as his helper.

8

ANSWERED PRAYER

Scott had a three-story townhouse that was part of a long row of other townhouses. Grace and the boys slept in Scott's bedroom on the top floor, which contained only one bed and a bathroom. Perry slept on the first floor which also had only one bed and a bathroom. The second floor was the main living area, the kitchen, and the living room.

Perry had a job lined up. He got work orders to fix computers or printers and do other kinds of technical work. It wasn't long before the bank repossessed their SUV. Although they were at the end of their financial resources, they bought a small car with lower payments for Perry to use for work. He soon began to make money.

Grace saw that Perry was still smoking, which enraged her. She found herself becoming a hard, hate-filled, angry, bitter person. She didn't have heated outbursts; instead, when she got angry, she cried. She also noticed that since they had moved to Texas, Perry seemed to calm down. He didn't seem to be quite as angry, so she set aside her plans to leave him.

Grace thought Perry was bearable to live with, and besides, she didn't want to leave him. She wanted a typical, happy family. She wanted the boys to have their dad in their lives. While he would still get mad at Grace once in a while, it wasn't as often.

Grace started going to a new church on the south side of Arlington. Although Perry did not want to go, he didn't have a problem with her going. She went there for a few months. On one Sunday, she heard God softly speaking to her heart.

"How can you stand here and pretend to worship me when you know you have been carrying anger in your heart for a long, long time?"

Grace was conflicted. She knew she was carrying bitterness and hatred in her heart, but she wanted to repent. She cried through the rest of the worship service and asked God to change her and help her to be a joyful wife and mother.

After the service, she had lunch with Perry and apologized for being so angry. She told him she wanted to be a joyful wife and mother.

He was impressed and said, "Now I know you're supposed to go to that church. That's where you're supposed to be."

About a month later, Perry came to Grace and apologized for the way he had been treating her. He said he realized that he had been breaking down her confidence and self-esteem.

He said, "You have a heart of gold. You are a precious child of God, and you are a beautiful daughter."

Perry apologized for all the damage he had done. Grace was surprised and was glad to hear such beautiful words. For a while, she thought Perry had changed. Life seemed to be better, and they seemed to be getting along better.

They enjoyed getting together with Perry's relatives. They spent time in East Texas with Perry's aunt at her lake house. They had barbeques with Scott and with Perry's sister, Patty, and her family. Although Grace enjoyed spending time with them, Perry did not seem to appreciate it. They spent their first Christmas in Texas with his grandparents. Grace was happy, and life was good.

After living at Scott's house for six months, they found an apartment in a town called Duncanville. Perry went back to Ohio to get their stuff out of his mother's garage. Their family of four moved into a one-bedroom apartment. Ben and Jimmy were now three and two, respectively. They brought immeasurable joy to Perry and Grace's hearts. Perry seemed to come to enjoy being around his family again. He played music and smoked marijuana with his cousin.

Grace had started going to a different church, one that had been recommended by Carolyn, who knew the pastor. Grace loved that church; it felt like home. The boys loved their classes, and that's where the family worshipped for the next several years.

Grace told her pastor that Perry was still smoking marijuana even though he had told her he would quit. The pastor recommended counseling but cautioned that other than that, he didn't know how to help. Grace knew there was no way Perry would go to a counselor.

She called up a dear friend and asked what she should do. Her friend advised Grace to throw him out of their home. While Perry was at work, Grace had the maintenance man change the locks. Then Grace took all of Perry's clothes, set them outside the door in suitcases, and locked the door.

When Perry came home from work, and the door was locked, he knocked on the door. Three-year-old Ben, wanting to be a big helpful boy, let Perry in. Grace tried to push him out, but she was no match for him He asked her why his suitcases were in the hall.

"I'm throwing you out."

"Why?"

"You said you would quit smoking and you lied. I don't want you living with us anymore."

Perry convinced Grace that he needed to stay and that his family needed him. He advised her to do some research on marijuana.

Grace did some research and was surprised to find that there are some legitimate health benefits to marijuana. It can help people think clearly and calm down and stay focused. It can relieve symptoms from some ailments. She was surprised to find that it was illegal; Perry told her it was because legislators were greedy. Perry told her he smoked marijuana because it helped him calm down. He said he had terrible anxiety and smoking helped him calm down so he could go to sleep. He also claimed it helped him to focus his mind and get his work done. That was the strangest conversation they had ever had.

Perry and Grace started finding some peace in their relationship. There were still moments of anger, but not like when they lived in Ohio. Perry was working, and Grace was home with her boys. She took the boys to church and also started going to a mothers' group at that church. Perry continued to smoke marijuana and hang out with his cousin and other guys who played music and smoked pot.

Grace's relationship with God was going strong. One desire of her heart was to have a daughter. She began to pray for a daughter, believing that she might have a daughter someday. Perry often said he didn't want any more kids. Grace told him she had faith she would have a daughter eventually. He just rolled his eyes and ignored her.

Two months later, Grace discovered she was pregnant. She was delighted and surprised. She knew right away that God had answered her prayers for a daughter, although it was much sooner than she expected. She used a pregnancy test to confirm her suspicions but hid the pregnancy stick until she thought it was the appropriate time to show Perry. She had to be very sensitive about when she talked to Perry in order not to anger him or stress him out. She walked on eggshells so she wouldn't disturb him.

Perry noticed Grace was in a mood. He asked her what was going on.

"I don't want to talk about it."

He coaxed her.

"I'm not ready to talk about it." He kept pushing her and prodding her until she finally said, "My period is late."

"Oh, well, I guess we'll wait and see and cross that bridge when we get there."

She was surprised by his lack of reaction. She went into the kitchen because she didn't want the conversation to escalate into a fight. Perry went out to the back patio where he spent a lot of time smoking and making phone calls. He saw her smiling in the kitchen. Grace was ecstatic she was pregnant, and Perry didn't appear to be angry. When he came back in, he told her he was glad she was happy.

He asked, "You're pregnant, aren't you?"

She admitted she was. She had the pregnancy test to prove it. Perry seemed to accept it and moved on casually.

Grace knew right away that this baby was a little girl and that her name would be Emily, after the Chupp family friend who was like a grandmother to Grace. Although Perry didn't like the name, Grace insisted.

During Grace's pregnancy, Perry told her he was afraid his daughter would hurt him like all the other girls he had known.

Grace tried to get him to see that all his other girlfriends were meant to leave him. She wanted to reassure him.

"I am the only one who was supposed to be with you. That doesn't mean that all girls will stab you in the heart and reject you. You haven't met our little girl yet, and so you can't make assumptions about her before she is even born."

Although their relationship was happier and more peaceful, when Grace talked about her family, she noticed that Perry always had something critical to say. He made fun of them or made derogatory remarks. He'd say how dumb he thought they were. Grace eventually stopped talking to him about her family because it just caused conflict. Although Grace was not aware of feeling sad at first, it became a weight on her heart.

The summer Grace was pregnant, she and the boys went to Ohio to celebrate her parents' fortieth wedding anniversary. All of the Chupp children had contributed to making an enormous, beautiful quilt for them. They had invited friends and relatives and had set up a tent in their yard. Grace hadn't seen her family for a year and a half and missed them. It was great to see everyone again.

When Grace returned home two weeks later, the apartment looked as if a giant party had been held there. Every dish and pan had been used and was sitting unwashed. The trash was overflowing. Every towel was dirty, and no laundry washed. Perry was conveniently unavailable to clean up his mess and left Grace and the boys to live in his filth. Grace cleaned it up because she hated the mess.

Grace didn't have spending money because Perry wouldn't let her have any. He was bringing in the income. It seemed they were always poor. They were always on a tight budget. Each week Grace bought groceries with whatever money Perry gave her to spend.

Once, Grace went grocery shopping and spent too much because she bought everything they needed instead of sticking to her budget. When she brought the groceries home, Perry exploded. He demanded she go back and get a refund. She took all the groceries back to the store and got a full refund. She was humiliated. They still needed groceries, so Perry sent her to a different store to get far fewer items. The next day, Grace's close friend bought a bunch of groceries for them and dropped it off at their door. That made a big difference to them.

It seemed they were barely getting what they needed. Perry wanted them to live on rice and beans. Grace was so frustrated because she was craving fruits and vegetables for herself and her boys.

Perry and Grace once again began having big fights, fights that left her feeling defeated and drained. One day, after they fought, Grace took the kids to the park to play. She felt so tired and emotionally drained that she lay down on a park bench. She just wanted to make all the fighting stop. An older woman saw Grace was crying and asked her what was wrong.

"My husband and I had a fight."

"You have to be strong, for your children."

Grace felt so weak and so defeated. She was exhausted. She tried to be strong, but it was hard because the people around her did not know anything of her struggles. She tried to present a happy face, but inside Grace was falling apart.

The family lived in Duncanville for one year, and then they moved again to a beautiful two-bedroom apartment in Richardson when she was seven months pregnant. Grace and the kids slept in one bedroom, and Perry took the other for himself.

One morning as Grace was making breakfast for the boys, she suddenly felt a small gush of liquid, she ran to the bathroom and realized her water had broken. She tiptoed into Perry's bedroom and woke him to tell him she was in labor.

He said, "Well, you'd better call somebody from church to take you to the hospital because I can't take you. I have to go to work."

Again, he made her feel unimportant and neglected. He hardly touched her or gave her affection anymore. He would prefer going to work to being with her, even though she was about to give birth to their third child.

Grace called a friend from church who said she could take Grace to the hospital that afternoon. Perry left and went to work. Grace was embarrassed that her husband wouldn't make time for her when she was about to deliver their baby.

Her friend came and picked up Grace and the boys. They dropped the kids off at their grandparents' house, then went to Arlington hospital. Her friend quickly prayed for Grace and the birth, then she left. Grace walked in alone and admitted herself. Perry wouldn't allow her to have a doula, or any friends or any relatives with her.

A few hours later, as the contractions came harder, Grace wished someone could have been by her side to hold her hand or encourage her or help her relax. She felt alone, but she held back the tears, trying to stay focused. She tried to relax and breathe through the contractions, but the pain became more than she could handle. The nurse offered an epidural, and Grace accepted it. Grace was then able to relax and manage the pain.

Seven hours after Grace arrived at the hospital, Perry came. He sat in a chair and looked at his phone.

"Why did you wait so long to come?" Grace asked.

"After work, I had dinner with the kids, and then I went home and took a shower. I came as soon as I could." He did not offer much support, but Grace was glad he at least was there for the birth.

Finally, Grace delivered her beautiful baby girl. Her name was Emily. Grace was delirious with exhaustion and joy. Perry stayed for a short time, and then he went home.

Life went on and Grace adjusted to having three kids. She had no one to help her at home. Perry was unavailable for Grace when she needed him, but she dared not voice that to him. She was more afraid than ever of angering him.

A month later, Joe and Carolyn came for a visit. There was going to be a reunion on Carolyn's side of the family. Perry planned not to go but told Grace she could go and take the kids. Grace drove with his sister, Patty, two hours North to Aunt Susan's lake house and spent two pleasant days there.

After they came home, Perry confessed to Grace that while they were gone, he had flown to Las Vegas and gambled and played blackjack. Grace was speechless. He was smiling as he told her how much fun it had been. He said he won $1,000, but Grace didn't know if that was the truth or if he just said that to make her feel better.

A month later, Grace had a minor surgical procedure. She asked Aunt Susan to come and hold baby Emily for her while she was in surgery. Again, Perry wasn't available for Grace when she needed him. He seemed to be dedicating more time to working even though he was self-employed. After the surgery,

Grace was in intense pain. She spent the majority of her days and nights laying down. The pain meds did not help decrease the pain but only made her more tired.

Perry was working long hours and did not take care of Grace. A neighbor offered to help her even though they had just met the day before surgery. It took Grace a month to heal from her surgery, and she was in extreme pain for two weeks of that month.

Grace enjoyed being a stay at home mother and doing fun things with her kids. She often took them to the park and children's events in the community room at their apartment complex. She became good friends with the events coordinator who also had a baby girl and a boy who was her sons' age. The two women frequently got together and let the kids play.

Soon, someone from the management office knocked on the door and asked Grace to come to the office so she could put her name on the apartment lease. Her new friend had innocently told the people in the office that Grace was Perry's wife. However, Perry wanted to act like they weren't married. He hadn't put Grace's name on the lease because he didn't want to pay the extra money. Perry panicked and asked Grace to visit her mother for an extended period. Grace was happy to do that. Perry got mad at Grace's friend and forbade Grace to speak to her anymore.

When Emily was four months old, Grace took the three kids to Ohio. They stayed at a hotel. It took two days to get to Joe and Carolyn's house. They were there for a few days. During that time, Emily became very sick and congested. Carolyn and Grace took her to the hospital. There they learned she had a respiratory virus, but because she was younger than six months old, there was nothing they could give her. In tears, they left the hospital.

The next day, Grace drove to her mother's. Emma gave her silver water to give to Emily. It released the mucus in the baby's throat, and she was able to cough it out. Within three days, she was doing much better, and the infection cleared up. Emma was welcoming, and her house seemed to have everything they needed. They stayed for six weeks. Grace loved having time with her family.

Perry called and said he missed Grace and needed her to come home, so they planned to return to Texas. Grace told him that he needed to clean the apartment before she came back. Perry told Grace that was why he couldn't live without her and missed her so much. He needed her to take care of the apartment because he felt that kind of work was beneath him. Perry wanted her to feel like he needed her and couldn't live without her. Nevertheless, he said he would clean the apartment for her.

When they arrived home, Grace could tell Perry had lived like a bachelor because every dish and pan and utensil was used and left uncleaned, sitting in a laundry basket beside the bathtub. Grace cleaned up all the things that Perry had used while he disappeared off to work.

Life went on, with Perry working a lot and Grace attending church and church gatherings. Perry ignored her unless he wanted her to show him that she loved him by fulfilling his sexual needs. He wanted her to prove that he was the most important thing in her life.

During intimate moments, he told her how to touch him, but he didn't act as if he was even attracted to her. Frustrated and disappointed, Grace talked to her pastor's wife Jan. She prayed with Grace and told her what God expected from a man and wife. She told Grace what Perry should be doing, but Grace knew Perry wasn't doing it.

One day, Grace was looking through Perry's phone and saw messages from a lot of different phone numbers. She saw that he had been texting and exchanging pictures with a lot of different women. Her heart started beating faster, and her skin felt cold and clammy. She felt like she was going to faint. Perry was cheating on her, and she thought that was the worst thing possible. She needed him to be there for his family, to provide income and love for them. She needed him to be a father to their children. Grace needed her husband. She didn't know what to do, as she had never read anything on how to handle a cheating husband.

Grace confronted Perry. He denied it.

"I have never cheated on you and I never will. Those women I talked to meant nothing to me. You are the most important thing in the world to me. Those women are just trashy whores, and I don't care about them. I am so thankful for you because you are a virtuous woman. I am so lucky to have you. I am the luckiest guy in the world."

He didn't apologize. Instead, he was angry that Grace had snooped on his phone. He thought she should stay out of his business. She knew Perry was watching porn, and doing things that dishonored her, but when she tried talking to him about it, he told her all guys did those things. He said all the right things to get her to believe in him again.

During the year they lived in Richardson, Perry managed to save five thousand dollars, and he seemed to be doing great financially. Grace didn't know about their good fortune, however, because Perry kept the bank accounts and bills and financial things hidden. He paid the bills and purchased what they needed. Often, he made big purchases impulsively without planning or talking to Grace. He was careless and ended up spending the money he had saved.

9

TWO DEATHS

When their apartment lease came up for renewal, Perry did not want to renew it, so they moved again to Lake Worth. In the fall, Ben started kindergarten. It was hard to watch their little boy carry his huge backpack and step up on that enormous bus to school. Ben enjoyed school. Jimmy and Emily went with Grace to the bus stop every day to wait for him to get off the bus.

Grace got her GED, the equivalent of a high school diploma, online. Perry encouraged her to do it, and she was proud of herself when she finished.

In their new apartment, again, Grace and the kids slept in one bedroom, and Perry had his own room. After they had been living in the apartment for several months, Perry moved his bed out of the bedroom and into the children's play area, filling the entire space. He wanted to use his bedroom as an office. He set up a couple of tables and computers, and he'd bought a large keyboard. He said he was going to record music in there. He told Grace how essential it was for him to play music and that it would help him calm down and release tension.

He also had two huge cabinets that he moved into the bedroom. They were as tall as the doorway and even wider. Grace soon found out why he needed the cabinets. Perry told her he was going to grow tomatoes and herbs in them, but he was growing marijuana. Marijuana is illegal in Texas. Grace didn't like the risk he was taking but felt helpless to stop him. He kept the cabinets locked.

Perry didn't want Grace to take their children to church. He said he didn't want Grace listening to another man. Grace didn't understand why Perry had a problem with the pastor, and they had almost weekly arguments about it. Perry either wanted her to stay home or to find another church. Grace told herself he was better than he used to be, but he was still far from where he needed to be.

Grace became involved in the church nursery and eventually became a team leader. She coordinated workers and made up the schedules. Grace made a lot of friends at church, including another mother named Molly. She and Grace bonded quickly and became good friends. Perry, however, forbade her to be friends with Molly because he and Molly had gone on one date ten years earlier and he believed Molly was crazy and a psycho.

Grace didn't believe him because she saw Molly worshipping God and the way she lovingly homeschooled her children. Molly made healthy decisions for her family. She was happily married and seemed to be doing very well in all areas of her life. She lived in a big, beautiful house. Molly reached out to help other moms and seemed to be a generous person. Molly was passionate about everything she did. She was loving and giving, and Grace admired her so much.

Molly reached out to Grace and gave her rides to church and helped Grace out many times. Molly was a prayer warrior. She seemed to have a very close relationship with Jesus, but Perry was not swayed by Grace's arguments, and he forbade her from seeing Molly. She never told Molly the reasons she stopped being her friend, and Molly was left feeling bewildered. Grace felt terrible about it. She felt sad to lose a dear friend because she was trying to prove to her husband how submissive and loyal she was.

One Sunday they had an especially vicious fight. Perry believed he was supposed to be her spiritual leader instead of letting the pastor do it. He believed God gave him direction and guidance for his family and that he was the mediator between God and his wife and children. Grace just wanted to run away and hide when Perry yelled.

She felt like it was a miracle that she and the kids were allowed to leave and go shopping after the fight, but she didn't go to the store. She went to her pastor's house. She sat down with the pastor's wife, Jan, and told her what had just happened. Grace wanted Jan to give her permission to leave Perry, but Jan wouldn't. She did say it was not God's will for Grace to stay in an abusive situation. Jan told Grace she should stand up for herself and be bold. She and Jan prayed together. Then Grace went to the store.

By the time Grace got home, she had been gone for several hours. Perry was just leaving in his taxi. He stopped beside her; he was sobbing. He apologized profusely.

"I was so scared that you had decided to leave. I wouldn't be able to handle it if you left. I wouldn't know what to do if you left. I'm sorry for losing my temper and having a fight. I'm sorry I yelled at you. I was wrong in the way I handled it. I'm so sorry for everything. Will you please forgive me? Please? Please forgive me?"

This type of tearful apology was nothing new. He yelled, they fought, and then he apologized. They made up again. Everything went smoothly until the next blow up. Grace thought he was trying to change. Perry said he knew he needed to change and he knew where he went wrong, but his heart never really changed.

Grace was blind to the cycle. Perry did the same things repeatedly under differing circumstances. He refused outside counseling. Although he told Grace to hold him accountable, he refused to be held accountable. Grace was scared to stand up to him when he was yelling, and even if she did, she knew he wouldn't listen to her.

Carolyn was concerned about Perry. Grace had confided in her that Perry was smoking marijuana again. Grace was afraid to tell her family because she knew they would be very judgmental. She felt she could tell Carolyn and she would be more accepting since Carolyn thought Perry was bipolar. Grace did not understand what bipolar meant, so she just dismissed it.

Bipolar disorder is a brain disorder that causes unusual shifts in mood, energy, activity levels, and the ability to carry out daily tasks. They may have difficulty finding a happy middle ground between severely depressed states and euphoric happiness. They are not balanced.

Perry was unbalanced. He got excited about an idea and talked very fast, as if he was in high gear. When he came down off of that high, however, it was terrible. He became irritable, had angry outbursts, and exploded at the slightest provocation. Grace never knew what was going to trigger him. When Grace tried to talk to Perry about what his mother had said, he dismissed it outright. He blamed other people for his angry outbursts. He blamed Emma for sticking her nose in his and Grace's business, and he blamed his family, Grace's family, and random strangers for his anger. Grace often reminded him not to direct his anger at her, and he would apologize, but he didn't change.

Perry said the reason he smoked marijuana was that he had adult ADHD. He was scatterbrained and had a hard time staying focused. He was forgetful and couldn't think calmly. He was fidgety and irritable and couldn't sit still. He preferred to stand. He said marijuana helped him calm down and sleep, and to think more clearly, but the truth was that it clouded his thinking. Grace just accepted his explanations and hoped that it would help calm his moods as well to keep him from blowing up more often than without it.

Grace weaned Emily from nursing at eighteen months old. Perry wanted her to go back to work. Grace was able to find some work taking care of elderly people at night. She loved it. It was like a vacation to take a break from the demands of being a mother and wife. Perry didn't do any housework while she worked. She still had to come home and do everything she had been doing before.

Perry wanted Grace to rub his feet nearly every day. She learned not to argue or talk back because she didn't want to hear how she wasn't being a good wife and not fulfilling his needs. She often tried to be there for him and fulfill his physical needs and sexual needs in spite of her exhaustion. She had a lot to do. She had three children to look after and a house to keep clean. Perry thought she should drop everything to take care of his needs. He wanted her to prove to him that he was her top priority, that he was number one in her life. She cried many, many times while rubbing his feet. She grew exhausted and discouraged.

Perry was immature and clung to Grace to assure her that he needed her so that she wouldn't leave. He kept her wrapped up in caring for him because he wanted her attention all the time. He wanted her to prove her love for him by rubbing his feet and giving him sex whenever he wanted it. He did not give Grace space from him or freedom to be with other friends.

He was very demanding and sang his own praises every day, giving himself compliments and talking about all the great things he did, yet he could not accept that he ever was wrong or made a mistake.

Perry was still working; however, he struggled with his health. He had minor surgery to correct a hernia. He stopped working during his recovery. Grace continued working while she was taking care of Perry and his child-like needs.

A few months later after his surgery, Perry and the kids went to Ohio to visit his mother. Carolyn had been quite sick for a long time, battling hepatitis C and liver disease. She was overweight and had health issues for a long time. She was on the waiting list for a liver transplant. She was tired of the battle and sometimes just wanted her fight to be over, but she wanted each of her children to visit her before she died.

Perry went to spend a week with Carolyn. He left his own children with Grace's mother. He spent time with his mother. Perry also visited each of Grace's sisters and delivered a bouquet of flowers to each of them in an attempt to repair the relationships. But it did not work. There had already been years of damage and Grace's sisters knew something wasn't right because he had a long history of being rude to them and accusing them of things that were not true. Grace stayed in Texas because she was working.

That autumn, both of the boys were in school. Ben was now in first grade, and Jimmy was in kindergarten. They loved going to school together.

Grace earned some extra money for watching two girls after school for two hours until their mother came home from work. Grace eventually got a full-time day job taking care of a disabled client, but she was at home the rest of the time. She did that for a few months until Perry decided to start working again. He began driving his taxi once more.

In October, Joe called to report that Carolyn had stopped taking one of her medications. She died about a week later. Her sister, Susan, had been there with her when she died. She had been such a warm, loving soul, a prayer warrior, a giver, and a nurturer. Their entire church mourned when she passed. She had ministered to so many people, especially women. They had a funeral for her in their church in Ohio, then they drove her to Texas and had another funeral with her family and long-time friends. She was buried in Texas near where her family lived.

Perry was shocked when his mother died. On the outside, he looked as if he was dealing very well, but he had not prepared himself for her passing. He blamed Joe and Susan for letting her die. Grace explained that it had been Carolyn's right to refuse to take her medication, and that she had known death would result. Death had been her choice, on her terms.

A few months later, Joe decided to take down Carolyn's Facebook page. Perry had a complete meltdown. He screamed at Joe on the phone. He told Joe he wished Joe had died instead. Perry said every vile thing he could think of while his children listened. Grace tried to calm Perry down and assure him she was on his side, but his rage made them shudder.

Grace knew Perry had anger issues. He smashed his guitar in a fit of rage. He justified it to Grace.

"Well, at least I didn't hit you. It's just an object, and we can replace it."

Around Christmastime that year, Grace decided to take the kids to the mall in Dallas to look at the lights. They decided to take their cousin Jake along, too, so they stopped by his apartment to pick him up. Perry and his cousin Marvin and some other guys were there. They usually played music and smoked marijuana.

Grace left with the kids. They enjoyed watching a movie on the DVD players on the back of the front seats. Grace took the kids to the mall, and they all looked at the Christmas lights. Mostly she just walked around and let the kids play.

When they returned to the SUV, Grace realized there was broken glass inside her vehicle. Somebody had broken in and stolen the DVD players, but nothing else. The diaper bag was in the back with her wallet was still in it. There was a phone on the dashboard, still plugged in. Perry's backpack was in the back with his laptop in it. The only things missing were the DVD players.

Perry admitted to Grace several months later that he never called the police and reported it because he knew who did it. It was one of Marvin's friends, who followed them to the mall. Grace was angry and told Perry she wished he would stop hanging out with his disrespectful and ungodly cousin. Marvin was divorced, and Grace respected nothing about him. He was lazy and drank and did drugs. He had been cited for drunk driving several times. He wasn't a good father or husband, and he mocked Grace for her conservative background.

Grace didn't know it, but Perry talked disrespectfully about his wife to his male cousins. He talked about her breasts, and he made fun of her, calling her dumb for listening to country and bluegrass music.

Perry and his cousins assumed that because Grace was from the Amish and she grew up in a small town and was sheltered most of her life, she must have been stupid. His cousins thought Perry could have chosen better than simple-minded Grace. Perry thought Grace needed him to make all decisions for her, but nothing could have been further from the truth.

Grace was not stupid, and she didn't need any help with making decisions. She often asked Perry before making decisions out of respect for him. He took that to mean he could dominate her. He was not respectful to her.

Perry was a misogynist. He was condescending to women, and he blamed his past girlfriends and his mother and sister for rejecting him and stabbing him in the heart. He belittled and degraded women, blaming them for his terrible behavior and using that as a justification for mistreating women. Perry blamed the women in his life for the trouble he was having in his marriage. He didn't want to take any responsibility for the issues. He believed his hatred for women was provoked and understandable. If Grace dared to question him or hold him accountable, he would turn it back on her immediately, pointing out her and other women's inadequacies.

Several months after the theft, Perry pulled out all his marijuana plants and showed them to Grace before he threw them in the dumpster. Grace was impressed. She thought the Lord surely had gotten ahold of him and he would at last change. Perry eventually stopped hanging out with his cousin when he realized Marvin was not doing anything good for him.

Around the same time, Grace's twenty-one-year-old nephew Bobby drowned while on a mission trip. He was Emma and Adam's oldest grandchild. It sent shock waves through the family. Grace wanted to be home with her family; Perry said they didn't have enough money for her to go to Ohio. At first, he said he was sorry and told Grace to send condolences to her family, but a few weeks later, Perry said he was glad that Bobby died because his mother, Esther, had told Perry he was in danger of hell fire many years ago. He had always carried a grudge against her for saying that.

Perry no longer had good relationships with anyone in his family. He didn't get along with his sister and called her every bad name in the book. He disliked her husband and mocked him for being short. He decided that since his mother was no longer alive, he didn't care to stay around his relatives. He told Grace he wanted to move to Colorado. He asked Grace how she felt about it. She had never been there but said she thought she would be okay with moving to Colorado. She imagined it would be about the same as moving to Texas. She didn't know many people in Texas before she moved there, and she imagined if they moved to Colorado, they could start going to a church and school there and find new friends.

They packed everything they couldn't take into their red minivan, into a storage unit. Grace packed up Perry's things and took them to his father's house. She packed her and the kids' belongings into the minivan, and everything else went into storage. Perry planned to stay with his father for a few more weeks and work and save up money while Grace and the kids went to Ohio for two months.

After everything was packed, they spent three more days with Perry at his dad's place, and then they drove to Aunt Susan's to spend three days there. The kids enjoyed spending time with their cousin Jake. The first night of their drive they spent in the Ozarks with some cousins, and the next day, they finished the drive to Ohio.

It was a wonderful reunion. It had been a year and a half since Grace had been home. They visited Bobby's grave and watched home videos. They picked blueberries with Grace's parents and went swimming and played with the cats. They visited a local zoo with Grace's sisters and had a mother-daughter breakfast. Perry communicated with Grace daily. He promised her that he wanted to find a church in Colorado where they could all go to together, as a family.

Grace looked forward to the move. In her mind, the future looked bright and full of adventure and promise. She and Perry loved each other and were committed to their kids and staying together no matter what.

10

ADVENTURE IS OUT THERE

In July, Grace and the kids drove the red minivan out to Colorado. There was a tire tread blowout on the first day and a flat tire as they entered Colorado on the second day. Perry missed Grace tremendously and the first night together was extraordinary. They stayed in a hotel.

Grace was excited to be with Perry again. He had promised they would find a church to attend together. Perry said they would try out Colorado for two years and if it didn't go well, they would leave.

The first week in Colorado, Perry decided Grace needed to call their families and ask for money because they had an unexpected expense, which was buying several new tires. He claimed they needed five hundred dollars. Grace called her relatives and his relatives. Her brother Kevin sent one hundred dollars and Perry's grandmother sent them two hundred dollars. Susanna offered advice on how they could get financial aid, which angered Perry. He wanted her to give cash, not advice.

Perry called her. "Hey, we are fine. You don't need to give us advice. I'm going to take care of my family and be the provider. Your advice is not needed or wanted."

As usual, Perry was rude and harsh, and he hurt Susanna's feelings. He carried a grudge against her from that time forward.

They stayed at a hotel for the first eight months. Their room had a full refrigerator and a kitchen sink and dishes in a cupboard, and a small cooktop which could cook one thing at a time. It was one room with two beds and a bathroom.

While she was in Ohio, Perry told Grace that the job he had been seeking was no longer available, so he needed Grace to start filling out applications and get a job. Later, he confessed the job he wanted was on a marijuana farm or working in an environment with marijuana.

Grace found a job as a caregiver with an agency called Live Home. They gave her 24-hour shifts, but not 12-hour shifts. To get the hours she needed, she had to work 24-hour shifts. Perry was not working at all. Grace was placed for five months with a client who had had a stroke. The woman was depressed and angry, and dealing with her was challenging. Many other caregivers didn't stay with her for long. The staff at Live Home were amazed that Grace was able to stay for five months, but Grace was used to dealing with difficult people.

After they had been in Colorado for several months, Susanna and her son Matt called Perry one day while Grace was at work. Matt and Jimmy were close and wanted to talk. Susanna handed the phone to Matt, and the boys talked for a while. When they finished speaking, Susanna hung up the phone. She had no desire to talk to Perry. When Perry took the phone, nobody was on the line. Perry called Susanna back, but she refused to answer because she had learned that phone conversations with Perry were terrible.

Perry was offended that Susanna refused to talk to him. He called Grace and berated her as he explained the damage Susanna was doing by not talking to him. Perry was mean and rude and vile.

Perry was active on Facebook. He had gone through Grace's family's private Facebook page and contacted all the members, making unfounded accusations against many of them. He was verbally abusive and criticized them.

He blamed all the members of Grace's family for the breakdown of their relationship. It caused upheaval for the whole family. The Chupp family was not accustomed to that kind of behavior. He tortured the entire family. They hurt for one another and became angry on each other's behalf. They assumed he was probably treating Grace horribly, but she never said so. It caused many of the family to worry and lose sleep.

Perry broke into Grace's Facebook account and read private things that she had shared with her mother and sisters. Perry called her at work and confronted her about her conversations. He told her she wasn't allowed to say to them the things she had, saying they were private between husband and wife. The messages were private conversations between Grace and her family, yet he was dictating what she could say to her family members. They had a terrible fight while Grace was at her client's house. She made excuses to her client for why she couldn't be in the room while she was on the phone. Most of the time she cried when she was on the phone with Perry.

Grace let Perry know he could not go on her Facebook account without her permission. She changed her passwords. Several times her client saw that Grace had been crying; it was because Perry called her up and was angry about something. He constantly picked fights with her while she was at work, yet she could not avoid his phone calls because he repeatedly called until she picked up the phone. He became outraged if she did not answer his calls. Perry told her she had to pick up the phone when he called, not considering it wasn't always possible when she was taking care of a client. He was very demanding of her time.

One night while Grace was at work, Perry told her there was a shooting at their hotel. A man had killed the front desk attendant, and a bullet had gone into the ceiling. The police came to their room to look for the bullet. It had burst through the floor just a few feet from where Emily was sleeping on the bed. Grace cried when he told her what had happened.

She hated that she was away from her kids so much. She was working five 24-hour shifts a week, and she missed her children terribly. She would have loved to stay with them, but Perry insisted she had to work while he stayed with the kids.

They fought once in a while. Once, Perry became so angry, he dug his fingernails into his scalp and drew blood. He held his breath until his face was deep red. He beat himself up and punished himself. He was destructive to himself, but he would never hit Grace.

Perry convinced Grace it was her job to help him deal with his issues. He was angry that his mother died. He missed her terribly and often cried for her, yet he had been disrespectful to her. Grace didn't know how to help Perry. She could only tell him what she would do if she was in his shoes, but it didn't help him at all because he seemed to be unable to make long-term changes.

After reporting to her boss, Candace, how stressful it was to be with her stroke client, Candace kindly placed Grace with a nice old man named Fred. Grace ended up working with Fred for three and a half years.

Perry homeschooled the kids that first year. He ordered a curriculum that arrived at their hotel room and made their small room even more crowded. The kids were doing well, but there wasn't a lot of work being done. It seemed to be sporadic, and Grace was not really involved at all because she was gone most of the time. Perry showed Grace the work the kids did to prove they were learning. He wasn't an effective teacher. He would give them their assignments but would not help them do the work.

They hardly did anything to celebrate Thanksgiving and Christmas that year. There were no relatives near them. In their small hotel room there really was no room for more gifts. The gifts that Emma had sent along for the kids were quickly thrown away by Perry.

Perry did fun things with the family once in a while. He took the kids sledding for the first time. They enjoyed driving to the mountains. The mountains reminded Grace of Psalm 121:1. "I lift my eyes up, to the mountains, where does my help come from. My help comes from the Lord, maker of heaven, creator of the earth."

Grace often reminded herself and her family and friends how much she and Perry and the children loved Colorado and how happy they were. Grace felt their concern for her and thought she should remind them that she and Perry and the kids were on a great adventure. It was why she loved Facebook; she could stay connected with people.

11

FROM GOOD TO BAD

After they had been living in a hotel room for eight months, Perry found them an apartment. This time, they put both of their names on the lease. They lived in that apartment for over two years. At first, the only furniture in the apartment was a king-sized bed, but soon they had a couch where the boys could sleep. Eventually, they got bunk beds, bookshelves, and desks. Perry didn't get a job until they moved into the apartment. Grace was providing all of the income but making none of the decisions.

Perry did make sure that he visited a doctor though, and he received a prescription card so that he could legally buy marijuana. Colorado residents needed to have a green card and proof of residency to purchase marijuana legally. Perry started working as an independent contractor, taking care of computers, printers, routers or internet problems. He was good at his job and had a high customer satisfaction rate.

During that time, it seemed Perry and Grace were finding a deeper level in their relationship. Over the next year, they fell more in love with each other. Grace finally started experiencing orgasms on a regular basis. Perry stopped watching porn. Their relationship improved and it felt great to both of them. Finally, Perry was focused on giving and loving and being gentle, and being the husband Grace had needed for so long.

While they had been living in Texas, Ben had developed a bad attitude toward Grace. He talked back to her and argued with her a lot. He acted as if he was her superior. If she disciplined him, he became angry, yelled at her, slammed doors, and attempted to break things. He cried and said she was mean and that he hated her. He whined and complained to get his way. He thought he was entitled to have privileges. When Grace talked to Perry about the problem, he said it was because she was a woman and Ben didn't like to take orders from her. Ben respected Perry, and they got along with no problem, but it was because Ben had picked up on the behavior of arguing with Grace and being disrespectful to her that Perry was modeling.

When they were in Colorado, Perry was around Ben a lot more and began to have problems with Ben, too. Perry had often been frustrated with Ben being a kid. Ben just wanted to have fun, but Perry wanted Ben to learn more responsibility and be tougher. He expected Ben to take care of his younger siblings. Perry expected more from Ben because he was the oldest and so Ben got more spankings from Perry. Perry wanted Grace to be the nurturer and give out lots of hugs and be the soft parent, while he wanted to be the disciplinarian and the hard parent. It certainly improved Grace's relationship with Ben. He was no longer disrespectful to her, but it was the beginning of a rift between Perry and Ben that would eventually cause irreparable psychological damage.

Perry was very particular about what Grace said on Facebook. He wanted to control what she said and who her friends were. She had to ask his permission before posting anything on Facebook to make sure it met his approval. Grace asked him to run his posts by her before posting anything, but he never did, even though he said he would.

When Grace talked to anybody in her family, they were not allowed to talk about him. Grace returned the favor by asking him if he could also not speak to her about them because most of what he said about them was negative. He blamed her for the rift between him and her family.

He unfriended some of her Facebook friends, people she knew who were actually her friends. He was often rude and argumentative on Facebook. He often got into arguments, insulting and calling people names, and falsely accusing them of various things. Perry spent a lot of time sending angry texts to people. He wanted to win every argument, but he always ended the arguments by unfriending and blocking people.

Perry held Grace accountable for everything she posted on Facebook and asked her not to post things about Christianity or God. He didn't want her to make a post about a religious holiday, but then he would post about the very thing he had just told her not to post. He lived by double standards. He attributed it to the fact that she was not presenting him and their family the way he wanted to be presented. Grace told him to stop trying to control her, but his anger and threats and accusations kept her compliant.

He loved to comment on posts that were political or religious and argue with the other commenters. He also loved to comment and argue with Grace's friends, and friends of friends. It was embarrassing. Most of her friends were Christians. Often, they would say they were praying, and he would pick on them, trying to convince them that praying was like practicing magic. He called it 'white magic,' and equated it with witchcraft.

Once, Perry's sister-in-law asked for prayer on Facebook because her child was sick. Some of her friends commented that they were praying. Perry proceeded to argue with her that prayers are a joke and not effective. He said if her child was sick, she should take him to a doctor instead of just praying and doing nothing. He embarrassed his sister-in-law in front of all her friends.

He also argued with Susanna on Facebook when she was very sick. He became angry at her for not going to a doctor when it was against her convictions. He insulted her because she asked for prayers. He was judgmental and had no problem telling people what he thought of them.

He friended many women on Facebook based merely on their sexy profile pictures. When he was confronted by them or by Grace, he justified his behavior saying he was paying them a compliment. Perry told Grace he could be friends with and work with women better than men. Men were competitive; women were nice.

He also wanted Grace to post positive things about him on Facebook on a regular basis. He wanted her to present him in a positive light and say good things about him. She posted about him being a great dad and how in love with him she was. She tried to present them having a great marriage and a happy family; otherwise, he accused her of being unfaithful.

"If you love me, you would stand in solidarity with me. I can't trust you if you don't tell me everything. You are sabotaging our marriage if you don't take care of my needs and make me the most important person in your life."

Grace wanted to make their marriage work. She was dedicated and committed to proving to Perry what a good wife she could be. She did not want to divorce Perry. Each time Perry did something that was controlling or manipulative, it would disappoint her, and she would contemplate whether that thing was worth her marriage. For instance, if he cut her off from a friend, she wondered if it would it be worth it to leave the marriage to retain the friendship. Each time, she let the friendship go, but each time her heart cracked a little more.

Perry also kept her in his control by apologizing each time she told him she was hurt.

"I love you to death. Gracie, you are the most important person in the world to me. You are the most beautiful girl in the world. I'm sorry I hurt you. I know what I did wrong. I know what I have to change. I know what I should have done instead. Will you hold me accountable if I ever do that again?"

He made her believe he was changing, but even if he changed, it wouldn't last.

Perry claimed to be very sensitive. However, that sensitivity only extended to his needs. When Grace told him what she needed, it didn't make a difference, but she was conditioned to believe he really loved her and that she was important to him. He always had an excuse why he could not give her what she needed.

Grace began to hide from Perry. She felt like she needed to protect herself and preserve what was left of her before he destroyed her. She felt Perry did not appreciate or accept her the way she was. She was still a country girl on the inside. She loved bluegrass music and going barefoot. She still had the foundation her godly parents had laid inside, but it seemed Perry resented that and held it against her. He did not appreciate her family or her upbringing. He believed he was better and smarter than her and her family. It was deeply hurtful to Grace. She accepted Perry the way he was.

Grace wanted to love Perry and to love her family. She assured Perry her loyalty was with him. She was committed to him and committed to working hard. She loved their children and their home and her job. Although she loved Perry and wasn't seeking to have a life apart from him, she kept up her guard.

Perry started his own business again. He talked the boys into being a part of his corporation and appointed them assistant positions. He took the boys' money as investments into his business, promising he would pay them back. The boys had saved up over thirty dollars, which was a lot of money to them and had taken them a long time to save. Perry never paid them back.

Perry was careless with money. He bought things impulsively without talking to Grace first, but he demanded that she ask his permission before she spent any money, even on groceries or gas. All the money she made went directly into their joint bank account. She didn't have any money of her own. Each time she wanted to spend money, Perry wanted to know about it first. Grace was a conservative spender, while Perry bought whatever he felt.

Perry had a separate bank account for his business. He managed all their money and paid all the bills. He decided the vehicle they purchased was going to be in Grace's name alone because his credit was bad. He made foolish financial decisions and did not know how to save. He knew how to create a budget, but he never stuck to it.

When Grace was working 24-hour shifts and came home for two days a week, the kids told her she was nice. Grace thought Perry was abusive to her but wasn't sure how he was about disciplining the kids. She knew he was tough and he demanded respect and obedience.

Perry had started making the boys, ages seven and eight, rub and massage his feet when they were in the hotel. After they moved, Perry asked Jimmy to stand on his feet and back. He often called the boys to rub his feet, because Grace was gone a great deal of the time. The boys did it together, and it was fun at first, but over time it became a dreaded chore.

Perry often made them do it at night when they were tired and sometimes after they had fallen asleep, sometimes after ten-thirty at night. Perry would make the boys get out of bed and rub his feet until he fell asleep. Grace still rubbed his feet often when she was home because Perry was so needy and demanding, but more and more she refused because she was exhausted. When that happened, he got the boys out of bed to do it. They had to use their elbows to massage his feet because their little hands became too sore and tired. They complained about the pain, but Perry wouldn't let them stop. He didn't even let them take a break. He often made them rub his feet for more than thirty minutes.

Perry manipulated them by playing the victim. He complained of leg cramps and digestion issues and pain. He wanted Grace and the kids to massage him and give him all kinds of attention. He often was sick and laid up in bed and wanted somebody to take care of him. He wanted them to feel sorry for him and forget the terrible ways he treated them.

Perry made the kids feel like he was more important than they were because he was an adult and they were just kids. They got the message that they weren't important to Perry, that they were obligated to rub his feet. He would often tell the kids that God was telling him to do things and giving him direction. but Grace and the kids could not confirm it. He believed he was hearing God giving him direction for his family as though his family could not discern the voice of God on their own.

Perry made the boys do the housecleaning and do a lot of things he did not like to do. Perry hated washing the dishes, and so he never did them. Perry made the boys clean the bathroom and kitchen. Perry was very messy and gross. He often left his phlegm sitting in the sink and instead of washing it down the drain, he let it dry. Perry peed in the shower and even drank his urine. He left messes for Grace and the kids to clean even though Grace often tried to get him to clean up after himself. She repeatedly asked him to clean the toilet on a daily basis.

Perry was an excellent cook. He made the best meals, and he enjoyed cooking. He had very high standards when it came to food, so his food was restaurant quality. He cooked homemade alfredo and the best cuts of steak. He loved making roast beef with vegetables. He always made a big mess and left it for someone else clean. Sometimes he made a huge breakfast that included biscuits and gravy, scrambled eggs and sausage and orange juice. They had some fun moments as a family, but they were not enough to heal the pain and damage to Grace's heart.

They had fun family outings. They went to the movies. They visited the Red Rocks Amphitheatre and the Denver Aquarium, the Denver Art Museum and the Children's Museum. They visited the Denver Zoo.

The next school year, they homeschooled their children again, but this time they used an online curriculum. Perry got a computer for each child. Emily was in preschool. Jimmy was in second grade, and Ben was in third grade.

Perry and Grace also enrolled in college at the local community college. Perry wanted Grace to get enrolled in taking online college classes so that they could get financial aid and grants. It was a way to provide additional money for them without Perry having to get an actual job. It wouldn't cost a thing. There would be enough money for all the textbooks and school supplies and extra left over. So Grace did it and took four classes each semester. She had a laptop which she took to her client's house. She did her school work while her client was napping or watching TV.

College was very demanding. She finished each semester with a GPA of at least 3.5. Grace wasn't trying to be at the top of her class. She was only trying to get the work done, and finish each class. Perry didn't try very hard. He skipped discussions and skipped doing a lot of the work.

For Christmas, Susanna sent a large box to Grace's client's house for the Lawrence family. It was packed tight with all kinds of wonderful things: a fluffy blanket, a scarf, some games, art supplies and all sorts of pretty and thoughtful gifts for each of the kids. Grace knew that Perry had a problem with Susanna, but she thought maybe if he saw what a kind and generous person Susanna was, it would change his feelings toward her. Grace also contemplated not telling him and saying the gifts were from her or her client. If she told Perry the gifts were from Susanna, it might make him angry. She was apprehensive, but she decided to be honest. He didn't even look at the gifts, just told her to send them back because his family didn't need Susanna's charity.

It broke Grace's heart. She kept the fluffy blanket but sent everything else back. It tore her apart that the man she loved most did not get along with her. Grace knew she couldn't keep the things Susanna had sent because she knew Perry would become angry and say she had broken his trust. He would then destroy or throw the items into the trash and make sure she couldn't get them back. She never told him that the fluffy blanket was from Susanna. She kept it at her client's house for several months, then eventually she told him it was a Christmas gift from her client's family.

12

I NEED GIRLFRIENDS

At the beginning of 2014, Live Home changed their policy and decided they would allow employees to work twelve-hour shifts instead of twenty-four-hour shifts. They were also ending their discount rate, which meant that employees would get paid a rate of nine dollars per hour. Grace could now work almost half her regular hours and get nearly the same pay she had been receiving. She decided to work just nights for twelve hours and then work twenty-four-hour shifts on the weekends. That would allow her to be home each weekday, which would allow Perry the freedom to work during the day. He didn't take advantage of the flexibility her new schedule allowed him.

Perry complained that he didn't get to sleep with her enough, but if she worked days, then he wouldn't work days. She refused to work both days and nights. He refused to work nights, and he refused to work more.

They looked for a church for the family to attend. Grace and the kids visited several churches before finding a big one they liked. The kids started going to Sunday school, and Perry and Grace went to the main service. They were invited to stay for a newcomers' lunch. After that lunch, Perry told the other church members that he would not be coming back because they believed that Jesus is the Lord.

Perry did not believe Jesus was God. He believed Jesus was just a man who died and went to Heaven. Not that He is God. He taught their kids to pray to God, not to Jesus. Perry demanded that they stop going to that church because he was afraid that if Grace and the kids went, the human-made doctrines would brainwash them. As he told Grace when she went to other churches, He did not want Grace to sit under the teaching of an ordinary man who was not her spiritual leader.

Perry believed he was supposed to be the spiritual leader of his home and his wife. He told Grace that God would speak to her through her husband or spiritual covering. There has a hint of truth in what he said, but he twisted it to make it reek of a cult mentality.

Of course, as soon as he made sure Grace stopped going to that church, Perry announced he was going to put away all religion and God and Christianity, and everything his mother ever taught him about God, and forget about it. He didn't want to talk about praying or reading the Bible, nor about going to church or having faith. He said he was a realist and just wanted to believe in things that he could see.

Grace wanted to be a part of the women's book study in the church they had attended for a few weeks. She argued and fought with Perry and finally convinced him that she should be allowed to go. It was only once a week, for six weeks. Grace loved it. She bonded with the women there. She was careful to share only positive things about her husband and not make him look any worse than anybody else's husband, but by the end, she felt like they felt sorry for her. They suggested classes for her and her husband to attend together. She knew that although it might be a good idea, it would never happen.

After several months of Perry banning religion from their lives, Grace lost her patience. He was supposed to be their spiritual leader, and Grace was supposed to be submitting to him, but he was providing no guidance. Grace thought she knew what was right and wrong, and about God and Heaven and Hell, but now she found only doubt.

Perry said, "Jesus is not the son of God any more than anybody else. Aren't we all sons of God? Anyone who believes Jesus is the Son of God is stupid. If you pray, you have to make things happen; you can't just sit back and pray and not do anything. You have to help yourself."

All of his statements negated a faith in God.

Perry would belittle and mock those who believed differently from him. If Grace dared to challenge his authority, he reminded her she was not following his lead, not submitting, and was on dangerous ground. He threatened to take the kids away from her. He verbally assaulted and chastised her for her beliefs, then ask her if she was too good to receive correction from her husband.

As part of her book club, Grace had read a book called "Misquoting Jesus," which shook her to the core. The book was a critical view of the Bible, examining the discrepancies, mistakes, and inconsistencies in the Bible. Some accounts of the stories of Jesus did not match one another. The book challenged the authors of the books of the Bible. Nobody knew who wrote the Bible.

"Misquoting Jesus" also challenged whether the stories in the Bible were myths or factual. For example, the story of Job, which includes a conversation between God and the devil. Job was a righteous man who had seven sons and three daughters. In one day, he lost everything. His story seems unlikely, but whether it is myth or true, the story still teaches valuable lessons. Who could prove whether God and the devil had a conversation? The likelihood that this story was true was slim, which shook Grace. What if parts of the Bible were stories? Which parts were true, and which parts myth?

Grace finished the book and was discouraged. She didn't know what to believe about the Bible anymore. Before she had gotten married, everything was black and white. She knew what was true and what was false; she knew there was right and wrong. She knew there was both a Heaven and a Hell. She knew there is a God who created everybody and loved everybody.

But now, she suddenly saw everything as grey. She didn't know what to believe anymore. She didn't know what parts of the Bible were true and which ones weren't. The strong faith which had always been her foundation was now crumbling. It eventually completely shattered.

Grace saw no point in continuing to read the Bible. She felt like her whole life had been a lie. Her beliefs and values, everything she had ever known, was based on the Bible, but now it was no longer strong and unshakeable as she had once thought.

She didn't talk about her doubts with anyone because she knew it sounded crazy to doubt the word of God, even though she wasn't sure it actually was the word of God if humans wrote it. She didn't speak to Perry about it, because he was also challenging her faith. He didn't want to believe in God anymore.

After the women's book study group ended, Grace longed for more female community. She tried to explain to Perry that women need other women. Women encourage each other in ways men couldn't or wouldn't.

"I need women, too. I want lots of girlfriends."

Grace said, "I need other women to be my friends and to connect with."

"I do, too."

"You're just interested in physical relationships and romantic relationships. My need is different. You don't need to be in more than one relationship with a woman. You are married and supposed to be faithful to me. I'm not unfaithful to you by being friends with other women."

Perry believed that he should be able to have many girlfriends and wives. He tried to convince Grace she was a lesbian, or that she should be. He accused her many times of being a lesbian. He hated people who were in same-sex relationships. He believed that if she wasn't following his lead, that if she dared to try to stand up for herself, she was surely a closeted lesbian. He thought if he could convince her she was a lesbian, he could justify having relationships with other women.

Perry wanted Grace to know that she had chained his heart and kept him trapped by being married to him, so he could not be kind to her or allow her to have other friends because she would not let him have relationships with women outside of their marriage. He wanted her to unchain him and let him be free to love as many women as he wanted. He said then he could be much kinder and nicer to her and the kids. Grace could only shake her head in sadness and disbelief.

In the midst of this on-going battle, Grace looked through Perry's phone and saw he had texted several women. She saw the pictures they had sent to him and knew Perry had cheated on her. She wasn't brave enough to leave him, but she was brave enough to tell him she wouldn't be intimate with him because she knew he had cheated on her.

"No, ma'am, I would never do that. I didn't do that. You're the only girl for me. You're the love of my life."

Again, he convinced her that he didn't know those women, they meant nothing to him, and she had nothing to worry about because he loved her. He told her what a good wife and mother she was. He apologized for causing her concern and assured her he would do nothing to jeopardize their marriage or risk losing her and the kids. Again, he roped her in, and again she forgave him.

Perry thought he was entitled to and was allowed special privileges because the rules didn't apply to him. When they went to a store, he would park in the fire lane in front of the store, and leave Grace and the kids in the car until he came out. Grace kept telling him not to do that.

He did that once when there were plenty of parking spaces to choose from, so after he went into the store, she moved the car to a parking space. Ben warned her that Perry was going to yell at her. Grace didn't care. She knew Perry wouldn't hit her.

Ben was right. When Perry came out, their car was in one of the first parking spots.

"Why did you move the car?" he shouted.

"It was parked illegally."

"I told you not to move it."

"You had no trouble finding it."

His rant built up into a huge fight, which left Grace and the kids feeling defeated. Grace regretted standing up and doing something right. She had to be very careful about what battles she picked because her decisions affected not only her but the kids. She had to keep things smooth and calm. Perry controlled them by using yelling and intimidation.

That summer, they made a trip back to Texas to retrieve their things from storage. On the way down to Texas, they stopped and met up with an old friend of Grace's named Becky. The women had known one another since they were nine. They had gone to the same church and youth group together. She was a very good friend. She had two kids.

They all met for pizza. Grace and Becky hadn't seen each other for 17 years, ever since Becky's family moved to Colorado when she was a teenager. Becky and Grace discovered they had similar lives. They were both homeschooling their children, and they had both tried public school for their kids, as well They were both caregivers and were both taking care of an old man at the same time. They laughed at the similarities. Their reunion lasted for about an hour. They took a few pictures, and then Perry and Grace and the kids headed down to Texas.

The family stayed with Perry's father, Scott, for about a week while they sorted through their storage unit and tried to sell a few things. Grace picked out the things that had sentimental value and things she wanted to use in their apartment.

They could only take back to Colorado whatever they could squeeze into their SUV, so they left six large plastic containers at Scott's apartment.

During the week in Texas, the kids attended Vacation Bible School at Scott's church. They didn't know anyone at that church and Perry would not let Grace and the kids go back to the church they had attended for four years. Grace was sad because she had some close friends at that church. She was also angry at Perry for the way he was trying to control her relationships. He was trying to cut off not only her friendships with women from church, but he was also sabotaging her relationships with her sisters and family. Grace's friendships were crucial to her. Grace had always said she did not want to get a divorce, but Perry's behavior was breaking her heart. She believed she would never be able to have relationships with her friends or family until Perry died.

Grace felt trapped. She told Perry how she felt and what she wanted and needed, but he did not even listen to her. He didn't care. He cared about his agenda. He thought they should cut ties and move forward and leave the past behind. His demand crushed Grace. She was angry and hurt. With tears, she cried out to God to let Perry die. She would rather be a widow than divorced.

The final day of Vacation Bible School was Sunday. The kids came out and sang songs. Perry and Grace sat with Scott and watched the kids do their program. After the songs, the preacher gave a sermon. Perry stood up in the middle and challenged the preacher. He began to argue with the preacher, but the preacher managed to answer his questions calmly and clearly. Scott was embarrassed.

After the service, Scott went home instead of having lunch with them as planned. Perry apologized to the preacher; he was gracious and forgave Perry, and even prayed with him.

When Perry called Scott to ask where he was, Scott said he wanted them to get their stuff out of his house, or he was going to throw it out. He wanted them to leave for embarrassing him in his church, so they went back to Scott's house and packed up their SUV and put the rest in boxes.

While Grace was packing, Perry and Scott had a screaming argument. Scott wanted them to leave, which Grace understood. What Perry did was inappropriate, but Scott's reaction was also inappropriate. They left six plastic storage boxes behind and packed whatever they could into the SUV, then headed back to Colorado.

The following school year, Perry again applied for college financial aid and was rejected because of his low GPA. He filed an appeal and was ultimately granted financial assistance, but again he did not finish the work and did not finish the school year. He only did enough to keep the financial aid. Grace did her school work. She did what was required and finished in good standing.

That same school year, they decided to send the kids to public school. They were living in a one-bedroom apartment. Perry had been a very impatient and harsh teacher during the previous school year. He often yelled at Ben to get him to do his school work. Ben couldn't think calmly to get his school work done. He was full of tension and worry, and he couldn't do his school work if he was afraid, which made Perry yell at him even more because he wasn't finishing his school work. Perry told Ben he had to do third grade over again because he was having trouble learning. He said Ben had a learning disability and that he had difficulty focusing, never understanding that he was the cause of Ben's inability to focus on his school work.

So for that school year, Ben and Jimmy were both in third grade, but in different classrooms. Emily was in kindergarten. The kids loved to ride the bus and loved making friends and playing at recess. Ben did great at school and was one of the best students in his class. He was chosen to be on a student-led committee group called Penny Harvest. He was selected because of his leadership qualities. Jimmy became involved in art classes. His picture won an art contest, not just in his class, but the whole school. His art was on display at the school. The kids were excited to be a part of the programs that each classroom did. They loved going to school and did very well.

Perry installed a security camera in the living room because there was an attempted break-in one night. Grace could see through that camera from her phone into the living room while she was at work. When she was at work, the things she saw through the camera were non-eventful. Often the kids were watching TV or playing video games or playing with each other. Most of the time, Perry was either in the kitchen or the bedroom. She could see the kitchen but not the bedroom. She did not ever see him be violent with the kids. She saw him talking to them. She saw the kids cleaning up the kitchen. She did not see things which caused her to be concerned or afraid for the kids. She trusted that Perry wasn't taking his anger out on them.

One night when Grace was going to bed, Perry wanted to have sex. Usually, she complied, but she decided to stand up for herself and let him know she was tired and wasn't in the mood. She worked hard every day, not only at her job. She also did all the housework at home, on top of her college schoolwork.

Perry got angry and pounded the wall with his fist. He left a big dent in the wall. He cried out for his mother. He got up and ranted and raved and threatened to find a prostitute at a bar because she wouldn't give him what he wanted. He was red in the face and was sweating and yelling. He didn't find a prostitute but went to bed angry instead.

Grace learned how to calm herself down and go to sleep because Perry was often angry and he would angrily jerk in bed as he tossed and turned. He often got leg cramps during the night and would become mad at her because it was her job to help him. She got up and massaged his legs.

That autumn was their tenth anniversary. They wanted to do something special to celebrate. It felt like they had reached a major milestone. They went downtown for some sushi, and then they went to buy Grace a piece of jewelry. She found a beautiful red ruby ring, surrounded by white sapphires. She felt like a queen, and she loved wearing the ring. Looking at the ring reminded her how far they had come. It felt like a reward for all she had been through with Perry.

Shortly after that, Perry's grandfather died. They made another trip back to Texas for the funeral. Although it was a sad occasion, it was a special time with relatives. Grace enjoyed seeing his relatives even more than Perry did.

That Christmas, they did not have a Christmas tree, and they celebrated without friends or relatives, just the way Perry wanted. They let the kids open their presents that Grace had gotten them and a few that Scott had shipped to them.

13

LOST FAITH, LOST RELATIONSHIPS

Grace went to the kids' school because it was a special day: Market day. She had helped her kids prepare things that they would sell in exchange for fake money. She went to look at each child's display in her sons' classrooms. When she came to Ben's desk, he was doing magic tricks. She put her hand around his shoulders and hugged him. He flinched and said his shoulder hurt because Daddy had hurt him that morning. He started crying. He couldn't even wear his backpack because his shoulder hurt too much.

Grace found out that earlier that morning as the kids were getting ready for school, Perry wanted Ben to change his pants. Ben wasn't doing it fast enough, and Perry decided to "help" him. He tried to take the pants off without opening them. They were on very tight. Perry was pulling on the bottom of the pants and Ben was upside down. He banged Ben's head on the floor several times trying to get his pants off. He also injured Ben when he grabbed him by the shoulder.

Grace was furious with Perry and told him that Ben's shoulder was still hurting. Perry insisted on talking to him without Grace present and then he apologized to Ben. When he and Ben had their talks, she had to stay out of it. He often justified his behavior, and he gave meaningless apologies.

There were other times Perry left hand-prints and bruises on the kids. Once he slapped Ben so hard, he left a hand print on Ben's cheek and another on his bottom. Perry spanked Emily and left a bruise on her leg. Jimmy tried very hard to stay on Perry's good side. He often lied to get out of trouble. The kids were so afraid of their father that if they were playing in the living room and they heard the bedroom doorknob turning, indicating Perry was coming out of the bedroom into the living room, the kids would hide behind or under any piece of furniture.

Grace quickly discovered that if she talked to Perry about something the kids told her he had done to them, he, in turn, got angry at the kids and they got a spanking for "lying" about him. Soon the kids were begging Grace not to tell Perry, but after a while, they just stopped telling her when he mistreated them. They kept secrets and learned to not talk about what happened to them because they knew if anyone found out, they'd get into more trouble. Grace felt terrible that this continued for as long as it did.

She knew she would get into trouble with Perry if she called the police. If he went to jail, the abuse would get worse when he got out. She was still trying to have a strong marriage. At times, she thought their marriage was getting stronger. Perry reminded her that she had to show him respect if she wanted respect from him. He wanted her to build trust with him, not tear trust down by exposing the awful things he did to her and the kids. He claimed he couldn't trust her.

She knew it would devastate Perry to be betrayed by her, his wife, best friend, confidante, and partner. She had always told him she was on his side, that she believed in him, and that she would never leave him. She had made promises before God, friends, and family that she would stick with him through the hard times. She couldn't turn him over to the police. She wasn't strong enough to do that.

Once in the middle of a fight in their bedroom, Grace started to cry, afraid that he was going to hit her. He was angry and yelling. She crossed the bed to try to get away from him. Perry cornered her and grabbed the ring on her finger and tried to pull it off. When she saw what he was doing, she took the rings off and laid them down. She told him she didn't want to wear his ring if he was going to treat her that way. She told him he was abusive, but he looked puzzled. Grace told Perry that she felt isolated and lived in fear. He only tried to convince her that she wasn't isolated and that she shouldn't feel that way.

When Perry yelled at her, spit flew out of his mouth landing on her face. His computer screen was covered with tiny little spit drops from him yelling on the phone while in front of the computer. He hardly ever brushed his teeth. All of their fights ended with her apologizing and groveling, begging for his forgiveness.

Perry had turned the garage into his man cave. He put foam pads on the concrete floor. There was a table on which was a computer, a printer, speakers and other equipment for recording music. A guitar stood nearby. The huge massage chair they all loved was in there, too. There was an inversion table on which he liked to hang upside down to stretch his back. He had hung about twenty file pockets on the wall to keep himself organized and also had a dry erase board.

Once, Grace went into the garage and saw on the computer that he had created an account on a website claiming to help married people find other people with whom to have affairs. Grace was hurt and angry, and wanted Perry to find her on there. She created an account for herself. She put her picture on her profile, hoping Perry would find her on that website and realize he should be pursuing her, not other women.

A week later, Perry found the profile.

"Why were you on that website. Grace?"

"Because I knew you were on it. I was hoping you would find me on there and we could have fun discovering and flirting with each other.

"I do not want you on that website. It's not the right thing."

"Then you shouldn't be on there either."

"Okay."

"So you need to shut down your account."

"Okay. I will close my account.".

She also closed down her account.

Almost a year after Perry declared himself a realist, he came into the kitchen and declared, "I've decided I'm going to be a Christian."

Grace didn't jump up with joy and congratulate him. She had become pretty cynical.

"That's great, honey."

She knew it wouldn't last. For the past year, he had been bashing her faith over and over. He was unstable, and it made her wonder what he would come up with next.

Grace grew up in a Christian home. She knew the difference between right and wrong. She knew there was a Heaven and a Hell. She knew God was real and he loved her. Things were absolute to her. Over the preceding year, Perry had belittled Grace and others on Facebook for praying. He had argued with her friends and friends of friends. He embarrassed her by causing fights and arguments when he mocked people for their religious beliefs and lifestyles.

She was not particularly excited that he suddenly announced he was going to be a Christian. She was angry because he had destroyed her faith. She had grown tired of battling to keep the truth straight in her mind. She had stopped believing. She had lost her faith. She didn't know what to think. Perry wasn't even aware of the destruction he had caused. They weren't going to church, they weren't reading the Bible, and now he wanted her to be happy for him. She couldn't be.

They didn't even fight about going to church anymore because she felt too much guilt about the arguments. She stopped trying to talk to the kids about God because each time he found out, he discouraged her. He found a way to discourage her at every turn, stealing every moment of joy.

At one point, Perry decided he wanted to follow the beliefs of Thomas Jefferson. He ordered a Jeffersonian Bible which contained only the words of Jesus. Perry began talking about starting a church called the Jeffersonian Church. He wanted to start a ministry to each first-born son. He believed there was a curse on each first-born son and he wanted to minister to that specific group.

Grace was skeptical. She wondered how he would minister to his chosen flock and why would people would want to join his church. Perry drew up a chart detailing how he would start a church in each state. Grace knew if Perry started a church and convinced people to come, it would be a disaster. He was not a good pastor or minister. He wasn't a good father or husband. He was not even taking proper care of his family, so she wondered how he could possibly think he could take care of a church. She knew it would turn into a cult.

Nevertheless, Perry talked about it every day. He tried to convince Grace what a godly man he was. He droned on about the doctrines, the pillars of faith, and the foundation his church would have. She just listened without comment, trying not to let him see that she didn't believe in him. He wanted his influence to spread out from his family into the community, and eventually into the nation. In his mind, there were only people who agreed with him and those who didn't. It was Perry versus the world.

He imagined a church of Perry in each state and having the pastors of his churches send him money every month. He asked Grace if she would be willing to travel state to state to start the churches. She was worried and scared of him starting a cult. If anything came of out his dream, she knew the end product was not going to be as he envisioned. He kept saying he wanted her help, but she didn't know how to help him since she wasn't the one with the vision.

"If we started this church, it would provide you with all the friends and social connections you need."

She didn't feel qualified to start a church. Grace had a strong instinct that what Perry wanted to start was going to be bad. He was a conniving, persuasive person who could potentially start something very wrong. Grace prayed for God to intercede and shut down Perry's grand plan. Soon, she saw that God was answering her prayers, just not in the way she expected.

The biggest issue between them was Grace's family. Perry seemed to hate her family. She couldn't talk about them or mention someone's birthday or mention someone's getting married without Perry saying a lot of negative things about people in her family.

One day, Grace was talking to her brother Kevin, who had just bought a house. Perry grabbed the phone away from her and started arguing with him. Kevin shouted right back at Perry. Grace was embarrassed by how immature her husband was acting. After the phone call ended, she told Perry he needed to apologize and make things right again. That attempt also ended in yelling again. She was disappointed and heartbroken.

Perry was very judgmental towards everyone in her family. Kevin got married and invited them, but they didn't go. Grace was afraid if she showed Perry the invitation, he would throw it away, so she kept it and attended the wedding via video call. She was at her client Fred's house while she watched the wedding. It was bittersweet.

When Grace's family asked her how she was doing and how things were going, she told them what Perry wanted her to say, that they were working towards building a life for their family in Colorado. The truth was they did not have enough money to go to Ohio to visit her family. Grace always spoke positively about Perry, telling her family what a good husband and father he was. Grace said the kids were happy and that they were all doing well.

Grace was careful only to speak to her family when things were going well with her and Perry. Grace knew she was keeping secrets from her family. She knew this was different from the happy life she had growing up.

Perry started an online conversation with Grace's eighteen-year-old niece, Jazzy, and claimed she wasn't biased toward him like the rest of her family. He said Jazzy was friendly and accepted him. He complimented her and told her how easy he felt it was talking with her. Her mother, Grace's sister, Esther, had a massive issue with the budding friendship.

Jazzy gave Perry some clear boundaries, and he crossed them. He managed to post a status about absolute truth on her Facebook page that did not reflect her beliefs. She deleted it and told him not to post things on her wall, inviting him to have a private conversation instead of a public argument. He acted innocent and as if he had done nothing wrong, but Jazzy had been very clear that she did not want him to post theological things on her page because he had been argumentative with her friends and verbally attacked them for their beliefs. He reposted it because he said he wasn't going to be shut up. She deleted it again. He texted her repeatedly trying to make himself look like a truth seeker.

He wrote to Jazzy.

> *You owe your Aunt Grace and I some respect, young lady. I'm going to correct you as your uncle right now. I'm what's known as an elder to you, young lady. I have tried to be kind to you, but you are trying to take a corrective tone with me, and that is not going to happen, young lady. If you have a problem with something specific I said, I will address it, but I am not going to sit here and play little girl games with you. Please stop harassing me. I have been very kind to you and your fiancé, which is well beyond what you deserve. If you are unsatisfied with the current treatment you are receiving from Grace and me, then please feel free to tell us where we have failed you. We have been nothing but be respectful to you, young lady, and I expect it in return. Good day.*

That wasn't all. His comments continued about how kind he was to her and how rude she was, simply because she did not want him to post his theologically religious opinions on her private Facebook page. She did not want any arguments, but Perry loved to debate religious philosophies. He wanted not only to show what a spiritual man he was, but also how smart he was and how stupid everyone else was.

Because of Perry's behavior, they did not get an invitation to Jazzy's wedding. It made Grace quite sad because that was one event for which she thought they could have gone back to Ohio. Perry said he would have liked to go to the wedding, but the following week he said he would never go back to Ohio. Jazzy's family didn't want him at the wedding, and Grace understood why. He was explosive and unpredictable. They didn't want drama. They couldn't risk him showing up at their daughter's wedding and ruining it, which is precisely what would have happened. They were right to be afraid of Perry and his instability.

Perry terminated his friendship with Jazzy and stopped communicating with anyone in Grace's family. Occasionally, she still talked to her mother and once in a while, her sisters. She spoke to them at Fred's house where she had time and privacy. She didn't let Perry know that she talked to them because she didn't want to reveal the subject of their conversations.

There was no love or respect in Perry's heart for Adam and Emma. He sent Emma many texts messages and told her what she could or could not do or say as if he were her authority. His behavior was atrocious. Once, Adam texted him back with the message, *We thought you were a Christian*. Perry exploded in anger. He yelled at Grace and said the most awful, vile, disgusting things to her about Adam. Grace could not handle his rage toward her wonderful, godly parents who had been nothing but kind and respectful toward them. Grace burst into tears, sobbing angrily.

Perry wanted Grace to cut off contact with all of his relatives on Facebook. His sister Patty and Grace were friends. Grace loved Patty, but Perry seemed to hate her and said vulgar things about her. When he found out that they had reconnected after he told Grace not speak to her again, he yelled at Grace.

"Patty is mentally ill and addicted to drugs and alcohol."

To calm him down, Grace had to unfriend all his relatives on Facebook and block his sister and her kids.

Perry unfriended and blocked many of Grace's friends on Facebook. She was friends with a happily married man who was a long-time friend. On one Facebook post, he teased Grace and Perry took offense. He insulted the man and then unfriended and blocked him from Grace.

Grace was angry that Perry considered his behavior acceptable. She didn't think that unfriending people on Facebook was worth ending their marriage over, but it made her mad.

She had spent years cultivating her friendships. She had lots of friends and relatives from all over. They were important to her, and she wanted to stay connected to them.

Perry was dominating and if she dared to oppose him, he became furious at her. She worked hard to stay on his good side. She didn't want him to accuse her of betraying him or not being loyal to him. He frequently asked her whose side she was on when he disagreed with one of her family members. She had to say she was on his side or he would threaten to take the kids away from her.

Perry spent a lot of time in the bathroom venting into his phone, having arguments with people on the internet and not allowing Grace and the kids to use the bathroom. He often made them come out of the bathroom while they were using it when he wanted to go in there. He was very inconsiderate of their bathroom needs and told them they just had to hold it while he was in the bathroom. Sometimes he was in the bathroom for hours, coming out only for brief periods, then going back in. He used the bathroom as his office. He was very pushy and demanding, and the kids were often scared of him.

When he came out of the bathroom or bedroom, the kids ran and hid because they thought he might be angry. Their apartment was small, and they didn't have many places to hide, but they'd find someplace until Perry calmed down.

It was one-thirty in the morning. Perry shook Grace awake.

"Grace, can I talk to you?"

"What is it? Is this an emergency? What's going on?" She asked, dazed, yet awake enough to be irritated that he had woken her out of a deep sleep to talk.

"I need to talk to you about your family."

"Let's go out and sit on the couch so we don't wake up the kids."

Once they settled on the couch, he vented about his anguish over why there was tension between him and her family.

"Why don't they apologize to me? They think they're so much better than me. The only way I can make it work with them is if they apologize to me. Everybody in your family owes me a huge apology. They have all rejected me and hurt me, and they have all ostracized me and excluded me."

He said he had tried to figure out how to get along with them for Grace's sake.

"Are you going to tell them to apologize or do I have to do it? Are you going to manage the relationships with your siblings or are you going to make me do it?"

"I can't force my family to apologize to you. I don't control them. Don't you think you caused this rift? Don't you remember that you yelled at them and were rude and argued with them? You need to apologize to them first because you have caused so much damage in the relationships. You have a lot of repair work to do."

"How am I going to apologize if they have all blocked me and are so rude to me? They are not trying to repair the relationships. They don't even want to talk to me. I can't even try to repair the relationship. Nobody wants to listen to me. They are all shutting me out."

The Chupp family was protecting themselves from Perry's insults and verbal barrages. They did not want to have conversations with him because they always ended badly. He was rude and mean to them.

Perry continued. "The only way to get beyond this is to move on with my life without them. They don't care about us. They don't want me in their life, so I have to cut them out of my life and move forward with the life I have here in Colorado and forget about them."

"OK, I accept that you can't get along with them. Some personalities simply don't get along well together. I can't make you apologize to them or make them apologize to you."

Perry blocked them all on Facebook and his phone. He also figured he could not get along with his sister Patty. Grace encouraged him to work out his relationship with his sister. They tried to have a friendly conversation. She said she loved him, but after having a couple of conversations with her, he blocked her because he decided it wasn't going to work out.

Grace talked with Susanna frequently while she was at Fred's house. Grace encouraged Susanna to make up with Perry and mend the relationship. During one conversation with Susanna and her husband, Grace asked her to apologize to Perry. Susanna refused to talk to him and she refused to apologize because she hadn't done anything to him. To protect his wife from Perry's hurtful jabs, her husband said he would not allow her to send any more letters or speak to Perry.

He said, "Why are you doing this? Stop talking to Grace. Why is it so important to you?"

"Because Grace is my sister. I love her, and she's worth it."

Grace started crying. Perry had tried to convince her that her family did not care about her, but she needed to hear that they loved her. It seemed all the people in her family were afraid of Perry, and now they were afraid to contact Grace. Susanna didn't know if she should call or not or write a letter or not. As with Grace, everything Susanna did was wrong, according to Perry.

Susanna was concerned that Grace and the kids were alright. When Susanna sent a card to Grace in the mail, Perry tore it up and threw it in the trash. Every attempt Susanna made to reach out in love to Grace, Perry found something wrong with it.

Grace asked Susanna, "So how are you going to mend it? I don't expect you two to be friends. You may never be friends; just have a conversation and apologize. I realize I have to accept the way it is. I understand why you won't talk to him. I don't blame you. I won't put pressure on you anymore. You don't have to do anything you don't want to do."

The sisters cried. Finally, Grace said, "What can I do?"

Susanna said, "Tell your kids we love them. I'm afraid that Perry is telling the kids bad things about me, and turning my name to mud."

Grace knew that was exactly what Perry was doing. In the end, they told each other they loved one another through tears and hung up. It broke Grace's heart.

Grace told Perry about her conversation with Susanna, and he got upset that they had talked about him behind his back. Susanna refused to speak with Perry on the phone and was stubborn about it. Perry saw how sad Grace was to lose her connection with Susanna, so the next day, he told her he's going to relent and let Grace connect to Susanna because he could see how important it was to her.

Grace asked, "How will that make you feel?"

"Happy as a lark."

"Yeah, right. I don't believe you. You're going to change your mind."

He said, "I know you don't believe me, but I'll put it down on paper to prove to you that I mean it."

He did not keep his word, not about writing down his promise and not about letting Grace talk to her family.

14

DEEP DARK DEPRESSION

One chilly spring morning, Grace came home from work taking care of Fred. Perry approached her.

"I have something to tell you. Last night, I was in the bedroom cleaning my gun. When I finished, I assembled and accidentally fired the gun."

"What! Are the kids alright?" Grace was furious.

"Yes, the kids are fine. They're still sleeping. The bullet entered the wall near the ceiling and passed through into the living room and through the opposite living room wall into the next apartment. See that hole up there?"

He pointed to a hole in the wall about a foot from the ceiling.

"Perry, how could you? Why would you even have a gun in the bedroom? What if you had hurt one of the kids? How would you feel?"

"As soon as I shot it, it scared me. I came out in the living room to check on the kids. The kids were scared because they thought I shot myself."

"Where were you when you fired it?"

"I was in the bedroom, laying on the bed, holding the gun and it accidentally went off."

"Perry, you know I'm already uncomfortable with you even having a gun. You are not even supposed to have it in the house. It should be in the garage. Promise me that you will keep the guns in the garage from now on."

"I promise. I'm very sorry. I shouldn't be cleaning my gun in the house."

Grace forgave him, but she also told him he could not buy any more guns until he sold some of the ones he already had.

A few months prior, Grace had reluctantly told Perry he could get a gun, for protection. He bought four guns. He excitedly showed Grace the best features about each weapon. He wanted her to learn how to shoot a gun. He practiced target shooting at the range. Grace wasn't interested. She didn't even want to touch the weapons.

A few weeks went by, and they almost forgot about the incident. One evening Grace made a delicious green curry Thai chicken dinner. After dinner, Perry laid his four guns out on the bed because he was preparing to sell two of them. There was an unexpected knock on the door. Grace and the kids stayed in the bedroom while Perry answered the door.

It was four police officers who questioned Perry about shooting his gun into the next apartment. He admitted he accidentally fired the gun and explained what happened, except he told them he was standing at the dresser when the gun went off. The police called Grace and the kids outside, and questioned them about their eye colors, what they liked to do, their ages and other light-hearted subjects. They asked each one about the gun accident, and they all told the truth. It was an accident that had happened while Grace was at work, the kids had been in the living room, and Grace felt uncomfortable having the guns around.

After the police went into the apartment and saw the guns on the bed, they told Perry he would have to go to court and pay a fine. The police questioned the family and stood around and talked for what seemed like hours before they left. Their visit left Grace disturbed and unsettled. She didn't feel right that the police knew things about them and where they lived.

Another week went by. The kids came home from school and said a lady had questioned them in the office. She had asked them if their father got angry often. They told her that their father yelled, but their mother never did. She questioned how they did in school and what their home life was like. She asked them if they got enough to eat and if they felt safe.

Perry got a call from the same lady the next day. She was from family services and she had come to the school and questioned the children. She wanted to make an appointment to speak to Perry and Grace and get to know their family.

Perry and Grace did not like that someone came to the school and questioned their children, trying to find dirt on their family, trying to find a reason to take the kids away. They were anxious.

The next day Grace took a note to the school and told the secretary that nobody had permission to talk to their children without hers and Perry's permission.

The secretary explained, "If Social Services comes in and wants to talk to a child, there is nothing we can do to stop them. Social Services has the authority to talk to whomever they want. However, we would be willing to call you and let you know it is happening. Everybody in the office was shocked that she wanted to talk to your kids because you have such good kids. We told the social worker we've never noticed anything of concern about your kids. They're happy and they love school. They're respectful. Ben is in Penny Harvest. Jimmy is always getting green slips for respect and responsibility. We had no idea why she was asking about your kids. We were sure she had the wrong family."

"It's my job to protect my kids."

"I will let the social worker see your note, and I will do what I can. I'll tell her to call you."

The next day, the social worker called Grace after she questioned Emily, who was five.

She said, "I have no concerns. Your kids were all well behaved and confident and not scared. I need to come and talk with you and Perry in your home."

Grace was glad to hear that but still worried to imagine what she was looking for. Perry wanted the house cleaned from top to bottom before the woman visited.

They hired a maid to come in and clean. When Laura, the social worker, came the following week, the apartment was spotless. Emily was home sick from school. The social worker asked them about their marriage and Perry yelling at the kids. He admitted he did yell at the kids on occasion.

She said, "I was surprised how well behaved the kids were. I asked the school personnel if they noticed anything of concern about the kids. They said they hadn't."

At the end of the interview, she concluded by saying, "I really don't see anything to be concerned about. I will probably recommend closing the case."

Grace knew they had dodged a proverbial bullet. She knew their home was chaotic and that Perry was abusive sometimes, but she certainly didn't want the social worker to know that. She didn't want to give the woman any reason to take away their kids.

The day before the social worker came, it was Adam and Emma's wedding anniversary. Grace wrote a note of congratulations to them on Facebook. Perry got upset about it and told her she should have posted it on their wall instead of on her status. He took her phone, went on Facebook and deleted her congratulatory post. Then he went through more posts and got angry about what he saw. Grace hated when he did that because then he got mad at her and they ended up fighting. To end the fights, Grace had to block someone to please him. She was still crying about it the next day before the social worker arrived to talk to her and Perry. She cried a lot, but she managed to hold it all together when the social worker was there and make it look like everything was just fine.

The next morning, as Grace was getting the kids ready for school, Perry said, "Grace, I've made my decision. You are going to have to block your whole family on Facebook because it is the right thing to do."

It was just a few days after he told her she could talk to Susanna whenever she wanted because he knew it was important to her, and it would make him happy if she was happy. Now he said, "They are not going to respect me, and this is the only way to get the message across to them that since they are shunning us, we are going to stop communication with them."

He had gone on Grace's Facebook and seen something that made him angry. "Since you aren't able to manage the relationships with your siblings, I'm going to have to do it. From now on, all communication will go through my phone, not yours." They both had cell phones so they could stay in constant contact with each other at all times.

Grace was angry, but she didn't feel safe expressing that emotion to him. She knew it did no good to argue with him since they had already had so many discussions about this. Perry did not allow the children to have contact with their relatives either. Grace dropped the children off at school, struggling to hold back tears the whole time.

When she got home, the floodgates opened, and she sat in the SUV and sobbed uncontrollably. Nothing seemed important anymore. She could feel herself slipping down into a deep dark depression. She felt so weak, so tired, broken, and sad. She was crumbling. She realized she didn't care about anything Perry said to her. She just wanted the pain to end. She wanted to die.

After she had been sitting there for twenty minutes, Perry came out.

"What's wrong?"

She was astounded by his obliviousness. He had torn out her heart, yet he wondered why she was crying. She didn't want to go into the house and hear him explain everything to her again. It was all too overwhelming. Perry led her inside and lay down on the bed with her and held her. She did not feel like cuddling, but that's what he wanted to do. Since she didn't want to anger him, she went along with it. She had school work to do and dishes and laundry, but she was not motivated to do anything. She just wanted to sleep. She couldn't make herself get up, so she stayed in bed for several hours.

Perry tried to convince her she had to cut off her family because it was the right thing to do. She felt powerless to do anything to stop it. There was no point in having another argument about it.

"I dared to open up to you and tell you it was important to me to stay connected to people. I told you this is how I am, and this is how you treat me."

Perry didn't care. It was all about making him feel better. He couldn't love her.

"I do not deal well with cutting people off. This is not something I would ever choose to do. I can't just cut people off and move on with my life like it's okay."

Perry acted like he was concerned about her, but it was an act. She didn't dare to tell him it was all his fault and that if he hadn't been such an a**hole to her family, they wouldn't be so afraid of him, and if they weren't scared of him, they would talk to him. If they spoke to him, he wouldn't have to cut them off from her. He had created the problem, and he should deal with it instead of punishing her.

Grace went to work with a sore throat. She was starting to feel physically ill from the repeated emotional trauma her body experienced. Perry called her during the night.

"I can't sleep because I can feel your vibes."

He vented his feelings about her family and explained again why it was best to cut them off. It made Grace feel depressed and broken. She didn't want to be pulled out of her restful sleep to talk about this painful subject again.

They talked for a while, and he said he felt better. Grace didn't. She was angry that he felt better and she was feeling completely emotionally and physically drained.

The next day Perry said, "I'm not going to let your sour mood pull me down. I'm not going to yell anymore because it doesn't do any good. I feel great and I'm in a great mood."

Meanwhile, Grace was in the worst depression of her life. She was mentally and physically ill. Every time Perry asked her if she was ok, she said, "No, I am not doing well."

He kept asking. The answer was always the same.

Grace started to resent Perry. She knew if she didn't talk to someone or start taking antidepressants, she was going to lose her mind. She was afraid she was going to have a mental breakdown.

At the end of the week, while she was at Fred's house, she called her friend Becky. At first, they made small talk, but the Becky started to reveal to Grace some things about her husband that sounded a lot like what Grace was going through with Perry. They began to realize their lives were very similar and Becky had been through the same thing Grace was going through. Grace was encouraged because Becky was able to give her wise advice and godly counsel. Grace was relieved to realize she was not going insane. Perry and Becky's husband did not know their wives' hearts. The women needed to connect to other people, especially other women.

Becky's friendship was a gift! She was there when Grace needed somebody to hold her up and encourage her. They confided in each other and told each other things they couldn't tell anyone else. They promised to pray for each other.

Grace began to think about standing up to Perry. She wondered what would happen if she stood up to Perry and told him she could not disconnect from her family because it hurt too much. Her heart was dying. She already felt dead. If Perry told her to leave, she knew she would consider it. She didn't want to stay with a man who did not let her talk to her family. She did not want to stay with an abusive man, one who cuts her and her kids off from their relatives. She never agreed to that, and it was unfair.

Perry was the one with problems; he was the one who couldn't get along with people. He couldn't even get along with any of his relatives. He didn't even know most of his Facebook friends in real life. Most of them were women who would take raunchy pictures of themselves to get attention. Many of them were from other countries, and they didn't even speak English. He didn't have any close friends. He had ruined all his relationships, except with Grace. She felt as if it was only a matter of time before their relationship was over. He kept threatening divorce, telling her to go back to her family. The reason she didn't was that she knew it would break his heart, but maybe that's what needed to happen

Grace realized she needed to let go of her marriage to get her heart back. It was a toxic relationship and Perry was killing her. She needed to be willing to walk out of her marriage to survive. Perry, who said she needed to submit to him, was killing her heart.

She had always allowed Perry the freedom to be himself, and dare to dream whatever he wanted, but he restricted her from expressing herself and being herself. That wasn't love; it was control and power and manipulation.

Grace told Perry, "You can try to make my family disappear. But I will always be connected to them. I will never forget them. They are a part of me."

"GRACE, THEY ARE SHUNNING US," he argued loudly. "Nobody in your family is calling us. They are all collectively ignoring us. You know it's true. They are all going on with their lives. They don't need us. They have each other. They have their large churches and small groups and close friends and family gatherings. They barely even think of us."

Grace knew it was true. If they did think of Grace and Perry, it was only to think about how mean Perry was and how frightened they were of him. Grace knew Esther was terrified of him.

Perry would not let go of the past. He had not forgiven any family members for hurts they had caused. He carried his grudges for a long time. Maybe time and space was just what they needed, but Grace missed her family. She hadn't seen them for three years, and she knew Perry was not going to allow her to visit any time soon. Her family had no desire to see Perry, and he had no desire to see them. Grace was the only one who wanted reconciliation.

Grace masked her sadness and tried to be happy when she was with the kids because she wanted them to be happy. She didn't want them to see how sad and stressed she was.

One Sunday, they went to the circus. Forgetting the tension for a few hours was great. The kids enjoyed the show. Perry left after the show started, but when he wanted to come back, the attendants would not let him in. Perry lost his temper and yelled at them. He went for a drive and left Grace and the kids waiting outside for an hour before he came back to get them.

Later that afternoon, Perry asked, "Grace, I need to know, are you going to stand in solidarity with me and support me if I started a church? Are you going to be on my side, do what I'm doing, and do what needs to be done to get this church started?"

Grace looked at her hands and confessed, "Perry, I can't. I can't carry on what you want to do. You want to reject my family, and I can't reject my family. That's not my personality. That's not who I am. I feel like you are trying to make me be like you. I can't do that. My heart was made to connect with people and love people and not be malicious and vindictive. I feel like cutting people off is vindictive. I don't want to do that. It hurts me. That was your decision, not mine."

"Do you realize what you are saying? Do you understand you would be losing your marriage?

"Yes." At that point, it didn't matter if he yelled at her or how mad he got. She knew she had to speak up for herself and say this was important to her.

"Look what you're forcing me to do," he said. "I'm going to have to take the kids and drive to Texas."

Grace thought to herself that if that was a threat, she would be glad to see him go.

"I'm going to fight for my kids. I will win custody, and you won't ever see them again.

She broke down crying. "I am desperate for a resolution. I feel hopeless. There is no answer. I don't want to fight with you."

He also broke down and cried because he felt like he was losing her. Of course, Grace cared about her children, but she thought the kids would be okay if they were with Perry because she thought his battle was with her, not them.

They ended up hugging and crying some more and apologizing, even though it did not feel like had they found an answer.

Grace said, "Let's stop talking about this, and go in the living room." She still felt extremely sad, but she wanted to spend time with the kids, hugging them and telling them she loved them.

With all Perry and Grace had been through, it felt like a miracle to her that they were still together. Perry had pushed her beyond what she thought she could handle. Perry felt like Grace had purposely pushed some of his buttons. Perry told Grace how badly he wanted to beat her up at times. They had been through terrible lows. Grace felt like she was losing her whole family to the conflict with Perry. They had all contributed to the problem but refusing to talk and solve things was not the way to heal anything. Grace wanted to heal. Perry said he wanted to reconcile.

Perry agreed to talk to Diane. The conversation went well, so Grace was permitted to speak to her sister again.

Grace thought she needed to get on antidepressant medication. She tried to concentrate on thinking positive thoughts to battle the negative ones. She tried to focus on her kids. She began to feel like Perry was on her side. He said he hated to see her sad. Being estranged from her family made Grace sad because there was nothing she could do to fix it. Nobody wanted to talk to Perry, so she had to stop talking to them. They didn't want to resolve things; it was quite clear. She had to move on. Depression made her tired. She wanted to sleep a lot more. She didn't want to think about so much sadness. She was glad when she finished the semester with high marks.

Once, when Perry and Grace were in a cuddling moment, suddenly he said he missed her family. That made her angry. She felt like she was not allowed to miss them, but he was.

"Don't mess with me. You've said terrible things about my family, and now you want everybody to forget what you've done and said."

Grace felt like he had damaged the relationships with her family and she couldn't imagine how it was ever supposed to feel normal again. He didn't want her to talk to them without him present, so how could it ever get fixed or resolved? Grace knew that as long as she was married to him, she would have to go without reconciling with her relatives.

Perry was worried that Grace was going to leave him. She saw him trying to be better, and it seemed his intentions were good. Grace could see he was desperately trying to keep their marriage together. He told her he felt like he passionately displayed his love to her, but she didn't reciprocate. While she didn't feel passionately in love with him, her love for him was steady and lifelong. Some days she felt animosity toward him. Grace felt like he had damaged her, so she felt justified in her anger towards him for him not making it work with her relatives. She felt it wasn't all his fault and they needed to work on their end of things and work towards a resolution.

One evening, one the way to work, Grace snuck a phone conversation with Susanna.

"Grace, are you alright?"

"Yes, everything is just fine." She didn't want anybody in her family to know what she was going through. Perry had made her promise to not talk about him.

"Is Perry around? Can he hear our conversation?"

"No, I'm by myself. Why don't you resolve it with him? He is willing to resolve things if you would only apologize to him."

"I will not speak to Perry. Every time I do, it ends badly, and I end up hurt and crying."

"How can you call yourself a Christian if you are not willing to resolve it with someone who wants to resolve things with you?"

Susanna felt hurt that Grace challenged her faith. Grace wanted to know how Susanna justified not being willing to resolve things with Perry when he tried to fix things with her. Susanna was stubborn and fear held her back. She had had enough experiences with Perry to know she could not and would not trust him. Grace felt like she had to defend Perry, but she also felt sorry for the damage Perry had caused. Grace felt conflicted and confused. Her relationship with her sister was now strained.

Perry brainwashed Grace, and so she defended Perry the way he wanted her to because she wanted to be the good wife. She thought that Perry wanted to do the right thing. She thought he wanted to change, and she believed that he was improving.

Perry was demanding. He had said he wasn't going to yell anymore because yelling didn't fix anything. If Grace wouldn't give him the love he needed, he told her she would need to help him find a woman who would love him. Grace gave him love but it seemed like it was never enough. Perry was never satisfied and wanted her to cuddle constantly with him and provide him with sex and rub his feet. He was always asking for attention. When she felt like she couldn't fulfill his needs, she gave up. She couldn't keep up with his demands. She gave him love when she could. He kept her focused on his needs, but he did not focus on her needs. He did not give her what she needed. He was a taker, and she was a giver.

It seemed like Perry was trying to make Grace be like him. He never accepted her just the way she was. Grace didn't feel understood or appreciated. Perry should have either moved on with someone else or learned to take her the way she was. He criticized her and scrutinized everything she did. He was judgmental and had a strong opinion about everything. At the same time, he was easily offended.

A few times Grace showed up at her client Fred's house to start her shift and was crying. The other caregiver was Bill, a tall, soft-spoken, compassionate gentleman. He noticed Grace was not doing well. Grace often spoke to Bill about how sad she was that her husband did not get along with her family.

"I'm sorry Grace. I'm here if you want to talk."

Bill would offer some perspective and psychology and talk about how people's self-images formed. He seemed to have a lot of insight.

Grace was thankful to have a wonderful friend like Bill who was there when she needed one. When she had first met Bill a year earlier, she was amazed at how soft-spoken and gentle he was. She had the quietest conversation she had ever had with a man. She told Perry afterward that she had met a man with a soft voice. Bill was divorced, but he still loved his ex-wife despite the fact she was married to someone else and seemed to hate him. Grace couldn't imagine why.

Bill listened to Grace talk about how her heart was breaking. He knew she still loved Perry and was trying to fix the relationship. He also understood that she needed to stay connected with her relatives. He offered to let her use his address, so she was able to receive letters from her sister. Perry never found out about those letters.

Perry judged the cards and letters that arrived at their home address from relatives. If the kids received birthday cards from Emma, Perry took a black marker and crossed off the words from their grandmother that said she was praying for them and that God loved them. Perry told Grace he did not want anything religious coming from her mother. He did not want Grace to say anything about God when they talked, which was difficult for her because she spoke of God every day. God was always present in her life. Other cards and letters from family members were checked for any religious words, and he would cross them off or throw them in the trash if they did not meet his standards.

15

BECOMING HOMELESS

Grace was out of college for the summer. The kids had a week of school left. Grace had prayed and asked God to stop Perry from starting the Jeffersonian Church. A few days later, they received a letter from the apartment management office notifying them that they had broken the lease by shooting a gun on the premise and they had three days to move out. They were being evicted.

Grace took time off from work and packed up their entire apartment in two days. They moved everything they didn't need immediately into a storage unit, and everything they needed to live was packed into their SUV. They stayed in a hotel. Grace continued to take the boys to school until the end of the school year. She continued to work. Perry stopped mentioning starting a Jeffersonian Church.

Perry declared, "I'm never going to live in another apartment again. I'm not giving one more dollar to those greedy-a** apartment lords."

After the boys finished school, the next week they stayed at a different hotel, five minutes from where Grace worked. Perry decided they should move back to Texas, but before they left, they wanted to go to Rocky Mountain National Park.

On Grace's day off, they drove through the park. They loved driving over the mountains, seeing twelve feet of snow, and looking down from the tops of mountains. It was breath-taking. Driving through the grand mountains, and being reminded of how small and insignificant they were, felt healing. They loved driving with the windows down and smelling the fresh, unpolluted, crisp air. The elevation in some places was ten thousand feet. It took all day to drive through to the other side. They stopped several times to walk around and take pictures.

Grace was concerned about moving back to Texas because Perry hated his sister and his father. He also hated his brother, who lived in Florida. Grace was afraid Perry was going to become even more mean and abusive. He said he wanted to move back closer to his dad just to make his dad miserable. Grace knew that was sadistic. He had a lot of animosity toward his family. She was sad when she realized she was not going to be allowed to have relationships with any of his relatives or her relatives.

Perry asked, "When are the antidepressant pills going to start working? When are you going to become happy and smiling?"

"They are working. I'm not crying every day."

He wanted her to jump out of bed and start doing cheers and pumping everybody up. She couldn't keep up with his unrealistic expectations. It had been months since she had talked to Esther, or Willie or Kevin. She had spoken to Diane earlier in the year, and Emma and Susanna more recently. Diane was pregnant with her first child.

What she didn't know was that her family was very concerned about her. They held a prayer meeting for Grace and Perry. They wondered if they should drive out and rescue Grace and the kids. The Chupp family had no proof that Grace and the kids were being abused, but they knew that they felt abused by Perry. He had exerted control over them, and they were afraid of him. He was rude and mean to them, and they suspected he was also mean to the kids and Grace, but none of them did anything but pray because whenever they talked to Grace and asked how she was doing, she always said things were going well. She hid the bad news from her family because she did not want them to worry and talk to Perry. If that happened, Grace knew Perry would become angry and it could end their marriage, which is what she feared most.

Over the next month and a half, they moved to a different hotel each week, looking for the cheapest deals. Grace continued to work as usual. Perry was not working. The kids were not going to school since it was summer break.

The first week in July, they decided to go back to Rocky Mountain National Park since they had enjoyed it so much. Perry wanted to find a spot not crowded with people where they could hike. They drove up to about ten thousand feet and found a mountain peak. They parked and decided to climb another thousand feet to the summit. They could look out a long distance and down on other peaks. It was a fantastic view. Perry gave them specific instructions to follow him, but Ben and Jimmy were fast climbers and were in front. There were many rocks to step on, and it was kind of like crawling uphill. They took breaks and looked around if they got tired. It was exhilarating.

As they neared the top, Grace and Emily climbed together. Grace saw Ben in front of her. He went one direction, and she went in another. Grace and Emily climbed carefully over some steep, jagged rocks and climbed on top of a huge boulder. It was challenging and dangerous. They had reached the peak. They sat on the rock and looked around. The stone was about seven feet wide. There was no room to walk around.

Grace said to Emily, "That was the scariest moment of my life."

From their perch, they could look down on all sides. For a moment, Grace felt proud that they had accomplished reaching the top. She and Emily sat at the top and felt the exhilaration of being there. She could see the boys in front of her on a grassy peak. She thought once they climbed on the other side of the boulder, they would be with the boys. The boys were also at the top; they were walking along a flat grassy ridge that was about ten feet wide.

When Perry saw where they were, he became angry that they had not followed him. He was afraid that they were going to fall. He quickly flew into a full panic attack. He was upset and concerned.

"WHAT ARE YOU DOING OVER THERE? Why are you putting your lives at risk? That's the stupidest thing you've ever done! Why didn't you follow my lead? You are scaring me. Don't you realize how easily you or Emily could fall? How are you going to get off that boulder?"

Grace figured it would be no problem, that they would continue forward off the other side of the boulder, and then she and Emily would be with them. She cautiously leaned her head forward and saw there was no way she could go ahead, as sharp jagged rocks were pointing up from ten feet below. Grace assured Perry she and Emily would go back the same way they had come. They did not even get a picture of themselves at the top.

It was scary to climb backward off of the boulder because one misstep could have resulted in a fatal fall. There were a few sharp, jagged rocks to climb over, and then they were safe. Perry was so angry that he did not want to stay at the top. He demanded they all go back down the mountain immediately. Grace was disappointed that they were not all together at the top of the mountain.

Grace apologized to Perry for scaring him. As she was climbing down her legs were shaking. For the last ten feet of the trail, Perry picked a dangerous descent with loose gravel that was quite steep. She told him that she did not feel comfortable about climbing down that part, but he ignored her. Grace fell and scraped her skin; Perry scolded her. She was crying and hurt. There was gravel in her shoes. When they were back in the car, Perry started yelling at her.

"Why can you just follow my lead?"

She was so baffled by his outburst because she hadn't been trying to assert her power. She had no problem following him, but she hadn't known if Perry was going to the peak. She thought he was behind her.

Grace apologized repeatedly and told him it wouldn't happen again. She was crying and wanted to get away from Perry and be alone and cry, but they had an hour of driving ahead of them. She never wanted to climb a mountain with him again.

Grace knew Perry was mad at her, so anything she said was going to anger him more. She was willing to do whatever she could to calm him down and make him stop being mad at her, but she couldn't. Perry kept saying he just wanted her to say something, but he was jealous that she was able to climb on top of that boulder, something he did not dare do. He secretly admired her strength but didn't have to guts to express that to her. Instead, he brought her down to his level by degrading her.

She blurted out, "I do not want to talk to you. I thought you were mean to me when I fell, and I do not think we should talk to each other right now because we are mad at each other. I'm sorry for what happened on the mountain, and it won't happen again because I'm never climbing a mountain with you again. I didn't want to say something because I don't have nice things to say. Are you happy?"

They drove in silence for a while. At Highway 25, Perry missed his exit because he was too involved in filming another driver. He was still angry at Grace and also at the other driver. Then he yelled at Grace for not telling him where the exit was. He asked her why she hadn't told him.

"Because I thought you knew where our exit was, and apparently what you were doing seemed to be more important."

Perry just kept yelling at her, asking the same questions again and again. They turned around and drove back to their exit.

When they reached the exit, he pulled over on the ramp and stopped. They were a quarter mile from their hotel. Grace thought that was her perfect opportunity to get out. She just wanted to get away from him and his yelling and constant questions and torture, so she opened the door. Perry grabbed her pants.

"LET GO!"

Perry was shouting at her, telling her to stay and Grace was yelling back, "NO!"

When he finally let go of her pants, she fell out onto the grass. By this time, he was in a state of panic, and the kids were all crying. They were all begging her to get back in the car. Perry said he would give her space.

"You are a liar! You lie to get whatever you want."

He was yelling at her that she was scaring the kids. She opened the door and told the kids to calm down, and she would meet them back in the hotel. She just wanted to get away because Perry would not stop yelling at her and she could not take it anymore. He finally convinced her for the sake of the kids to get back in the SUV, and he promised he would give her space at the hotel, so she got back in, and they drove to the hotel.

Perry did not leave and give her the space he promised. Instead, he went into the bathroom for a long time. She just continued to do what she usually would, and she fixed the kids peanut butter and jelly sandwiches.

Grace knew that when Perry yelled, she couldn't communicate with him in a healthy or effective manner. She thought that Perry might understand the damage he caused by screaming at them, and he would stop, but he never seemed to learn. Just as he calmed down, something else would anger him, and the cycle of yelling would begin again. He accused Grace of provoking him or said she deserved it for being so stupid.

Perry accused, questioned her, criticized her, scolded her, judged her, and belittled her. It was torture. He went on and on, saying the same things again and again, just in different words. He could keep a conflict going for hours, but she just wanted to avoid it. When he asked her a question, he did not stop to let her think and answer the question. By the time she knew what she wanted to say, he was off on another subject. She couldn't get a word in edgewise. He dominated their talks and constantly interrupted Grace.

Grace often felt angry at Perry, but she did not feel safe to express that anger to him. If she did, he would often become even more upset. He thought his anger was justified, but not hers. Perry used fear to control Grace and the kids. They walked on eggshells around him because they did not want to do anything that would give him a reason to be mad.

They continued to stay in hotels for close to six weeks until Perry took the kids and their only vehicle and left for Texas with the understanding that he would look for a job. Grace worried he might be mean to the kids when he became stressed, but the kids never reported anything. She was also glad to get a break from Perry. On her days off from work, Grace could walk all over town and visit friends. She spent the nights at her client Fred's house. Her co-worker Bill took a vacation and let her work all the days he was gone. She was able to visit a church and make some new friends.

Ten days later, Perry and the kids came back. They had decided they did not want to move to Texas. They missed beautiful Colorado and the cooler weather. Perry bought two small tents and five sleeping bags. Instead of staying in hotels, they decided to camp. They purchased some cooking supplies and found several campgrounds.

At first, camping was fun. It was peaceful to be in nature, away from the city traffic and noise without television and sometimes without internet. Perry played his guitar and wrote a song from time to time. The kids would play games and watch squirrels and chipmunks. Perry wanted to teach the kids how to fish, but he always did the fishing and made them observe, which was frustrating for the boys because they wanted to fish, but Perry always held the fishing pole. They built campfires and told scary stories. Perry and Grace slept in one tent, while the three kids slept in the other.

They found a remote campground up in the mountains at Golden Gate Canyon State Park. It was at a high elevation, so it was a bit cooler. Perry said he was using the time in the mountains to do a lot of thinking. He said being in the mountains was healing for him. Grace also wanted some healing. She thought if she could get some distance from him, maybe she could start to repair herself. She was on an antidepressant so at least she wasn't crying every day.

Their first night camping, Grace had a painful and honest conversation with Perry. It felt good to get some things off her chest. She was angry at Perry for a lot of stuff, mostly for making her separate even more from her family than she already was. She was scared of his reckless driving and the way he put their lives at risk. She was furious that he wasn't working more. She was enraged that he shot his gun in their apartment and that it resulted in them being homeless. She was angry that he got so mad at her and the kids.

When they were camping at Aspen Meadows, he was a jerk, yelling at Grace and the kids for not packing up the tents and sleeping bags right.

Grace finally couldn't take it anymore and spoke up, "It sure doesn't seem like you love us by the way you're speaking to us."

Perry sat down and asked all of them if he should leave and let them live life without him. They all stood around awkwardly, nobody saying anything. They were all afraid if they said what they really felt, that it would be nice without him around, it would make him angry. Nobody wanted that.

Finally, Emily said, "I don't want you to go." Ben and Jimmy agreed.

Ben said, "It doesn't feel like you love me when you tell me to shut up."

When Grace was alone with Perry, he asked, "Do you want me to leave?"

She thought it would be nice not to have his anger, meanness, and rudeness around. "I just don't understand why you can't be nice."

"I know I can be a hard a**. Take it or leave it."

She said, "I have taken it and taken it and taken it. I've been taking it for ten years. Why can't you be nice?"

A couple of weeks later, she asked him, "When can I unblock my family? When will it have been long enough?"

"How long will they continue to ignore me?" he responded.

Grace realized he would spend the rest of his days trying to block her family out of his life. He didn't care how it affected her. He didn't realize what a jerk he was. She needed friends, girlfriends, and sisters, for her health's sake, for her mental health. Everything was his decision, and he didn't care about anyone but himself.

Grace sometimes dreamed of being in a relationship with someone who let her talk to her family as much as she wanted. She would be with a nice guy who respected and understood that she needed friends.

Grace harbored so much resentment and hostility toward Perry. She blamed him for not getting along with her family. He didn't have any friends. He didn't even get along with his own family. Everybody in her family had lots of friends, and they got along with almost everyone—except Perry. Perry was the common denominator in all the failed family relationships.

One evening, Perry said he was feeling negative vibes from her. She confessed that she was feeling bitterness toward him. She said she missed her family and she wanted to talk to them.

"You can talk to them whenever you want, on the condition that both of us have to talk to them."

She already knew that nobody in her family had any desire to talk to Perry, so she knew that would not be acceptable to them. She had to talk to her family members for her own health. She had to be able to reach out and tell her sisters she loved them for herself. Grace knew Perry would never understand. She knew he would never allow her to talk to her sister, to unblock her family. He would go to his grave holding on to his principles. He didn't care.

There were bears in the area where they were camping. The ranger warned the campers to lock up food and not sleep near food. During one of their stays at a campground, a bear came into the camp and bent the steel lid of a dumpster locked with a bar. The bear got trash and food out of the dumpster and scattered it around, leaving a big mess. Grace feared a bear would come and eat one of her children. The nights up in the mountains got cold. In August, she would wear her winter coat and hat and snow pants and sleep inside a sleeping bag to stay warm. The kids didn't get as cold as she did.

Grace's birthday was in August. Bill brought a big, beautiful, chocolate cake to work along with pies and other desserts. He told Grace she could take the cake home to her family and they could all eat it. Grace was grateful and was happy to have a birthday cake. When Perry came to pick her up, she held the cake in her lap.

Once Perry realized the cake she was holding was from Bill, he accused her of cheating on him and having an inappropriate relationship with Bill. He took the cake away from her and set in in the middle of the parking lot, on the concrete, and drove away. Perry was sure Bill was trying to win her over by giving her food, but Perry said, "I'm doing you a favor by preventing you from eating sweets."

Perry and Grace decided to see if they could get a motorhome. It would have to be under her credit because he had destroyed his. They looked for motorhomes on the internet and found a few at a reasonable price. Perry and Grace tried to sell their large items in storage so that we could buy an RV. She was starting a new semester in college, and she would also be homeschooling the kids. She was getting some grant money from college that they would be putting that toward a motorhome.

They found an RV at a dealership south of Denver. They went and looked at it, and Perry liked it. Grace went inside and applied for financing. While she was waiting, she got an email denying an application for funding on another RV. Grace was worried and knew that if she couldn't get financing, they were doomed to remain homeless. The finance manager kept asking her questions and talking to somebody on the phone. Suddenly, the bank had approved a loan for twenty-six thousand dollars, which was enough to purchase the motorhome.

They were excited and could hardly sleep that night. Ben, Perry, and Grace were all in the car talking at three in the morning because they couldn't fall asleep. The next day they got insurance, and two days later they drove the RV off the lot.

They went to their storage unit to get bedding and kitchen supplies for the RV. Perry suggested they wash all the bedding before they put it down since it had been in storage. When Grace got to the laundromat, she realized it was only pillowcases, so she washed those and washed the clothes, too. Perry asked her to get dinner at Wendy's. By the time she got back to the storage unit to drop off the food and unload more stuff from the car, she knew she would only have time to switch the laundry to the dryer before she had to go to work. Perry was furious with her because she still had not washed the bedding. She told him she had to go to work.

He took away her keys. "You are not going to work until you finish the laundry. You cannot leave all this on my shoulders. You had one job and you need to complete it."

"I hate you so much right now. You are such an a**hole."

Perry forced her to unpack boxes until she found the bedding. She was angry because he could have emptied the boxes while she was at the laundromat earlier. She wanted to pack up the RV, but she didn't get to do that at all because she ran out of time and had to go to work.

Becky called while Grace was driving to work. It felt good to talk to Becky. She was so kind and understanding and supportive. After Grace spoke to Becky, she dried her tears and called Perry to apologize. Later that night, Perry called and said he had gone to the laundromat, but it had closed. Again, he blamed her because she started the laundry and she wasn't there to complete it, and now he had to clean up her mess. Grace asked Perry if he thought he bore any responsibility for not getting to the laundromat before it closed or looking in the boxes in storage for the bedding while she was at the laundromat. He refused to accept any responsibility. They had several long conversations that night.

She admitted she struggled with some things, like camping, not talking to her friends and family, and being homeless. She also revealed that she sometimes wondered what it would be like to be with a different man, one who got along with her family, who had a house, who was kind to her, who was soft-spoken, like Bill, but she didn't mention Bill specifically.

Perry was already suspicious Grace was cheating on him. He had asked her several times if she had sex with Bill; her answer was always the truth – no. He didn't want Grace to bring home food from Fred's that Bill brought because he thought Bill was giving it to her as gifts.

She started thinking about how much she loved her kids and how she wished she was in the RV with them. Although she was still angry with Perry, she told him she loved him and that she was thankful for the RV. He got the laundry back the next day, and they all settled into the RV.

Over the next few months, she continued working, taking care of Fred. She was also taking four online college classes and homeschooling the kids. Perry did not help with the kids at all. Ben and Jimmy were in fourth grade, and Emily was in first grade. They would sit at the table in the RV and she would help them do their schoolwork. Many times, Perry would be in the bathroom or laying on the bed, but he did contribute in other ways. He maintained the RV. He did the oil changes and kept things running smoothly.

Perry needed to be in Colorado Springs for a short project, so on Grace's days off, they took the RV and headed to a campground in the mountains near Colorado Springs. Grace called Becky, and she and her husband and one of their daughters agreed to come to see the Lawrences at their campsite. She was so excited to see her again finally.

They both knew from previous conversations that their husbands had a few things in common. They built a bonfire and roasted hot dogs and burgers. They had a great time. Becky and Grace were so happy to get to talk. Their husbands spoke to each other and got along great. They found they had a lot of interests in common and had a lot to discuss. They both had the same temperament. Becky and Grace giggled, secretly hoping this would mean they could see each other more often. They enjoyed that evening. Grace loved being around a dear friend who understood her situation and helped her feel better.

After Perry's project ended, they returned to the Denver area. Grace went back to work, and Perry parked the RV in a park or campground or parking lot. He and the kids would stay with the RV while Grace took the SUV to work.

Perry was still doing contract jobs once in a while. Grace was with the kids in the RV during a gig he had in Aurora. She needed to fix some supper for the kids before she went to work, so she heated cans of clam chowder. Perry came into the RV and flew into a rage.

"I bought that clam chowder for me. I got other soup for you. The clam chowder was mine, not for you." Then he insulted her and called her names.

Grace apologized but told him to deal with it. She jumped into the SUV and drove away before he could stop her. He scrambled into the driver's seat of the RV and started following her, but he forgot his briefcase was sitting in the parking lot, with his computer inside. In his haste to chase Grace, he drove over his briefcase, and that was the end of his computer. Perry was angry and cried over his mistake.

They got bikes for the kids and Grace. They enjoyed the many biking trails that are all over the Denver and Longmont areas. One day they were at a park in Aurora. The kids were outside biking while Perry and Grace were inside the RV fighting. She was discouraged. He yelled at her, and she screamed back. Sometimes if she yelled at him, he would calm down and tell her to calm down. They sat at the table and tried to talk it out, but it did not help her feel better. He wanted her to see that he was a good guy and trying to fix their marriage, but all she needed was to end the conversation and go to work.

Perry would not let her go to work. He brought the kids into their fight. He asked them to choose between him and Grace, where they wanted to live. She couldn't believe he was doing that to the kids; they looked so sad. She did not want to split up, but he was forcing the issue. The kids told Perry they wanted to live with him. That made Grace sad. She believed he had somehow convinced the children that he was a better parent than she was. She felt very alone, realizing if they split up, she would have to leave without the kids.

"You are not leaving until we work this out. My marriage is more important than your job."

When she got into the SUV, he also climbed in and would not get out so she could go to work. He made her call into work to say she was going to be late; then they talked more. She was desperate to leave and get a break from him. She believed he would calm down after she left for work. Finally, after an hour, he let her go. She was still crying when she arrived at work.

Bill was there and noticed she was crying. He said he was there for her if she wanted to talk. Bill stayed another hour to listen to her. He offered his perspective in a very gentle way. He was such a comforting friend to her wounded heart. It helped to have a friend who would listen to her when she felt so alone.

She wondered if Perry had done anything inappropriate to any of the kids, especially Emily. One night, Grace was putting pajamas on Emily, and Emily said she did not like to put on her jammies to go to sleep. Grace asked her why. Emily told her that once Perry took off her jammies, and she was naked sleeping with him. She knew it because she had diarrhea and made a mess on her hand because she wasn't wearing any underwear or anything.

Grace confronted Perry and asked him why he would sleep with Emily naked.

He became angry, "She said that? She is lying! I would never do anything inappropriate with my daughter. I can't believe you would think of me that way. Don't believe her. Emily, come here. You are getting a spanking for lying."

Emily burst into tears and said, "I was just joking."

Grace boldly announced, "Listen, nobody is getting a spanking." Grace wondered if Emily was joking because she knew her daughter usually told the truth.

Grace and her children were learning that telling the truth was dangerous. Lying became a way to defend themselves from Perry. They were all afraid of his wrath. They found it was often necessary to lie to Perry to keep him calm and keep themselves out of trouble.

Winter came, and they were at a campground in Longmont. There were several inches of snow. The RV had heat, and they kept warm. They made a special little meal for Thanksgiving.

There was no turkey, but they did have green bean casserole, which was a favorite.

Perry talked about finding a piece of property to purchase so they could park on land they owned. Grace wanted a piece of land that was not anywhere close to fracking. She knew how dangerous and unhealthy fracking was. There were hundreds of fracking sites in Colorado, and she could count a hundred just on her way to work. Fracking is when water is pumped into shale rock to fracture the rock and release methane gas, which generates fuel and energy. It's a big money scheme. They looked for land all over Colorado, but since people had been moving to Colorado by the thousands, there was nothing affordable.

Colorado had recently legalized the recreational use of marijuana. There were marijuana stores almost on every corner. It was legal for anyone who could prove residency to buy and use marijuana recreationally. Marijuana came in many forms, including oils, sprays, gummy candies, drops and dried so that even children and animals could use it. There was not enough housing for all the new residents. The prices on apartments and homes went sky high.

Grace and Perry looked online on all kinds of sites for land or homes, but even a little shack on undeveloped land cost upwards of two hundred thousand. There were thousands of homeless or desperate people in Denver. Everywhere they went, they saw people standing on the street, holding signs, asking for food, money, jobs, or help. Grace saw people camping beside biking trails, and she saw homeless people wherever she went. People would approach her in her car and ask for money. She did help out and give a little here and there.

They decided they needed to look for land outside of Colorado. They looked for property in other states and finally found cheap, undeveloped land in Arizona. There was no fracking in Arizona. They decided once Christmas break was over, Perry and the kids would go to Arizona and look for land.

One day, Perry lost his sunglasses in the Walmart parking lot. He stood in the middle of the parking lot looking for them until Ben found them about ten feet away. Perry was mad at Grace because she hadn't helped him look for the glasses. They went back inside the RV, and he yelled at her. Grace tried to talk to him, but Perry said she was combative and aggressive and argumentative. He also told her to shut up, so she shut up. Grace shut down, and yet, he continued to berate her and verbally assault her and said that she was abusive to him.

She began forming a plan in her mind to leave Perry. She knew it would hurt the kids, but she had to get away from him. She knew their marriage wasn't healthy or safe. She knew in her heart of hearts that it was over, but she was scared to tell him that. He had already said he would fight for the kids. She just wanted to get away from him.

When Perry and Grace were alone, and the kids were watching a video, she told him she didn't want to be married to him anymore. He didn't seem surprised. Perry told Grace he had been feeling animosity from her for some time. Grace admitted she had been carrying around pain and sadness for a while. She tried to hide it and be strong and pretend like nothing was wrong, but it was killing her. Grace told Perry he was too restrictive with her and that sometimes she just wanted to do whatever she wanted to do, be friends with whomever she wanted, talk to whomever she wanted. She wanted to listen to music of her choice and have her own beliefs.

"You're an a**hole, Perry."

"And you're a b**ch."

"I guess at least we're being honest with each other."

Part of her wanted to move forward with him and make future plans, but another part was afraid of him and wanted to get away from him to protect herself.

"Why didn't you talk to anyone about all of this?" he asked.

"Who would I talk to? I don't talk to anyone."

"You can talk to me."

"But you're the one who hurt me, so how would that help? I can't trust you."

"It helps to talk things out."

"I don't feel safe talking to you. It's better to keep things to myself because I don't want to hurt you or make you angry. That's never my intention. We are incompatible, and I don't feel safe talking to you."

Some nights when she was at her client, Fred's house, Perry would call her in the middle of the night to talk. He called her one night to tell her he wanted her to stand up for him to her family, to say to them that she was on his side.

"Perry, I've stood up for you lots of times. The reason people in my family don't like you or don't want to talk to you is their own experiences with you. You have yelled at them. My mom hung up on you because you were yelling at her and making her cry."

"Well, I was hurt because she cut me off from what I wanted to say. She doesn't listen to me, and she interrupted me."

They talked for over an hour. Grace tried to be a friend and listen to him, but Perry was only trying to convince her to move on from her family without actually saying it. He believed he was more progressive than she because she was hanging on to things from the past, like her family. She tried to explain to him that she was connected forever to her family, but he thought it would be healthy for her to cut them off.

Perry wanted Grace to write to her sister Esther and demand an apology. Diane had talked to Perry and was kind, and he accepted her, but Esther thought Perry was wrong for Grace and she was terrified of him. When her daughter Jazzy had gotten married, they were not invited because the family was afraid Perry would be disruptive at the wedding. While that was hurtful, Grace understood because Perry was unpredictable and untrustworthy. He was aggressive, mean, rude and angry. He wanted Grace to tell Esther that he and Grace and the kids would like to come to Indiana for a visit but that they would not be seeing her. Esther had offended him, and he was going to punish her by keeping her from seeing Grace.

A little later, Grace received a text message from her mother saying she was thinking of Grace and that she loved all of them. Grace sent the text to Perry, thinking he would like to know that Emma loved him. He called Grace immediately.

"Tell your mom to back off and stop harassing us."

"I can't say that. I can't say things that hurt my mom. I can't do that."

"You are not my friend. You are not standing up for me."

Perry hung up but called back later, and they talked more. By the time the sun rose, Grace's mind had turned to mush from him telling her what she should be doing and thinking. As soon as she got home, she went right to sleep.

Perry loved to talk to her during the night when her brain was tired, and she couldn't think straight.

He never seemed to get tired. He would be awake all night because sometimes his brain couldn't shut off. He overreacted to things and became overwhelmed. The coping mechanism he had for dealing with all the emotions and thoughts was to talk to Grace.

Susanna called Grace one day when she was home in the RV. Perry had her phone, so he answered the call. He just asked her if Grace could call her back. Susanna was surprised to hear Perry's voice and did not want to talk to him. Later, when Grace wanted to call her back, Perry insisted that he had to be on the call. Grace called Susanna's number and Ron, her husband, answered the phone.

"Can I talk to Susanna?"

Then Perry spoke up, "This is Perry, how are you doing Ron?"

Ron hung up. Ron had seen his wife crying and distressed for days after her conversations with Perry. For months afterward, Perry acted like he was all hurt that Susanna and Ron rejected him, and he used that against Grace. He told Grace that was proof they didn't want to repair the relationship.

Perry made it clear to Grace that she was supposed to disconnect from her family and leave them in the past. It devastated her to think about not having a relationship with her sisters. She was close to her family, and it made her feel devalued to realize that Perry did not understand what healthy relationships were.

She wanted to be the good wife, but she didn't know how. She thought if she could counsel Perry on how to patch up relationships with her family, he might see God's truth and change his mind. She wrote a letter to Perry, inspired by God as if she was Perry's guidance counselor. The letter was dated December 2015.

Dear Perry,

It's your guidance counselor here. I think I know how to help you. You have some issues you are facing with your wife's family. You have felt hurt by her family members. You have felt shunned and rejected by them. It's been years and you still carry these hurts with you. I know you would like to move forward and not have to deal with these people anymore. But in your process, you have been hurting your wife and kids. Please read this entire letter before reacting.

First of all, let me say I'm sorry they hurt you. I'm sorry they rejected you. I'm sorry for how messed up this has gotten. Your way of dealing with these problems is not helping your wife. Now your hurt has spilled over to your wife, and now you are hurting her. So your methods are not working.

I know about your past. I understand your parents neglected you. I know you did not get what you needed from your parents and I am sorry about that. I'm telling you I'm sorry because you will never receive an apology from your parents. They did the best they knew how at that young time in their lives. They made some mistakes which left you feeling left out, forgotten and neglected. You did not deserve that. I'm sorry that happened to you. Now that is not your wife's fault. She wasn't there when those things happened in your past. She came along much later.

From what I understand, you married your wife, and there were some misunderstandings, some offenses, some negative interactions between you and some members of her family. Is that your wife's fault? Did she cause that to happen? No. From what I understand, you had some conversations with members of her family that went wrong. You felt threatened, you felt hurt, you felt offended, and you reacted. You yelled at them. Let me tell you something. The moment you yelled at some-one in her family, you may not see it as a big deal, but they did. They did not know how to deal with your rage. You caused them to feel scared and felt the need to protect themselves. Perry, the way to communicate with someone is not to yell at them. The moment you yell at them, suddenly, you're an enemy. You're the opponent. You have made your-self someone of whom they need to be frightened. The people in her family did not marry you. They did not promise to put up with your rage. They do not have to sit there and take your yelling. That is not their obligation. If they feel threatened by you, which I'm sure they did, they have a right to withdraw from you to protect themselves, which is what they did. They disengaged, not to hurt you, but to defend themselves against your anger. They realized you're too volatile to be around you. They were afraid if they invited you to a wedding, you would become disruptive. They were afraid to talk to you on the phone because you had yelled at them and they could not say what they wanted to say. You were louder than them. You see why yelling is not a good form of communication? If they are not yelling, you are forcefully louder than they are and you have an advantage over them. It's unfair. You get to say what you want, but you don't listen to them. You interrupt them and talk louder than them; you don't give them a fair turn to speak.

They don't feel like you listen to them. Your style of communication is damaging.

You need to find a way to repair the damage you have done. You have a responsibility in this problem. Your wife did not cause you to yell at them, nor did she cause them to say things that offended you. She did not cause them to hurt you, nor did she cause them to feel hurt by you. The damage in these relationships is between you and the members of her family. So please stop telling your wife to fix your problems.

I'm going to give you step by step instructions on how to heal this. Your method of fixing this is not working because it is hurting your wife. She feels as if you are slowly killing her. But I will address that in the next section.

1. The way to fix these issues is for you to write a letter. A phone call will not work. It must be a written form of communication. It can be a text, an email or a card or letter. You need to send a letter stating how you felt hurt by them. You need to state explicitly what they did that was offensive or hurtful.

2. Then you need to say how that made you feel. This requires softening up and opening your heart, which may not feel good, but it must be done to heal the hurt. This means becoming vulnerable.

3. Then you need to talk about your reaction. Specifically, you need to state why you felt the need to yell. This is important because it is important to them and they need to hear it.

4. Then you need to apologize for your role in this issue. They need to hear an apology from you, and you need to say it for yourself as well. This is important in the healing process.

5. Then ask for forgiveness. It may not magically make everything better right away, but it will start to resonate with them. It will go a long way in fixing this.

6. Request that they respond to you. State why you would like a response. Give them an avenue to respond to you. Do not demand it. The key here is to be soft.

I wanted to help you solve this because I hate to see you hurting and blaming your wife for this. She did not cause this. She is not the one who has a problem with her family members. She would like to be able to see her family. But you do not want that happen because you are making your problem her problem. Do not punish her because you cannot get along with members of her family. Don't blame her for your inability to fix your problems. The responsibility lies with you, not her. You have to admit you are a passionate person. That is not her fault. You created this situation. That is not her fault. She only married you because she loves you. She never meant for you to get hurt. She never intended for anyone to get hurt. The only thing she ever wanted was for everyone to get along and love each other.

It's not right, and it's not fair to tell your wife that she can no longer see or talk to her family members. She is an American citizen. She has a right to be on social media and be friends with whomever she wants. She has a right to love whom she wants to love. Just because you are her husband does not mean you can tell her if she can be on social media or who she can talk to or have as friends. When you do that, you are hurting her. She has a soft heart, and your actions are slowly killing her soft heart and turning her into a hard-hearted person. Then you look at her like she's a freak and call her "Cool Hand Luke." That's not right. If you don't like "Cool Hand Luke," stop turning her into "Cool Hand Luke." If you want her to remain soft and warm, let her blossom where she blossoms. When you tell her to cut off friendships, you are causing her to become cold and hard, and in turn, you are hurting yourself.

Here's an idea. Give yourself a gift. Give your wife a choice to decide to whom she wants to talk.

Don't give her the chance to say you forced her to do anything. That way she cannot have the opportunity to hold any animosity toward you. You will be giving yourself a gift of a softhearted wife you will have never seen before. She needs relationships outside of you and the kids. Don't ask me why; she just does. That's how she is wired. That's how she was created to be. By you squashing that, you are squashing her beauty, her kindness, and her softness. Does that make sense? If you do this for your wife, watch how she will slowly detach from others and start to cling more to you. You can't hold on to her with a closed fist. Open your hand and give her freedom and watch her coming back to you. She will. She loves you.

Sincerely,

Your Guidance Counselor

When Perry saw the letter, he called Grace at work.

"Did you write that letter? Or did you copy it from somewhere online?"

"Of course I wrote it! How could I have copied it from somewhere? It was specific to your situation. It's all about us. How could I have found that online?"

"It doesn't sound like you."

"That's because it's not coming from the timid me that doesn't stand up and speak the truth because I'm so afraid."

Perry didn't believe that God could give Grace wisdom or guide her. He yelled at her and disregarded the letter.

Perry also wanted Grace to get off of Facebook but she fought him. He thought it was healthy for her to get off of Facebook because that's what he had done. Again, she tried to explain how important it was for her to stay connected to friends, but Perry wanted her to make new friends in Colorado and dump the old friends. He thought she should let go of the past. While this seemed to be a good idea, in theory, it felt like isolation. She wondered how she was supposed to find new friends when they weren't going to church, and she was doing an online school program. She only saw the few people she worked with, other caregivers and her client and his family members. She was so thankful for her friendship with Becky, the one relationship Perry never tried to take away from her. She realized that since Perry didn't want her on Facebook, she would have to keep that hidden from him because she needed to stay in contact with people. She felt alone.

For Christmas, there were several packages from family members. Perry's sister Patty had sent them gifts, which included models for the kids to assemble. Perry's father had sent toys for the kids. Emma sent more toys, jewelry, a book and Christmas lights. Susanna sent gifts, as well. Perry threw Susanna's package in the trash. He gave the rest to the kids, who were so happy to feel like they had Christmas. Grace could feel the love put into the gifts and she knew their families loved them. She was angry that he had not kept the package from Susanna. But she put on a smile and tried to make the best of it. They all made a thank you video to send to Emma.

16

LIVING IN SATAN'S ARMPIT

It was January 2016. Perry and Grace had decided he and the kids would take a trip to Arizona to check out a piece of land they were looking to purchase, someplace where they could park the RV. Grace was planning on staying in Colorado to keep her job so that they could transition to Arizona without a gap in income. She was going to continue to take care of Fred, whom she had been taking care of for three years. Perry intended to find and land a job in a month. Once Perry found employment, Grace would join him and the kids in Arizona.

The first day off from work after Perry and the kids left, Grace visited Becky. They spent some time visiting Becky's mom, which was a pleasant reprieve from their stressful lives. They were free to talk about how awful their husbands had been to their families. They discovered both of their husbands were smoking marijuana and understood how their lives were even more similar. When Grace ate dinner with Becky's husband and daughters, she was struck by how awkward and quiet it was at the table until Becky's husband finished eating and left the room. After he went, they all relaxed and watched a movie together.

Grace also visited her cousin who lived south of Denver, the only relative she got to see during four years she lived in

Colorado. Grace did not disclose to her cousin what was actually going on in her marriage. They were cordial and friendly, and her visit was short.

Grace enrolled in her final semester of college. She would graduate with an associate degree. She was delighted that the end was finally in sight. She had only gone to college because Perry wanted the financial aid so he wouldn't have to work. She was exhausted.

Grace was taking a different psychology class each semester. She wanted to learn as much as she could about people, and especially Perry. She found psychology fascinating. It helped her to figure out why people were the way they were and why they did the things they did. She tried to understand Perry. She realized Perry had had an insecure attachment to his mother when he was a baby. When he was older, he had been hurt and neglected, which caused him to have relationship problems as an adult. Perry never saw a counselor, and he never forgave his parents. Instead, he chose to carry grudges and seek revenge. He hurt other people because he was hurt.

Grace missed the kids a lot while they were in Arizona. She was concerned about Perry being kind to the kids. She talked to him every day and got to talk to the kids a few times a week, but he was always around, so she couldn't get honest answers from them. She knew he was often impatient with the kids. He didn't want them to eat Cheetos because their fingers got covered with cheese dust and he got angry and yelled when they did.

He threw away the kids' toys. Emily had a backpack containing her little-stuffed animals that Perry threw away. He thought it was time for Emily to let go of those toys. She was six, and she was heartbroken. Some of Ben and Jimmy's toys were also thrown away, the Lego blocks and other small toys. The toys didn't take up much room, but Perry didn't want to see toys around. He kept saying he was a minimalist.

He threw away Jimmy's markers and colored pencils and crayons. Perry kept saying the RV did not have room for crafts, but the truth was, Perry hated the mess they made.

Once they were in Arizona, Perry also sold their bicycles. They had only had the bikes for a few months. They had enjoyed biking on the many bike paths in Colorado. Perry didn't have a bike, but Grace and the kids had loved to go biking. He thought he would be able to get some money out of those bikes, but he only got one hundred dollars for all four bikes. He replaced the bike rack on the back of the RV with a small platform which was attached to the hitch. The shelf held the generator.

Perry had bought a new generator because the one that came installed in the RV had stopped working. Instead of fixing it, he just bought a new one.

Perry spanked the kids, but not for being defiant. He spanked them when he was angry; he spanked Emily for eating the last two strawberries; he punished them for making mistakes. Perry beat the boys for not cleaning the kitchen and the bathroom correctly. Jimmy didn't make the chicken pot pies correctly, so Perry spanked him. Perry pinched Ben's cheek so hard he left a huge, purple bruise under Ben's eye. Jimmy slept until eight o'clock one morning and got spanked, while Emily's transgression was accidentally breaking Perry's briefcase. The kids made a mess with their paints, so Perry spanked Jimmy and Ben.

Perry had too many rules. He made up new rules every day. He was not consistent or stable. He made up rules to suit himself. He treated the children terribly. He was not gentle or patient. Grace felt terrible when she found out later how he treated the children. The kids often made the meals, and they always did the cleaning when she was gone. Many times, Perry prepared food, but only for himself. He ate while the kids watched him, and only when he finished would he fix food for the kids.

After a month, Perry had found a piece of land, but his job search had not even begun. In February, they decided to meet at the halfway point so they could all see one another. They met in Pueblo, Colorado and they slept in the RV and enjoyed being together. It was only for two days, and then Grace went back to work and college.

In March, Grace took five days off from work and went to Flagstaff, Arizona, to purchase the land. They met with a realtor and closed on the property and got the deed. It was Grace's first time in Arizona. She was so happy to be with her family again. They celebrated the boys' birthdays and had a good time being back together. She had a twelve-hour drive back to Colorado, so she took a more scenic route through the mountains.

When darkness fell, she was still in the mountains. She didn't realize that in the mountains, the roads became icy sooner than roads at a lower elevation. It was also foggy because it had been a warm day, but when the sun went down, it quickly cooled down, and it began to snow. She was on curvy and hilly roads. Not all parts of the roadway had rails. She was going about forty miles an hour downhill around a curve when she lost control of her SUV and started sliding on the ice. The car started spinning around. She pumped the brakes, but they didn't engage. The SUV kept sliding downhill backward.

After what seemed like forever, her rear bumper came to rest against the median rail, which prevented her from sliding into oncoming traffic. God had prevented her from hitting anyone else or sliding off the road. She restarted the engine and was able to drive out of her predicament. Her wheels had never left concrete. As she continued driving to work, she saw six more vehicles that had been in accidents. Some were upside down. She was grateful the damage to her SUV was minor.

Grace was excited about buying their land and someday being able to build a home there, but she was also sad because she felt like she was losing her connection with her Ohio family. It seemed those relationships were dying and she was grieving. Perry reminded Grace they had to make sacrifices to live out there. She was going to have to sacrifice her family. Emma had already told her they would never come out west, and Perry had already told Grace they were never going back to Ohio. She was as sad as if they were dead.

In April, Perry finally got a customer service job in Phoenix, three hours from Flagstaff. He started training, which was to last for three weeks. During one of their evening phone calls, Perry told Grace that the RV had gotten sideswiped. He said it was parked and nobody was in it when it happened. The driver's side mirror was gone, and some of the side paneling was gone too. The tail lights were messed up, and the left side tail lights were out. When Grace talked to Emily, she asked Emily if the RV was parked or if it was moving when the accident happened. Emily said it was moving. Grace did not confront Perry. She wanted to know the truth, but she did not want to get Emily in trouble.

Perry was deceptive. He wanted Grace to get the RV insured since it was uninsured at the time of the accident. He wanted her to get only the minimum insurance for the RV, as if nobody was driving it or it was in storage. He also wanted her to be named the only driver of the RV so that they could pay less. Perry wanted Grace to tell the insurance company that he couldn't drive, and he was not going to operate the RV. The truth was, he was the exclusive driver of the RV. She lied for him.

Perry promised her that once he got a job, they could call Emma and have a conversation together. It had been a year since he had told her to block her family on Facebook. She knew she could have a conversation with any of them whenever she wanted but it had to be on his phone, and he had to be part of the discussion. During the past year, she had talked to Emma only once.

Perry and Grace made a three-way call to Emma. He wanted to tell Emma he had gotten a job in Arizona and that Grace was working in Colorado. He talked about school and what they were doing. Perry dominated the conversation. Grace said maybe two sentences to Emma and the conversation felt awkward. Emma did not say much, either, but at least there was no yelling. Grace thanked Perry for allowing her to have a pleasant conversation with her mom, even though it was far from satisfactory.

A few days later, Emma texted Grace and said that she would like to talk to just Grace because Perry had degraded and insulted her in the past, accusing her of things that were not true. Grace showed Perry the texts from Emma to show him how Emma felt and how he had hurt her. He called Grace and yelled at her, trying to get her to admit that Emma was being childish. Grace refused. He was enraged. They were on the phone for over two hours.

The next morning, Perry called her up again and continued the barrage. He tried to convince Grace that Emma was the one who was ruining her physically and mentally. Perry wanted Grace to admit that her mother was acting childishly. Grace didn't want to say it, but he bullied her until she said it.

Grace realized Perry was bullying her. She knew she was going to need to let go of her marriage if she was going to stand up for herself. If she dared tell him she wanted the same rights and freedom that she gave him, Perry would end the marriage. She became very anxious and worried. She had trouble sleeping at night. She cried most of the time. She was not praying or reading the Bible. Her faith in God was shattered. Perry had said awful things to cause her to doubt in God and stop believing that God cared or heard her prayers, which discouraged her from praying. She turned to hypnosis to help her relax and go to sleep. She felt hopeless.

She sought counsel from Becky. She told Becky about her situation.

"God does not want you to feel oppressed, Grace."

"I want to stand up for myself and my rights, but I'm afraid it could end my marriage. I feel like I am a shell of who I used to be. I hardly know who I am anymore."

Becky didn't sugarcoat anything. "It very well could end your marriage. My first marriage ended when I stood up for myself. Then you'd have to battle for the kids, and since he has the kids with him in Arizona, he could get custody of them."

Becky advised Grace to wait to have this battle until they were together in Arizona.

Grace felt anguished, knowing the kids were in his grip and she did not want to go through a divorce. She just wanted to be able to talk to her mother. She felt trapped. Becky comforted her and prayed for her and gave her some encouraging scriptures. She was such a pious friend. Grace cried even more because she knew she had to do something difficult.

At the time, she had another client, a sweet old lady named Janet, to whom she became close. Janet advised her to stand up for herself. She told Grace she would never let anyone tell her she couldn't talk to her family. Grace cried a lot because she was scared of Perry. Grace thought she should take Becky's advice and wait until she got to Arizona to stand up to him. She was afraid she would never see her children again if she didn't.

Perry told her that Emma was sending him texts and he felt like they were moving in a positive direction. Grace felt encouraged by that, but when she talked to her mother without his knowledge, she learned that he hadn't told her about a conversation he'd had with Emma that had gone bad. The only thing he said to her was that a mother-in-law should shut her mouth and open her purse.

"Grace, have you given your mom your new phone number?"

Grace knew if she was ever going to stand up for herself, she had to start sometime. "Yes, I just talked to her."

He shouted, "WHAT! WE HAD A DEAL! WE HAD AN AGREEMENT!"

"That was your agreement, I never agreed to it. I am a human, and I have the same rights as every other human. I get to talk to my mom, just like everyone else."

Perry threatened to take the kids away from her. He said, "If we split up, I'm going to get custody of the kids, and you will never see them again." She had always dreaded getting on Perry's bad side because she was so afraid he would take the kids away from her and hurt them or turn them against her. She knew how vindictive he was. If he felt he was injured or wronged, he would take revenge.

She tried to stand up for herself, but he kept trying to talk her back into letting him control the relationship with Emma. Grace tried to explain it to him.

"I just can't. It's killing me inside. My heart is breaking. I miss my mom. I want to be able to talk to her."

Perry told the kids he and Grace were getting divorced. The kids were crying. Grace could see he was already brainwashing them. He bullied her into conceding to him. He asked her over and over and over again if she would let him manage the relationship with her mother. Grace told him she was afraid he would not let her speak to her family again.

"That's not true. We are going to speak to them together."

That wasn't acceptable to Grace. She felt alone and isolated in Colorado, and not to be able to talk to her mother and relatives was devastating.

"OK, you win Perry. You get to control the relationship with my mom." A piece of her died as she said it. She was numb and exhausted. They were both crying. They both felt broken down.

The next morning, Perry called her. In a low, tired voice, he said, "Congratulations, you've won. You manipulated me, and you won. How does it feel to be the winner?"

Grace could hear the anger in his voice. She did not feel like she had won. She felt like Perry hated her.

Over the next week, they continued to battle over her decision to talk to her mother without his permission. He told her he had to control the relationship with Emma because he felt she was influencing Grace. He did not want them to talk about him. He thought it would be best to keep them apart so that he could manage the relationship. He did not like that Emma sometimes told Grace she prayed for her, so he felt he had a right to block her from their lives. Grace tried to tell Perry how she felt, and he said she was playing the victim. He accused her of being sensational when she cried.

Finally, Perry told her he had been convinced by God to let Grace hold the reins in her relationship with Emma. She could call her whenever she wanted and talk about whatever she wanted. He trusted her. He had been texting Emma and had talked to her. He understood it was what Grace needed and it was the right thing to do. It seemed his heart was sincere.

"How do I know you're not going to change your mind again?"

He reminded her it was in writing because he had sent it to her in a text message. "You were right, and I was wrong."

Thirty minutes later, he called her again and said, "I was just fired from my job for stepping out and making that phone call to tell you that you could talk to your mom."

He was crying. Grace felt terrible and told him he could have waited until after work to call her so he wouldn't lose his job. She already knew it was against the rules for him to take phone calls while he was supposed to be working. She tried to comfort him.

Once Perry told her she could have a relationship with Emma, Grace started feeling better. She started feeling more love for Perry because he had allowed her to love her mother again, whereas before, she believed he wanted her to have animosity toward Emma. Her heart was opening again so she could love Emma and love Perry.

At the beginning of their marriage, Perry had asked her if he could have multiple wives. She was not okay with that. Throughout the years, he had expressed that he wanted to have girlfriends. He thought she was controlling him and emotionally abusive to him by not allowing him to have girlfriends. He shut down his heart and did not let himself love anybody except her and the kids. He understood that if he had romantic relationships, that would be very hurtful to her and that was not something he wanted to do. It was not his intention to hurt her.

Perry begged her to let him have relationships with other women. He said he had shut down his heart for her and couldn't love her as much as if she would release him to pursue other women. At this point, she was so glad to be able to have a relationship with her mom without interference from Perry, she was willing to do anything.

"I'm going to set you free to seek other relationships because I trust you. I think you should have friends outside of just the kids and I. I think it's healthy for you to have friends and be social."

Grace did not think he would fall in love with another woman; he just wanted freedom. Neither of them wanted to be chained, and they both gave each other the freedom to have outside relationships. That caused his love for her to grow, too, because he felt his heart was open to love again. They were both able to love each other more.

Throughout their marriage, consciously or subconsciously, he had justified berating and verbally abusing her because he thought she was emotionally abusive to him by not allowing him to have other girlfriends or multiple wives.

A new dilemma arose. Perry was supposed to have a job so that Grace could quit her job and join them in Arizona, but he didn't get another job. Grace continued working until the end of the semester, taking care of Fred, and doing her schoolwork.

At the beginning of May, Grace left Fred and packed up the SUV and headed to see her family in Arizona. She was ecstatic. She was graduating with an Associate of Arts degree. She finished college, and she was going to see her family. It had been about six weeks since she had seen them.

Grace assured Perry they would both look for jobs when she got to Arizona. Perry had been in Phoenix. Since he did not have a job, they decided to meet on their land in Flagstaff. They were both excited and couldn't wait to see one another. She called her mother, and they talked and laughed. Grace told Emma how great it was that they were all going to be in Arizona and that she felt hopeful things would be better. When she arrived that evening, the kids were so happy and hugged and squealed and laughed. They showed her what they did on the land and things they found. They built a bonfire and had a great time. It was nice to be together with her family.

Over the next three weeks, Grace noticed Perry was drinking a lot. He was drinking a bottle of whiskey in two days. She also saw he was sleeping a lot. She asked him what was going on. She had never seen him drinking this much, and she was concerned.

He said, "I'm going through something and I can't talk about it right now."

Perry and Grace looked for jobs. They decided to look for jobs in the Phoenix area. Perry looked for customer service, or sales or telephone jobs. She looked for caregiver jobs. The second week, they had some interviews lined up, so they headed to Phoenix. By the end of the third week, Grace had found a job taking care of a man named Tucker who used a wheelchair. He lived an hour and a half outside of Phoenix in Prescott. She stayed with him for four days and nights a week, and then she had three days off. She made five hundred dollars a week.

Perry and the kids stayed in Phoenix where the temperatures rose to one hundred ten to one hundred fifteen degrees Fahrenheit during the summer. Prescott averaged about fifteen to twenty degrees cooler than Phoenix. Perry tried to find a job, but nothing worked out. Grace needed him to have an income because without it they could not make RV payments or pay for insurance. One position after another didn't work out.

Perry wanted Grace to claim the accident damaging the RV happened when the RV was parked. Since she was supposed to be the only driver, he wanted her to tell the insurance company the accident had happened since she arrived from Colorado, but the accident had already happened a month before. She made the phone call to the insurance company with Perry sitting across from her, telling her what to say. She gave them all the information Perry instructed her—date, time, circumstances. It was all false.

They were approved to get the RV repaired. Perry wanted the check to come to him so they could live on that and pay their bills. They took the RV into several shops to get an evaluation for the insurance company so they would not have to pay anything out of pocket. One of the shops even said they would pay for the family to stay in a hotel for two weeks while he fixed their RV. The insurance money would go directly to whichever shop repaired the RV, but Perry argued and hemmed and hawed because he just wanted the money. He was afraid that if they left the RV in a repair shop, they would not get it back because they were not making payments on it. Grace grew frustrated because the RV did not get fixed.

Perry was frustrated because he wanted the money from the insurance company. He thought one shop was shady. He didn't have a good feeling about the other shop, either. He couldn't find good reviews on them. They continued to live in a wrecked RV with no driver-side mirror, no left turn signal, and no tail lights. They could not drive after dark. Some of the side panels were missing. The slide-out that expanded the living room and gave them eighteen inches more space inside stopped working. Life became more and more stressful.

In June, on Father's Day weekend, they made a trip to Durango, Colorado in the RV, so that Perry could buy more marijuana. They made a fun trip out of it. They decided to visit the Grand Canyon on the way back to Phoenix. It took all day. Once they got there, Perry would not let them jump out and go walking around. Instead, he insisted Grace had to spend time alone with him in the bedroom while the kids waited in the living room.

Perry wanted her to do some special favors for him before they could look at the Grand Canyon. He made several videos of her performing the intimate things he asked. Grace agreed to it but told Perry he needed to delete the videos by the end of the day, as she didn't want the kids to find the videos and pictures. Perry monopolized her time. He even took a nap as the afternoon wore on.

Grace and the kids were mad at Perry, but they had to do what he wanted, or he would get angry. They all knew that when he got angry, he became vindictive and it could get worse. Finally, in the evening, they were permitted to get out of the RV and look at the Grand Canyon. It was breathtaking and awesome. They took as many pictures as they could. They were only there for maybe two hours.

They had to get back to Prescott by dark because it was illegal to drive without tail lights after dark. They needed to find a place to park the RV for the night. Grace had to be back at work the next morning. Perry was planning to start a new job the next day, but that night he received a call from the guy who had hired him, letting Perry go before he even started. Perry spewed his anger at Grace and the kids.

Grace continued to work for Tucker for another month while Perry couldn't seem to find a job. She felt sorry for the kids, stuck in the RV in that awful heat. They had the generator and the air conditioner running twenty-four hours a day. The kids were allowed to play at a park whenever they stopped near one, but they became overheated and tired and quickly drank up the water they had bought, and then Perry got angry at them for drinking too much water and would not let them drink anymore.

Perry controlled how much water the kids could drink. Money was tight, and they bought all their drinking water. If the water supply was getting low, he cut the kids off from drinking any more water. The kids became desperately thirsty from the heat. One day, Jimmy and Ben found a water bottle in the loft which was their bed. The bottle had some water in it. They stuck it in the freezer to get it cold. Perry found the bottle and claimed it as his own, so the kids didn't get any of it.

Once, the kids were very thirsty, and it was raining. They set a cup outside to gather some rainwater to drink, but it was too dirty. Another time when they were very thirsty, they drank the tap water used for the toilet, shower, and sink.

Grace had some cousins that lived close in the Phoenix area, but she never contacted them. She was sure Perry would never approve, and she was also embarrassed that they were homeless and living in an RV. She didn't want anyone to think she was pitiful, desperate, or needy. She would have loved to see her relatives, but she was also too ashamed and afraid to reach out.

During another fight, Perry slammed the side door on the RV so hard that he bent the edging on the door and the door got stuck shut. Grace and the kids were inside. They tried kicking the door open, and it took quite a bit of effort before they were able to free it. The door was so damaged, they could no longer open the door from the outside. Fortunately, the front doors were still in good working order. Perry and Grace talked to try to work out their disagreements. As much as they tried to fix their problems, it seemed to overwhelm them. The talks did little to repair any of the damage.

It was July and very hot in Phoenix. They felt like they were living in Satan's armpit since that was probably the only place hotter than Hell. Perry finally found a job.

The generator built into the RV had given out. Perry found a new one that he rigged with a gas line from the gas tank. He found a way to add gas to the generator by holding a switch inside the RV. After ten minutes of holding the switch, the gas tank on the generator would be full.

Perry did that so that if the kids were in the RV during the hot part of the day, the generator could keep the air conditioner running to keep the kids comfortably cool. The kids would not have to go outside of the RV to restart the generator. They also bought the kids a phone, so that if the generator did stop, they could call Perry and he could go out to the parking lot and start the generator for them because he did not want anyone to see the kids unsupervised.

One day, Jimmy was holding down the switch, and Perry came and moved Jimmy's arm. The switch broke. Perry pushed Jimmy, who fell to the ground. Perry was so angry at Jimmy that he slapped him. He got on his knees and leaned over Jimmy and continued to hit both cheeks, calling him names and blaming him.

One night while Grace was at work, a policeman knocked at the door of the RV. As Perry was talking to the police officer, the boys were peeking out the window to see what was going on.

The officer asked Perry, "Do you have any kids?"

"No."

"Then why do I see them looking out of the window?"

After the policeman left, Perry beat the boys for looking out of the window. They had made him look like a liar and made him look bad.

Grace was trying to get a job closer to Perry and the kids. She started orientation at Walmart. She was supposed to go to a clinic to get a drug test. While Perry was going to his first day on his job, she was going to the clinic. On the way, the air conditioner for the trailer stopped working. Although the front air conditioner still worked, it would quickly become sweltering in the RV.

When Perry came to the RV, he blamed Grace for the air conditioner giving out, and he demanded that she fix it. He called her stupid and an idiot and said she couldn't do anything right. She telephoned a shop, but they said they couldn't do it that day. They gave her an estimate on the cost to fix it.

The air conditioner burned out because they had been using it non-stop. It was small and not meant to run continuously. Perry got the air conditioner going that night by fiddling with it, so they had air conditioning that night, but the next day the air conditioner stopped working again. They took showers in the RV and ran errands in the SUV. They drove the RV to a place where they could leave it parked for a few days.

They went into Wendy's to get cooled and have something to eat. They were low on money, which was their normal state during those days. They hadn't made an RV payment for a couple of months and hadn't paid insurance either. Grace was making just enough for food and gas and a few other essentials. It was just too hot to stay in the RV. The temperature outside was one hundred ten degrees. The digital thermometer inside the RV only went up to ninety-nine degrees, and it was stuck on ninety-nine. It was much hotter than that inside the RV.

Perry decided Grace had to call Emma and ask her for money so that they could fix the air conditioner. Grace hated doing that, but she was desperate, and Perry was demanding. He reasoned that since she must have broken the air conditioner, it was her responsibility to call her mother and ask for money to fix it. They were out of options. Perry had worked one day at his new job, and Grace was trying to get a second job.

She called Emma. Grace explained the situation and asked if Emma could send them some money. Grace cried as she described how hot it was and how they were both trying to get jobs. Emma wondered if they were using her for money. Emma explained that the whole family loved her and wanted a relationship with them, but they were afraid of Perry. Grace apologized for how things had turned out between Perry and her family. She tried to make it right, but Perry had no desire to fix any of it. Emma said she would pray about sending money. She wanted to help them out.

Then Perry decided since it was too hot to stay in Phoenix, they would take a trip to Durango, Colorado, to buy marijuana.

"You've got to be joking. Are you serious? I just asked my mother for money, and you want to get more marijuana. How irresponsible! We haven't been able to make RV payments or get insurance, and you're just thinking about marijuana."

Perry explained that someone had given him three hundred dollars to go and get the marijuana and so it would not cost him anything to make the trip. Grace inquired more and found out he met a girl on a website who needed marijuana and was willing to pay someone to pick it up. She had already given him the money. So all they needed to do was pack up the SUV and lock up the RV and go.

Perry had texted his cousin Marvin already and told him about this girl who had given him money for marijuana and said he had made a beautiful friend in Phoenix. Then he'd sent a picture of her. Marvin asked, "What about Grace?"

"We're still happily married. This girl is just a friend."

Grace should have known this woman was Perry's new girlfriend. She didn't give it much thought. She was too busy thinking about how to please him and focusing on her family.

They headed out of Phoenix, and they slept in the SUV that night. She was able to get some sleep even though she was irritable, grumpy, and moody. Perry was not a happy camper either. They made it to Durango, where it was cooler and pleasant. Perry went to do his business while Grace and the kids played at a park beside a river. They had a picnic and a very relaxing time.

Soon after lunch, they decided to head back to Arizona. They decided to go to Flagstaff, to their land, which was about halfway between Durango and Phoenix.

They talked about taking the RV into an RV repair shop and then letting insurance cover the cost of fixing it, but they realized that would be pointless because they were behind on their payments. The bank would repossess the RV, and then they would be homeless. Their conversation had become heated, and Perry was losing his patience. They pulled into a parking lot. Perry called her stupid and an idiot and said she wasn't logical. He was driving recklessly and jerking the wheel. He drove over a curb and drove very fast and aggressively. Grace was hysterical.

"STOP IT! Just stop! Stop! Let me out."

Perry stopped, and Grace got out. He apologized and said he had been very stressed out and had not been sleeping well. They went to the grocery store and got groceries for supper. Then they headed to their land. They loved being back on their property. There were no structures, and it was dusty and dry, but it was peaceful and quiet.

Perry spread a tarp on the ground and started throwing everything that was in the trunk on the tarp. He was angry that they had markers and paper for the kids to do art on the road, and mad that the cooler had leaked and gotten the pillows and blankets wet. He swore at the boys as they were trying to help and doing everything he told them to do. The boys set up their tent while Perry criticized everything they did. He had apologized to her less than an hour ago; now his apology meant nothing.

Grace confronted him when all she wanted to do was get away from him. "You need to straighten up your attitude."

"You are not following my lead. You're not working fast enough and not doing things the right way."

Grace and Perry finally got the trunk organized and the tent set up, then they grilled their supper and cleaned up. That night the kids slept in the tent, and Perry and Grace slept in the SUV with the back seat folded down.

The next morning, they headed back to Phoenix and back to work. Emma had decided to send a check. It was enough to fix the air conditioner. Perry was able to fix it.

As soon as they fixed the air conditioner, the generator stopped working. It was a only a few months old, but evidently, Perry had not been changing the oil as often as he should have and the engine seized. They were out of money again, and at this point, they were ready to give up living in Phoenix. They did not have the money to fix the generator, so they decided to go back to Flagstaff. It was cooler there and they loved staying on their land; it felt like Heaven. Perry drove the RV and Grace drove the SUV, and they went back to Flagstaff.

17

A BAD SITUATION BECOMES WORSE

Once they got to Flagstaff, they heaved a giant sigh of relief. It was a balmy eighty-two degrees, and the air gently wafted through the windows of the RV. They were finally home and at peace and they could all get a good night's rest.

The first night, Perry gathered them all together and apologized for taking them to Phoenix in the first place. He admitted that God had brought them to Flagstaff and provided this land for them. Instead of trusting God to help them find jobs in Flagstaff, Perry thought he would be able to find a job in Phoenix quickly. He had been relying on himself instead of trusting in God. He apologized and said the RV was wrecked because he was being disobedient to God and trying to run his agenda.

Perry admitted that the day the RV got wrecked was the first day they had headed to Phoenix. He had been driving to his first day of work and was behind a slow-moving truck pulling a horse trailer. Perry pulled out to pass, and the horse trailer started speeding up. Perry could not get around him with a thirty-foot RV. Then another vehicle came from the front and both Perry and the truck braked, and Perry could not get behind the horse trailer in time, so the oncoming truck sideswiped Perry. She knew Perry drove recklessly and did not have regard for his children or consider that he was driving an RV and not a race car. The kids knew he had lied to her and the insurance company.

Grace was still taking care of Tucker, but she was also applying to a bunch of jobs in Flagstaff. She wanted anything she could get so she would not have to drive two hours to work. One week when she showed up at Tucker's, he had hired somebody else in her place and let her go. It was unexpected and disappointing. He paid her for the week even though she did not work.

She went back to Flagstaff and aggressively started pursuing employment. She also filled out applications for Perry. She called places for both of them. A fast-food restaurant in the middle of downtown Flagstaff hired her, and she also got a part-time job as a caregiver. She started working at the restaurant right away, and she loved it. She was excited about getting to work around young people, and she enjoyed the fast pace and all the activity. She was making minimum wage.

One evening, when they were leaving the park, Grace noticed the trunk light was on. She asked Ben to jump out and close the trunk. Inside was a large, three hundred-gallon bag of water which they used to fill the water tank in the RV. When Ben opened the trunk, the edge of the water bag unfurled, and Ben closed the lid on the bag of water which made a small hole in the bag. Grace had to drain the water because she had no way to stop the flow and she didn't want to flood the trunk. She let it flow onto the ground. Perry came back, wondering why they hadn't followed him.

Ben was scared. "I'm going to be in big trouble. I already got spanked this week for breaking dad's computer."

Grace told Perry she had closed the trunk on the bag and it ripped a small hole in the bag. She apologized. She was willing to take the blame because she didn't want Perry to spank Ben and she knew he wouldn't hit her. She had asked Ben to close the trunk, so she felt responsible. Perry's face filled with rage and frustration, and he started crying.

"I can't trust you. You don't take care of sh*t. I can't believe you're that irresponsible."

He wailed and sobbed. He had bought that bag so they could bring water to the land. She got it. She knew that the bag was essential.

"I was the one who closed the trunk on the bag, and I'm sorry. I'll never do it again."

They finally drove away from the park to a parking lot of a closed business. They couldn't go back to the land because the recent rain had made the ground too soft for the RV. It had recently gotten stuck in the driveway, and they had had to call a tow-truck to come to pull them out.

Once they were parked, Grace sat down with Perry to apologize and spend some time with him and listen to him vent. She put her arm around him and offered to hug him, but he pushed her away and rejected her. Grace got up and started washing the dishes while Perry went on and on about the water bag. He told her she either had to replace the water bag or repair it. He said to feel better he needed a date by when she was going fix the water bag.

She named a date a year in advance from then.

"That's not acceptable," he fumed. "You need to pick a better date."

"I can't give you a date. I don't know when I can have the bag replaced."

After much browbeating by Perry, she finally named a date that was six months away.

Perry walked up to her and leaned into her face and huffed, "Stop being a smart ass."

She wanted to get away from him. She tried to push against him and go into the bathroom, but he wouldn't let her go, so she pushed open the side door and went outside. Perry followed her.

"Stop following me."

He kept coming. Grace was faster than him. Every time Perry started running to catch up with her, Grace ran faster.

"Grace, Come back. Grace. Grace. Grace! Grace! Grace!"

She ran to the hotel next door.

She kept telling him to go away and leave her alone.

"Stop following me. I apologized for ruining the bag. I offered to fix it. That wasn't good enough. I gave you a date. That wasn't good enough. I feel like you want to be mad at me and hate me. Everything I do for you is not good enough."

"I'm sorry Grace. You're right. I only want to talk to you. Please come back. I need you. The kids need you."

"Stay away. I can't talk to you,"

"Please, Grace, I'll stop yelling. I'm sorry. Let's talk it out."

By the time she was in front of the hotel across the parking lot, she was crying, sobbing, and feeling frustrated. Perry took her hand and pulled her back to the RV. She jerked her hand away. She felt like he was trying to control her. They went back, sat in the SUV, and talked. They came up with a date that was a month out to fix the water bag. Although they didn't know how to resolve their issues, they nevertheless talked a little bit, and they felt better.

They were low on money. Grace's first check from the restaurant was sixty-six dollars and that was supposed to last two weeks. Her first check from her caregiver job was thirty-four dollars. She was worried about how they were going to get groceries and money for gas, but God always provided.

Her manager gave her a free bag of twenty expired frozen cooked chicken patties. Grace was grateful. That provided several meals for them. Perry threw them on the grill, and they ate just chicken patties without buns or vegetables. The food tasted delicious.

Grace turned forty in August, and Emma sent a check in the mail for forty dollars. Grace was grateful and relieved. That forty-dollar check was a big deal, and it meant a lot to her. It helped them get enough food until her next paycheck. She also made a few dollars in tips—usually no more than fifteen dollars a day—and that helped them get through the tough times. One of her co-workers gave her ten dollars; it provided her with enough gas to get to work again. One day they only had fifteen dollars to get groceries. Another day they had to get groceries with only eight dollars. They didn't have enough money to put gas in the RV, and they didn't have enough money to do their laundry. They kept the RV parked on the land and only used the SUV to run to town. Many times the kids were hungry and didn't get enough food to satisfy their hunger.

Perry finally found a job with Jiffy Lube and started in August. Grace called more places and filled out applications for him, and he got a part-time job as a taxi driver. Perry worked mostly nights at the taxi company. He was tired and claimed he was going to die because he was exhausted from driving at night. He always found something about which he could complain.

One night, he drove the taxi out to their land at eleven o'clock. He did not rest during the day. He thought he would sleep at night while he was on duty. As he drove on their land, he heard one of the tires go flat, but he needed to come in and use the bathroom. While in the bathroom, he reported to the dispatcher the tire went flat, but he lied to her and told her he was at a wooded area. He fought and argued with her for quite a while. He also told her he was using the bathroom. His story was inconsistent, and the dispatcher confronted him for lying and fired him. However, she was not the boss and did not have the authority to fire him.

Grace went with him to park his taxi car on the side of the road, but there were no woods for miles. The trees were small and few and far between. The next day his boss called and said he could still work there, but Perry decided to quit. His taxi job lasted less than two weeks.

Perry also worked at Jiffy Lube but that job was physically demanding, and he couldn't make it. After coming home from work, he would lay down and complain about how sore he was and how hard the job was. He soon grew tired of it.

He became friends with his Jiffy Lube supervisor and confided in him about his marriage. His supervisor kindly told Perry if he needed to take some time off to work on his marriage, it wouldn't be a problem. He could come back to work when he was ready, and he'd still have a job. Perry worked for fewer than two weeks, then never went back again.

Each time Grace asked him why he wasn't going back to work, Perry told her he did not want to talk about it, and he did not want her to nag him about it.

"Why did you quit?"

"I didn't quit. I'm still employed there."

"When are you going back to work?"

"Whenever I feel like it. It's my decision, and you need to stop nagging me and let me take the lead. I can take off as much time as I need."

A few weeks went by, and as they were sitting around the table one night, Emily innocently asked, "Daddy, when are you going back to work?"

Perry jumped up and yelled, "DO NOT ASK ME THAT AGAIN! I'm offended you would even ask me that. Listen, it's my business when I get a job. I can go back whenever I want. Stop being annoying!"

Grace was angry that Perry exploded at Emily. Something was wrong with him.

Perry wanted Grace to enroll in college for another year so that they could get more financial aid. Grace made it clear to Perry she was done with college. She was tired of college. She had been in college for three years, and now she was working two jobs. She wanted to focus on homeschooling the kids, instead.

Life with Perry was stressful, and she felt tired all the time. Grace felt like another year of college would be too much for her. Perry promised her he would take on two of her four classes so she would only have to do the work for two. He promised once they got the financial aid they would be able to make the payments on the RV and get the RV repaired.

Perry also made it clear to her that he did not want her to go to college to get a degree. It was only to get the financial aid.

"You take college way too seriously and neglect your family and me. You spend way too much time doing school work. You make it your highest priority."

Nevertheless, he was upset at her for wanting to quit because that would cut off their financial aid. He expected them to get nearly four thousand dollars in financial aid.

So reluctantly, she enrolled in four classes in an online community college. She was angry at Perry for forcing her to do it. She couldn't understand why he couldn't hold a job so they could pay their bills and make it work.

One night, they had a fight that started because Perry wanted Grace to take a shower before he would have sex with her. She got up at one-thirty in the morning to take a shower. When Grace got back into bed, she was no longer turned on. Perry called her a cold fish. He said they weren't compatible, and verbally berated her and blamed her for all their problems. He went on and on until he got up, turned on the lights, and got the kids up.

Perry told the kids that they were splitting up and they needed to choose between Mom and Dad. The kids picked Perry. They were afraid they would get a spanking if they wanted their mother. Grace felt so defeated, but she also had a feeling they were scared and were not being honest. She also struggled with the idea that the kids favored their father. Grace knew that Perry had brainwashed the kids or somehow won them over, and she felt so alone. She felt as though she would have to leave without the kids. She felt like it didn't matter because they would rather live with Perry than her. She was trying to understand how this happened. How did the kids all make the same choice? The fight dragged on for several hours.

In his rage, he broke his glasses, then started crying because he knew they did not have enough money to replace his glasses. He wanted Grace to tell the kids how she felt. She was confused and conflicted because part of her still loved Perry, but part of her thought the marriage was ending. The kids were confused.

Finally, at about four-thirty that morning, they all went back to bed, but there was no sleep for Perry and Grace. Every time she reached out to him, Perry rejected her. She scratched his back and rubbed his shoulders, but he continued to rebuff her. His feelings were hurt. He likened her to a dirty whore and said she was frigid and cold and said things that made her feel awful. He called her "Cool Hand Luke." Grace was ready to end her marriage, but she didn't want to leave the kids with Perry, and she still couldn't figure out exactly how to go.

At six o'clock, she got up to put another blanket on the bed because she was cold. Perry got up and said he was going to take her to work because he wanted to use the SUV. It was her first day with a new client named Rachel. As he came out of the bathroom, he warned her he wouldn't be a nice guy that day. Since he was honest, she took a chance on being straight, as well. She was standing by the bed.

"Perry, you're a f***-up."

He couldn't believe she said that. He asked her to repeat it to the kids.

She said, "I want to leave." Grace was fed up. She put on her jacket and went to grab the keys, but they weren't hanging where they usually hung by the door.

She went out to the SUV. Perry followed her outside. It was locked, and Perry held all the keys in his pocket.

"Unlock the door," she pleaded.

"Not until we talk about your issues. We need to talk about our marriage before you go to work. Our marriage is more important than your job. You need to fix your issues."

"I don't know how!" she cried.

She stood beside the SUV and discreetly called 911. She held the phone in her hand but didn't have the nerve to talk to anyone. She was desperate. Their fight continued.

Perry said, "If you can't respect me, you can just leave." He continued to yell at her and wouldn't let her in the SUV.

"Open the door," Grace begged.

Perry refused. He just stood there and continued to yell at her, blaming and criticizing her. She was crying because she felt hopeless and helpless. She felt like nothing she did was good enough. She was broken and felt like she would never be whole again.

After several minutes, she hung up the call to 911 because she did not see the point of keeping someone on the phone. She started walking down the driveway. Something had to change. She knew Perry would stop her. Perry came and stood in front of her and blocked her. She crumpled to the ground. Grace felt too weak to fight. She was sobbing. She did not care that she was in the dirt.

"Grace, get up and stop being so dramatic. You're such a drama queen. You're just trying to be sensational," he scolded her. "Come on."

"You don't love me," she cried.

"Yes, I do," he huffed impatiently.

"You are a f***ing liar. You say whatever you want to get your way," she told him.

"What are you talking about?"

"I know that you quit your jobs but claimed you got fired. I know you quit because you didn't want to work anymore. I know that you lied about the RV getting wrecked. You've lied about so much. I knew you lied about how you treated the kids."

He wanted to argue with her. She knew it was time to be honest. She got up and started walking down the road even though she knew she wouldn't get very far. She felt like Perry didn't want her anymore. She just wanted to disappear. She couldn't stop sobbing. He came out on the dirt road and started following her.

He called after her. "GRACE! GRACE! Come back!"

She kept walking. She wanted someone to come down the road and take her away. Perry caught up with her and grabbed her hand. His voice became softer and kinder.

"Where are you going?"

"I want to leave. I want to go back to Ohio."

"Why"

"People are kind to me. People love me there."

"You're ungrateful for what you have here."

He pulled her back to their driveway. When he let go of her hand, she hung her head and cried. Perry drove the SUV up beside her and told her he was taking her to work. Grace got in. They both cried as he drove her toward town. Their issues were too like a briar patch—thick and tangled.

"I don't think we can save our marriage at this point. There's been too much damage. I think we've crossed the line of no return," Grace whispered through her tears.

Perry had been hurting her and the kids and everyone around him for twelve years. Even if the damage could be repaired, it would take years. She knew he would not talk to a counselor.

When Perry dropped her off, he told her he loved her. Thirty minutes later, Grace's phone range. It was the police. They were at her property. They had received her 911 call, and they were checking to see if everything was okay. Perry arrived just after the police did. The kids were in the RV, and his marijuana was on the hood of the RV. The police did not say anything about that.

They asked Perry what happened. He told them he and his wife had fought. The police called Grace and asked her what happened.

"We had a fight. It was about sex, but it's over now."

The officer asked, "Do you feel safe to come home again?"

"Yes, I do."

"Do you want to press charges?" She did not want to press charges and make Perry angry. She knew he would not trust her anymore and it would be her fault if the marriage ended, so she said no. They assured her that if she ever had any concerns, she should call them right away.

After that phone call, she went back to her client and pretended everything was alright. Even though Rachel was almost blind, she could tell something was wrong with Grace. Later, she expressed to a friend that something was wrong with her new helper and she seemed to be very sad.

Perry came and picked her up to take her to her next client's house. Of course, he was angry. Even the kids were angry at her for making Perry upset. Perry thought the police would try to take the kids away from them, but Grace was desperate and didn't know what else to do. Perry made a point to let her know God was on his side because God protected him from getting arrested. The SUV's license plate was expired, the kids had been left alone, and marijuana had been sitting out on the hood of the RV. The police did not seem to notice any of that. Perry was mad that the police had been to his property and knew where their family lived and that they had issues.

Perry dropped her off at her next client's house, but not without some extra drama first. He threatened not to take her. He made her call the office to cancel her next service, but since she was not able to speak to anyone confirming it, he reluctantly took her to her next client's house. Once Grace was there, her client's granddaughter stopped in and started talking about her upcoming wedding and what a godly man her soon-to-be husband was.

As Grace sat listening, she couldn't help crying. Although it was unprofessional and unexpected, they were Christians and were gracious. Grace started thinking back to when she thought Perry was a godly young man. She remembered the feeling of being young and in love and hopeful about the future. She cried when she remembered thinking Perry was the one God had sent to her, something she had doubted for the last several years.

When Grace went through difficult times, her faith was shaken. She didn't know if what she used to believe was true. She didn't know what to feel anymore. She had started to doubt God and instead thought she was meant to leave Perry. She thought it would be better for him if she was not in his life. She encouraged him to find another girl. She was also really missing her Ohio family and often fantasized about going back there for a visit.

Grace still loved Perry, yet her heart was sad with him. It was a confusing time. She had started to doubt everything. When Perry picked her up that day, she expressed to him that she was feeling sad. He became upset with her.

"You should not be feeling that way. You should be thankful for where you are."

"I'm sorry, Perry. I am thankful for our RV and our land and my jobs and everything. I'm also sorry for doubting God and not knowing what to believe. I'm confused. I don't know what to believe anymore. I doubt my faith. I'm also sorry for calling you a f***ing liar."

"Well, I'm glad to hear you say that because it helps me to understand where you're at mentally."

They both cried. Grace was mentally and physically exhausted, so she went home and took a nap.

During those difficult times, she would lay awake at night worrying. *What if Perry didn't get a job? Why didn't he feel the need to work and provide for his family? If he didn't get a job, she was going to have to take the kids and go to Ohio. It would be great if she could take the kids to Ohio and live with her parents. She knew her parents would let them stay there. Grace knew her parents loved her, even though Perry tried to tell her no one loved her as much as he did. How amazing if the kids could be around their grandparents and their cousins, and see what a loving family is! How fantastic it would be if they could play with their cousins and get to know their relatives! They would all have a better life there than they did in Arizona.*

She could picture it all in her mind. She could imagine the kids playing in the yard. She could picture them playing with their cousins. She could see them living in her parents' house. She could envision them in the bedrooms. She knew there was a better place. She knew people loved them. Perry would not willingly let her go.

Sometimes they had the opportunity to leave Perry if they drove off in the SUV and left all their clothes and personal belongings behind. But how could she manage to pack up all their stuff while leaving Perry's things with him? She told herself to stop fantasizing because it seemed unrealistic. It was never going to happen. She felt trapped and hopeless.

Perry told Grace several times she could leave, but not with the kids. She wasn't going to leave without them. She still loved Perry, and they still had moments of love and joy. She did not intend to divorce him. She was trapped. She could not leave because Perry would never let her take the kids. She knew he would fight for the kids. He fought about everything.

Grace did not want to get on Perry's bad side again; she knew what it looked like, and she needed to keep him soft and close, but that was dangerous, too. All the verbal abuse had damaged her. Perry was the most vindictive person she had ever known. She did not want to be on the receiving end of his wrath. She kept trying to appease him, but it was difficult. There were times she felt like dying, and she just wanted to give up. She was so tired of all the fighting and stress. She was physically exhausted.

The bank holding the RV loan called Grace about overdue payments. She begged them to give her until September to make the payments. She knew by that time the financial aid would have come through. They wanted her to surrender the RV to them so they could repossess it as there had been no payments since May, and it was now August. They were also uninsured and should not even have been driving the RV.

The condition of the RV was deteriorating. The drawer floors buckled under the weight of the dishes and cups. One of the drawers' front panel had come off. Every time they drove, one of the kids had to hold the board in place so the things in the drawer wouldn't fall out. Eventually, they just emptied that drawer. Perry didn't even try to repair it.

He threw away things he thought were taking up too much space, including things Grace and the kids wanted and used. He threw away the art supplies.

Grace was still using Facebook once in a while, but she made sure she did it secretly. She did not have the Facebook app on her phone. She had to log in and log out and erase her history so that when Perry grabbed her device, he would not see Facebook on any pages. She was very careful not to post things so in case Perry did look at it, he would not see she had been active. She felt disconnected and desperate to talk to someone who cared.

Grace was mindful about what she said. She always spoke about how great life was for them, how excited they were to move to their new land and press forward on a great adventure. If someone pressed further, she would reveal more, but she was choosy about who she trusted. Everything she said about Perry made him look good. Grace defended Perry and hid how bad things were. She felt isolated.

Sometimes she would unblock one of her siblings on Facebook just to see their pictures. She would have to block them again when she finished peeking into their lives.

Perry told her, "You should pray and ask God to help you move forward and heal from the past. You should ask God to help you let go of people and the past."

It was difficult to voice that prayer, but she did pray and ask God for healing.

One day, Susanna, fearing for Grace's safety, texted her asking if Grace was alive. Grace replied that she was okay and everything was fine. Diane also worried about Grace and texted her asking her if she was ok. The whole family was worried. They felt in their gut something was very wrong. But they didn't know what.

Grace was afraid that if anyone ever found out how badly Perry was treating her and the kids, he would blame her, but she knew he was revealing himself by his behavior. She received messages from people she didn't know who said Perry had bullied them and that they were concerned about how he was treating her. Grace deleted those messages, telling herself that those people didn't know Perry. He had a good heart, and she knew how soft he was with her and the kids.

Sometimes he was rude and yelled and called people names in public. She defended him but inside she knew he was abusive. Grace was desperate and conflicted.

While Grace was at work, Perry and the kids spent most of their time on the land. Perry had a truckload of gravel delivered to their place. Grace and the kids picked up the big rocks and threw them on the driveway. Ben and Jimmy shoveled the gravel onto a deep wagon with four wheels, and then they hauled it to the driveway and Perry raked it out. It always bothered Grace that Perry made the kids do the hardest work while he did the easy part.

Perry was lazy. When he did work, he praised himself or complained about how hard he worked. He rewarded himself by taking some extra time to lay down to recover from actually working. One day he spent about seven hours taking apart the middle console of the SUV and fixing the heater which made a clicking noise. He needed to install a new part. He did a great job by saving them a lot of money by doing it himself instead of taking it into an auto shop.

He constantly bragged about what a great job he had done on any given task. Grace was thankful and praised him, but he continued to congratulate himself after she thanked him for his efforts and hard work.

"Yup, I'm your awesome guy. Man, I worked so hard. I saved us at least seven hundred dollars. Listen to that. You hear that?" He turned the fan all the way to high and smiled. "No clicking. Wow, I worked so hard on that. You have no idea."

One evening, after Grace came home from work, Ben and Jimmy were outside. They were supposed to be working, picking up rocks and putting them in the wagon. Somehow, one of them pulled the pin out of the handle which attached to the shaft. The pin was dropped and got lost in the dirt on the ground when the boys were wrestling or fighting. They couldn't pull the wagon without the handle. Ben blamed Jimmy for losing the pin.

Perry lost his temper and hit Ben with his belt. He called him a moron and an idiot for dropping the pin and told him he couldn't come inside until he found the pin, not even for dinner or to sleep.

Both boys dug through the dirt with their fingers. Perry told Jimmy to stop looking for the pin and just let Ben look for it. Perry was raging mad. He roared off in the SUV.

Grace went out and told Ben if he didn't go inside, she wouldn't, either. She grabbed a rake and started combing the dirt. Within a few minutes, she found the pin and put it on the wagon handle. Ben, feeling worthless, walked away.

Perry came back shortly. Grace was angry with him. She continued to help the boys work on the driveway. After they emptied their load of rocks, Perry said he wanted to talk to Grace and Ben together. Ben sat in the backseat and Grace sat in the front seat of the SUV.

"Grace, how should I handle Ben?"

"I'm not sure what you expect me to say."

"I think we should send Ben to military school.

Grace asked Ben how that made him feel.

Ben said, "Sometimes I just want to run away, and I think about killing myself."

Grace said to Perry, "You're acting as if you hate him. It doesn't surprise me that Ben wants to run away or is thinking suicidal thoughts when you treat him the way you do."

Perry had called Ben worthless, stupid, and slow. He berated him and put him down.

Grace told Perry, "If you call Ben a jerk, you're a jerk. If you say you want to hit Ben, I want to hit you. If you call him stupid, you're stupid. If you hurt my child, you are hurting me. Whatever you do to him, you are doing to me. Don't you realize how the things you say affect him?"

Perry admitted Grace was right. He apologized to Ben, but it hardly made up for all the damage he had done over the years with his emotional abuse.

Grace noticed the light was going out of eleven-year-old Ben's eyes. He didn't cry, even if he got spanked. Ben had become tough, just like Perry wanted. Perry seemed to hate how immature and irresponsible Ben was, like any child, and how he just wanted to have fun and play. Perry was turning him into a tough, little man.

Ben learned how to bury his emotions. He did not seem happy anymore. The kids were isolated. All they had was each other. They had no friends from church or school or a neighborhood or park. They didn't have any of that in their lives. They just had each other.

However, Grace had two jobs, so she got to interact with people and make friends at work. Perry wanted the boys to jump up when he commanded them to do something and run to do what he wanted. When Ben ran, it angered Perry that he didn't run faster. Perry turned to Grace and with hatred in his voice, asked, "Why does he run so slowly?"

She said, "Well, he's just like you. He's your son. Why does that make you so angry? Why does it seem you hate him?"

Perry didn't have a good explanation.

The boys did the best they could to please Dad and to cheer up Mom. They knew she was sad because she missed her family. They tried to clean up the RV for her at times. They picked flowers for her and made coffee for her. She loved the kids so much, but carried so much sadness with her every day. She masked it the best she could. They tried to have fun times and do fun things as a family, but there were not many free fun activities.

A few weeks later, Perry was bringing Grace home from work, and they were driving down the road with the RV water bag on top of the SUV. They had gotten the tiny hole repaired, and they were using the bag again. He was driving aggressively. Soon after he turned onto a road, in a fit of rage, he jerked the wheel to pass the vehicle in front of him. The water bag flew off the roof and landed in the ditch with a huge splash.

Grace exclaimed, "The water bag fell off!"

Perry's wasn't concerned. The only thing he cared about at that moment was showing the other driver that he was going to be in front. He didn't even stop. It was ironic that Perry freaked out when Grace made a tiny hole in the water bag two weeks before. But when he caused a huge hole in it, he couldn't care less.

The next day Grace stopped by the broken water bag and picked up the belts and ropes. She left the water bag. It had a two-foot hole ripped into it from the impact of hitting the ground while full of water. That was the end of the water bag. Every time they needed water, they had to take the RV into town and fill the water tank with water. Sometimes they took showers as they were filling up the water tank so that they could take more home.

Grace's client, Rachel, asked Grace about her family. Grace told Rachel that Perry was not working and did not allow her to contact her relatives.

Rachel said, "He is not a good father, and he is not a good husband. He needs to know your family supports you. He should not try to stop you from talking to them."

She encouraged Grace to talk to a lawyer. She told her it was free to speak to a lawyer and find out what her rights were. She didn't understand why Grace didn't just leave.

Grace kept Rachel's words in the back of her mind. She never had the opportunity to talk to a lawyer. Perry often took her to work, and most lawyers didn't work after five o'clock, so Grace did not have the chance to arrange a meeting. She did not want to disrupt their lives unless it was necessary. She kept on working, trying to make it on minimum wage.

One evening, as she was getting off from work, Perry texted her about what to pick up before she came home. His texts were not explicit, so she went to the store and bought a can of vegetables for dinner because that's what she thought he was telling her. When she got home, he was furious that the only thing she brought home was vegetables. He had wanted her to buy the other items he mentioned. He insisted she needed to apologize to him for misunderstanding his texts. She did apologize, but he wanted her to admit she f***ed up and wanted her to apologize over and over.

She headed to the store again. The whole time she was driving to the store, Perry kept sending her angry texts. She stayed away for an hour and a half because she was afraid to go home. She knew Perry was still going to be mad at her, and the fight was going to continue, but she went back because she was afraid he would come looking for her.

Once she got home, Perry and the kids had already eaten, and she had lost her appetite. It was after nine o'clock. She sat on the couch. Perry verbally berated her and wanted to argue. She did not have the energy to deal with him anymore. Grace just wanted to lay on the couch and sleep, but Perry insisted she had to go to bed with him. She was afraid of what he would do if she disobeyed, so she went to bed. Perry came and laid down with her. She wanted peace, but Perry wasn't about to let her have any.

He grabbed her butt and jabbed his hand into her crotch. Grace cried out in pain. She tried to push his hand away. She told him to stop because he was hurting her. He was very rough with her. He turned on the flashlight on his phone and shone it into her face. The light hurt her eyes. He continued to question and accuse and berate her. It was torture.

Then he called the kids in and had them watch her, while he berated her until she felt worthless. He made her feel like everything was her fault and she began to think it was better if she died. She wanted to leave Perry because then he would not be able to yell at her anymore. She was so tired of fighting. Her mind was so tired and confused she could not keep her thoughts straight. She cried and begged Perry to stop. She just wanted to leave and get away from Perry. When she tried to get up and go, all three kids hugged her and laid on top of her. They were all wailing and crying loudly, begging her not to leave.

Grace was so desperate to get away from Perry, she was willing to do anything, but the kids were laying on top of her. They wanted her to stay with them. She realized the kids were scared of Perry. They clung to her desperately. All she could do was sob hopelessly.

Eventually, Perry calmed down, so Grace and the kids were able to calm down. It was close to midnight. The kids went to bed. They were finally, peacefully lying in bed.

In the dark, Perry said, "Someday, I can see myself just punching you in the face. I'm just going to let you have it."

How had she ended up married such a monster and how could she get away from him? Who was this crazy man who said he loved her? Grace felt like she was going insane. She was scared of Perry, but she didn't know how to leave him.

They weren't able to pay for two phones, so Perry's phone ran out of service. They both used Grace's phone. They called the phone company and made a partial payment with the promise that they would pay the rest later. They were trying to figure out how to make it until the financial aid came in. Perry refused to get a job. He believed he could not get a job and be a good employee without marijuana. Perry said he needed marijuana to help him focus and calm down and think clearly, so as soon as the financial aid came in, he planned to drive to Colorado and get the marijuana, and then he could get a job.

Grace was angry that Perry was going to get marijuana with the money that they needed to pay bills and provide for their family. She wanted to have a rational discussion about what they were going to use the financial aid for when it came in. Perry told her he was going to use three hundred dollars to go to Colorado to get marijuana. She let him know that she wanted him to have a job to support himself if he was not going to provide for her and the kids. She knew it was not illegal to buy marijuana in Arizona, but it felt like she was only working to support Perry's habit.

One evening, Perry and the kids came to pick her up from work. As they were driving, Perry again brought up that he wanted to have multiple wives. He thought Grace would do well to have some sister wives so that there were more women to compete for his love. Perry thought it would help her to love him better. He did not think she showed him enough love. She refused to even talk to him about it because the kids were listening in the back seat.

Finally, she asked, "Perry, how, in your mind, would this even work? You don't provide for the family you have. How would you provide for even more people?"

"Don't you see? The wives would provide the income."

"What if one of the wives gets pregnant? What if they all get pregnant? Then nobody would be working."

He thought Grace should treat him like royalty. He called himself a king sometimes. "You would be the top wife and could be over all the other wives."

That wasn't what she wanted. She could only shake her head and wonder if her husband was crazy. Perry tried to convince her that it was alright and it was biblical and it was natural.

"Look at a herd of cows. A bull will only mate with a cow one time. There are many cows for one bull. Cows do not mate for life. Look at King Solomon. He had multiple wives, and he was the wisest man who ever lived. Look at the chickens—one rooster, many hens."

"Look at penguins and swans. They have one mate for life. God created one man for one woman," Grace retorted.

Perry wanted to argue with her. He knew how to argue. He knew how to win arguments. He loved to win fights. He could talk faster than her. He knew how to convince people of almost anything. He could talk himself into a storm. He knew how to stir up drama.

Finally, Grace said to him, "I'm not playing your game. I want you to know that if you get multiple wives, I'm not going to be your wife anymore."

Grace had to get her Arizona driver's license. They drove the RV into town, and Perry dropped Grace and Emily off at the Department of Motor Vehicles so she could get her license. She was standing in line when Perry called her. He never considered whether she was in a public place when he decided they needed to have a private conversation.

He was enraged. "Did you delete the pictures and videos we made in the bedroom?"

"Yes, I did. I gave you two months to delete them and get them off your phone because I don't want the kids to see them. You promised you would get them off your phone, but you didn't keep your promise. Don't worry; I emailed them to you."

"Grace, it didn't work. The internet is too spotty. My phone won't send a large file when I'm not on Wi-Fi, and it froze up my phone. Now I can't do anything on my phone because it froze up because it can't send the file."

He was supposed to fill the RV up with water. Instead, he came to the DMV again to pick her up. She was not able to get her driver's license that day. He was going to put everything on hold till they went home and made those videos again. He forced her back into the RV and headed back to their land.

"We're going to go home and re-shoot those videos right now! You have no right to go on my phone and delete my files!"

Grace started crying and said that she did have a right to delete those pictures and videos. She was in them, and she didn't want them on his phone. He was furious. They had not accomplished anything they had planned to do in town.

He asked, "Are you planning to divorce me?"

"No."

He must have thought she would delete those files if she was planning to divorce him so that he could not blackmail her.

When they got home, she did not want to be anywhere close to Perry or the bedroom. For some reason, he did not force her to do it. He was angry, and she was crying, it wasn't a good time to do it anyway.

That night, when they were lying in bed, Perry asked her, "Are you planning to leave me?"

She answered honestly. "No."

She wished she was, but there was no way she could form a plan. Their lives were unstable. They didn't have enough money for her to feel like she could formulate an escape plan. Perry was always with either her or the kids. She felt hopelessly trapped.

Perry made it clear their family was never going back to Ohio. When he told the kids they would never see their parents get divorced, Grace wondered if that was to comfort them or because it meant he would rather kill her than face a divorce.

Whenever Perry vaporized marijuana, he always had a coughing fit. When Grace heard him coughing, she knew he was vaping. Sometimes when he coughed too much, it would cause him to have diarrhea.

Early one morning, Perry had gotten up and gone outside to vape. He had sudden bouts of diarrhea, and he had made a mess in his pants. He came into the RV, woke Grace up, and told her to bring him a trash bag. Perry had walked past the trash bags on the way to the back of the RV where she was sleeping. He stood in the doorway of the bathroom with the door open. Carefully, she tried to make her way around him, but it was difficult because the hall was narrow and if the bathroom door was open, nobody could pass through. Perry refused to move. Grace tried to squeeze around the door and was about halfway around when he suddenly slammed the door in her face. She cried out in pain.

He half-heartedly apologized. "If you hadn't been moving so slowly, this wouldn't have happened. I thought you were past the door. Why were you moving so slow?"

"I couldn't move any faster because you were blocking me. Why didn't you get out of the way?"

The kids heard the crying and yelling. They woke up and saw how he treated her. He apologized, but blamed her at the same time.

Perry was out of control. He was spanking the kids while she was at work, yelling at them and treating them as if they were in the military. He excused his behavior, saying he was tired, or he was sick, or someone provoked him. He made the kids do extra work. They had to rub his feet daily while he laid in bed and slept. He walked around naked in front of the kids. He even made them massage his feet and do his leg stretches while he was naked.

Ben was beginning to realize he did not love his dad anymore. He wanted to run away and was contemplating suicide. Perry did not know the psychological damage he was doing to Ben. Although he treated Grace and the kids all badly, he treated Ben the worst, calling him names and belittling him.

It was a dark time, even for the kids. Emily, who had just turned seven, felt alone because they had no friends. They weren't going to church or school. They felt isolated. Perry caused Emily to feel as if she was always wrong, which made her feel as if she was worthless.

When Emily turned seven, the family was too impoverished to buy a cake or presents, but Grace made cookies. She made a special cookie sandwich with crème in the middle for Emily. After dinner, Grace and the kids sat around the table and sang Happy Birthday to Emily. Perry did not want to join them. He was lying in bed, watching videos. He did not feel it was important to celebrate his daughter's birthday. It was the saddest birthday Grace had ever seen. There were no presents to open.

Jimmy felt like he could never be good enough for Perry even though he tried very hard to please him. Sometimes Perry accused them of doing things they did not do. Perry put some important insurance papers in one of the cabinets. The next day, he couldn't find the documents because he had forgotten where he had put them. He had the kids look for the papers. When he found the papers, Perry accused the kids of hiding the documents. "Don't ever do that again," he told them.

Ben felt suicidal with Perry getting mad at him day after day for nothing and everything. Perry yelled at him and made him feel guilty for things that weren't his fault. Ben turned his hatred towards himself. Ben felt hopeless because he believed his father was never going to change. He thought he could never get out of this situation. When Perry spanked him, it hurt not only physically, but emotionally as well. Perry made Ben feel like a failure when he said great things about Jimmy and compared him to Ben. Perry made fun of Ben and mocked him when Ben couldn't do things that Perry could do. Ben stopped crying. He wouldn't complain even if Perry beat him.

The kids all felt afraid of their dad. They felt isolated and trapped. He treated them terribly and belittled them and spanked them. There was nothing they could do when their mom was at work. They just had to do whatever their father told them to do. When Grace returned home, Perry softened up, became gentler and more affectionate, and was not as harsh.

It seemed the core issue of Perry's anger arose from his childhood. He felt neglected and rejected by his parents. He carried that hurt into adulthood and never forgave them, causing a root of bitterness to grow in his heart. Sometimes the pain he still felt about that hurt came out as rage because he believed crying about it made him look weak.

Perry's anger was also a result of his addiction to porn and sex. As a child, he received the message he was unlovable and unworthy of love. As a result, he comforted himself with porn and sex. His self-loathing turned into anger, and again, his hatred and disgust at himself came out as anger at others.

The secrets Perry held inside of his porn and sex addiction brought him guilt and shame. The guilt and shame grew and grew inside like a cancerous tumor, and eventually, it spilled over into every area of his life. It turned into anger, and Perry vented his anger on his wife, children, and anybody else who was close.

He apologized because he knew his behavior was wrong, but he was living in a way that contradicted his values. He loved and valued his wife and kids, yet he was hurting them. He realized he had to either change his behavior or his belief system, and it caused him to be in a constant state of confusion, conflict, and guilt because he felt he couldn't change either one.

Perry tried to rationalize or normalize his behavior or minimize or deny how bad it was. He told Grace that all guys looked at porn. He told her he was so thankful for her because she wasn't like those trashy whores. He threatened to find a prostitute if she didn't have sex when he wanted. He blamed her for making him angry. He rationalized his behavior towards her, saying that at least he didn't hit her or cheat on her. He often said he was still a good guy because he was able to quote scripture.

Grace tried to talk to Perry to tell him to calm down and to stop being angry. She wanted to help him. He said he did not like to fight with her, but it seemed it was impossible to have a calm conversation with him because whenever she tried to talk to him, he became easily upset. Sometimes he'd have a panic attack and overreact. He said he was going to calm down and be nicer.

Sometimes, she lay awake at night and thought, *What if Perry doesn't get a job? I would have to leave him. I have to take the kids with me. I wish we could see my family. He will never let that happen.* She felt hopeless and depressed.

Grace tried to think positive thoughts, move forward, make the best life she could for her family, and be the best wife she could be for Perry so he would not complain and get mad at her.

Grace mentioned to Perry that she recognized he had some psychopathic and sociopathic tendencies. She told him he did not seem to recognize or understand emotions in others. He did not seem to care about what other people were feeling or thinking. He cared only about himself and his agenda. He acted as though he did not love his family, despite saying that he did, every day. Perry agreed and admitted he had struggled with mental illness.

Perry told Grace she was the most beautiful girl in the world. He also told her how awesome she was and how thankful he was that God had brought her into his life. Perry said those things as a way to keep her with him. He used words to control her. He didn't love her. He loved the way she made him feel good. He used kind words to compensate for how mean and rudely he treated her. He knew he did not treat her right. He liked the way the kids did things for him. He was not a giving person. Perry was a taker, and he used them.

Perry was thoughtless and cold and unable to be empathetic. He did not care about the feelings of others, nor did he realize that his actions hurt others. He saw himself as the victim and blamed everybody else for hurting him.

Psychopaths are not able to detect fear in people's faces. Perry could not see the fear in Grace's and the kids' faces. He showed a lack of embarrassment and guilt. He was not afraid of anything, even consequences. Psychopaths blame others for events that are their fault. They are also pathological liars. They are overconfident and think too highly of themselves.

Grace realized that the descriptions of sociopaths and psychopaths described Perry perfectly. He was impulsive, especially when he was angry. His anger could be triggered by anything or by nothing. His rage was dangerous. He became easily angered, offended, or hurt, but then he escalated it, got even angrier, argued even more, and became filled with hate. He talked and talked and dragged things out. He made fights and arguments last for hours. He loved to argue. He wanted to feel like he could win every quarrel. He usually won every argument by bullying the other person.

18

HOW SHE ENDED IT

Perry was not doing well. He was stressed out. He was mean and rude. Grace could sense he was more overwhelmed than usual and tried to talk to him about it but having a conversation with him was always risky because she never knew when he was going to be triggered and start to argue.

It was September. The financial aid had finally come into their bank account. That meant four thousand dollars was in their bank account. Their request for food stamps was approved, and they could finally start making payments on the RV. They could get the RV repaired, and they could get another water bag. They could pay their bills. They could get insurance.

Perry was focused on going to Durango, Colorado, and getting marijuana and he planned to do it on Grace's next day off. She was upset about that, but there was not much she could do to stop him. She already told him how she felt. Her next day off was Wednesday, September 21.

On Sunday night, September 18, Grace noticed she and the kids were sick with something. They all seemed to have either a cough, a fever, a sore throat, or a rash. Perry and Grace made love that night.

The next night, Monday night, Perry drove her to work. They were alone, and Grace could tell he was feeling stressed out.

Perry began, "I haven't been feeling good about myself lately because I realize that I probably have some mental illness—like sociopathic thought patterns." He began to cry, "I don't feel like I am what I'm supposed to be; I'm not what you deserve. I've been going through something, and I'm not even sure I can talk about it. I know I take out my anger on you and the kids and I'm sorry. I should be venting through some other avenue, not taking it out on you. I know you don't love me anymore."

"Yes, I do, I love you. I enjoyed making love with you last night. How did you like it?"

"It was all right. I wasn't really into it," he drawled nonchalantly.

She hugged him when they arrived at her client's house where she was spending the night.

"I know you are stressed out. It's going to be okay. Can you do me a favor and be kind to the kids?"

They talked about him feeling stressed, that he was too angry and frustrated, and needed to recognize it was his problem, not the kids', so he needed to be aware of not taking his anger out on the kids. She hugged him goodbye.

The next morning, on Tuesday, Perry came and picked her up and took her from the client's house to work at the restaurant. She worked until about five o'clock in the afternoon. After work, Perry and the kids came and picked her up. Perry told Grace he was going to Durango the next day, Wednesday, on her only day off, and he wanted her and the kids to go with him.

She began to cry. "No. Perry, that's my one day off to get things done. I have to go to the library and do my school work. I still haven't bought the kids' school books. And all of us are still sick. I don't want to go to Durango." She was angry. She dreaded going on a road trip with him so that he could buy marijuana.

"I need you to go along and make phone calls to the insurance companies so we can get insurance. We need to do that together."

Grace wondered why he couldn't do that while she was working all day. She dreaded working with Perry and making phone calls with him. He would tell her to make the phone calls, but they would be on speaker so that he could hear the entire conversation and he could instruct her what to say. Usually, he'd get mad at her or the other person on the phone, and then he'd grab the phone away from her and be a real jerk to either her or the other person. It always ended badly.

She begged Perry not to make her go to Colorado. She was crying. Then they got back in the SUV and went home. She asked him if he had yelled at the kids.

"Why are you asking?"

"Because you're angry and in a bad mood."

"Well, I'm trying to have a better day. I'm working on it," he growled.

The next morning, Wednesday, Grace awoke around four o'clock because Perry was up.

"How are you feeling?"

She was exhausted and had a sore throat. "I feel awful."

He was anxious to go to Colorado. "Fine, you don't have to go with me. While I'm gone, I want you to clean up the RV and then take it into town and fill it up with water and dump the tanks and put propane gas in it and fuel it up."

He also gave her instructions on going to the library and getting on the internet to find auto insurance. He explained what she should look for and how to find prices.

He said he would take the SUV to Colorado. Then he said, "I wish I could trust you."

Grace wondered why he was concerned. She thought she was trustworthy and thought he could trust her. He was going to take the only phone they had that still had service so he could call insurance companies.

Grace went out to the SUV and got her purse and hugged and kissed him goodbye. She told him she loved him, but he did not return her sentiment. They planned to meet back at their land at four o'clock that afternoon since they would have no way to contact each other.

Grace went back to bed and slept for a few more hours. When she woke up, she and the kids had a peaceful morning. They happily cleaned up the RV and put everything away. She drove the RV into town and filled up the water tank and the fuel just as Perry instructed. They went to Walmart and got a stuffed toy for Emily and a game for the boys because Grandma Emma had sent Emily some money for her birthday two weeks ago and she still had not gotten a birthday gift. Perry had a problem with birthdays. He did not see a reason to celebrate a person for doing nothing. He did not think they should make a big deal about birthdays.

Then Grace went to the library. But before going into the library, they decided to have lunch. They ate ramen noodles, the cheapest meal on the planet. While they were eating, Grace thought she should try to explain Perry's behavior to the kids, so they understood it wasn't their fault.

"Your dad's parents hurt him, and he's never forgiven them. He felt neglected by his parents. He felt they were not available for him when he needed them. It has turned him into a hard, mean man. It's not your fault he's been mean to you. Can you tell me what's been going on while I was at work? What happened yesterday?"

Ben said, "Jimmy and I both got spanked with the belt yesterday. I got hit because Dad was outside grilling and he wanted me to bring a spatula. Once I got into the RV, I could not remember what he wanted me to get. Dad came into the RV wondering what was taking me so long and said, 'I'm going to beat you until you remember what I told you to get.' Then he took off his belt and beat me and kept on hitting me until he finally told me he wanted the spatula. I think he gave me at least ten lashes."

Ben continued. "Jimmy got spanked because he went to turn off the generator, and he did it wrong. I thought Dad wouldn't spank Jimmy, but he got spanked even more than me, probably fifteen lashes with the belt." Jimmy looked ashamed and slid down in his seat like he wanted to hide under the table.

They also told Grace about the trashcan that Perry had vomited into that week. She had often reminded Perry he needed to clean the trashcan and clean up his mess. He took the trash can outside. Perry had made Jimmy clean out the trashcan. Perry put soap and water into the trashcan. Without a rag or sponge, he forced Jimmy to stick his hand into the vomit-water and clean out the can. Grace was disgusted. Jimmy slid further down in his seat, trying to disappear under the table; he was embarrassed.

Ben turned to his mom and said, "While you're at work, Dad is mean and terrible to us. He treats us like we're in the military. He wants us to run to do our work and shovel gravel for the driveway. When you come home from work, he's completely different. He acts all sweet and affectionate."

The situation was awful. It was so much worse than Grace had thought. She remembered her client Rachel's words and knew she had to talk to a lawyer.

"Why did you say you wanted to live with Dad when he made you choose between him or me?"

Jimmy said, "We were scared to say we wanted to live with you, Mom. We were afraid he would beat us."

"How do you feel when Dad is mean to you?"

Emily said, "I felt like I'm a bad person."

Jimmy said, "I feel like I can never do anything right and never be good enough to make him happy or proud of me."

Ben said, "I feel depressed and like I want to kill myself. I want to die or run away and disappear."

Grace's heart broke. She knew exactly how they felt. She realized she needed to open her eyes. She could not keep making excuses for Perry's behavior when she could see the damage he was causing. At that moment she knew she had to protect her children.

After lunch, she told the kids to wash the dishes and take showers while she went into the library to do some schoolwork. She didn't do much because she kept thinking about talking to a lawyer. She posted a comment in only one discussion in one of her classes, and then she looked online for a lawyer. There was a lawyer one block away.

At three o'clock that afternoon, she drove the RV over to the lawyer's office and parked behind the building. The kids stayed in the RV and played Battleship, the new game they had just bought. Grace went into the lawyer's office and asked if she could talk to a lawyer. As she was waiting, she realized she was petrified. She was fighting tears. She was trembling. She had no idea how much her life was about to change.

She couldn't believe she was sitting in a lawyer's office. If Perry knew where she was, he would be furious. She didn't want to get divorced. She just wanted to get some advice. She just wanted to know what her rights were. Perry treated her and the kids terribly.

It seemed to take forever while she waited in the lobby. Didn't the lawyers understand it was urgent that she speak to someone? She knew she only had a short time window before Perry would come home and realize they weren't there.

Finally, a nice-looking young man, Noah, came out and invited her into a conference room with a big, beautiful, wooden table. She sat down and told him everything. She explained to him that Perry had been abusive throughout their marriage, that they were living in a motor home, that Perry wouldn't get a job, and that they were uninsured. Grace detailed how Perry was keeping her and the kids from her family, that they weren't going to church. She spoke of Perry beating the kids and explained that the kids would be safer with her family than with him. She told Noah that Perry traveled to Colorado regularly to buy marijuana, and how he forced her to go to college so they could live on financial assistance. She was crying and trembling. She realized it sounded pretty awful.

"So, what are my rights? What advice can you give me? What should I do?"

"So, you are married, right?"

"Yes."

"Then you have the same rights as he does. You can take the kids and go to Ohio. You can get an order of protection and go to Ohio today. Don't go back to your land."

Her thoughts started racing. Today? She hadn't planned anything. What about her jobs, what about money?

She asked the lawyer about their money. It was in the joint checking account.

"You can take all the money out. It's your money."

"How do I get an order of protection? I don't even know where the court is."

He pulled up a map and showed her. It was three blocks away. She was scared. It was nearly four o'clock and time for Perry to meet them back at the land.

"I don't want to get divorced. I don't know if this is the right thing to do. I don't know if I can do this."

The young man looked her in the eye. "You can do this. You're a strong lady."

Grace didn't feel strong. Tears ran down her face and her chin trembled. She felt weak and scared. She hadn't planned anything. She was doing this to protect her children.

One of the last things the lawyer said to her was, "Normally, our consultation fee is one hundred and twenty dollars, but we will waive that for you today, so you don't have to pay anything." Grace thanked him profusely.

The last question she asked before walking out was whether she could leave Perry's clothes and a few of his possessions so that Perry could pick them up. She knew if she dared to go back out to their land to leave his things behind, if he saw her, he would never let her leave. If she was going to leave, she had to do it without seeing him again. The lawyer refused to let her leave anything for Perry at the office. She left crying and trembling, but there was also a glimmer of hope in her heart.

She entered the RV where the kids had been playing their game and waiting. She drove the three blocks to the justice center.

Ben spoke for all the kids. "Where are we? What are you doing? Where are we going?"

She didn't tell them because she was uncertain and scared. If Perry showed up while she was gone and the kids told him what she was doing, he would take them and leave forever.

"I can't tell you right now, but I'll tell you when I come back." She was worried that Perry would come into town looking for them. The court was not close to any of the main roads, and she wasn't sure she had ever driven past it before. It seemed to be in a maze of back streets. That was comforting; if he did decide to come into town looking for them, he would probably not go the small side streets where they were.

At four o'clock, she parked the thirty-foot-long RV away from the rest of the traffic so she would not get into any tight spaces and she walked the long walk into the justice center. She filled out an application for an order of protection. She had to explicitly list the things that Perry had done from which she wanted to be protected. She wrote down some of the times he beat the kids and was mean and yelled. She detailed how her son felt suicidal and how her kids felt they did not feel as if they were ever good enough for him.

After turning in her application, she sat in the hall and waited for what seemed to be a very long time. She was very nervous thinking that Perry was arriving at their land and he could very soon come into town looking for them. A judge appeared and invited her into the courtroom.

Grace cried as she detailed the abuse they were suffering from Perry. She explained that she had just talked to a lawyer and was following his instructions. She planned to leave for Ohio today. The judge said that Grace needed to get custody of the children. She said she would grant Grace the order of protection but instructed her to turn Perry's copy over to the police station which was right across the road. They would serve the order of protection to Perry and then it would be effective. If she did not turn the order of protection over to the police and if they did not serve it to Perry, it would not protect her. Even if she called the police, they could not enforce the protection order until they handed it to Perry.

At five o'clock, Grace walked out of the justice center holding her order of protection and Perry's copy which she was to hand over to the police. For a moment, she wondered if the kids were still in the RV or if Perry had discovered them and taken them and left. She had a sick feeling in the pit of her stomach.

She climbed into the RV. The kids were there. Her heart lifted.

"Mom, where have you been? Where were you? What is taking so long?

"Okay, now I can tell you what I've been doing. I talked to a lawyer and told him everything. I talked to a judge, and I got an order of protection. Daddy is never going to hurt you again. We are going to Ohio today. But first, we have to stop by the police station, so I can drop off Daddy's order of protection so they can give it to him."

The kids were stunned. Initially, they didn't believe her. Then they started smiling, but they were shocked. They began to cry. They wondered if they would ever see their dad again.

They drove to the police station. Grace walked into a small lobby. She couldn't see anyone, but she heard a voice ask what she needed. She explained she had an order of protection for

Perry Lawrence. The voice told her to slide it under a window. She left, never having seen a human being.

The kids started getting excited.

"Will we go to Grandma Chupp's house? Are you getting divorced? Will we ever see dad again? If he gets married, I'm not calling his wife 'Mom.' I don't want to live with Dad. I want to live with you."

Grace stopped by the bank and withdrew five hundred dollars. That was the limit she could withdraw from the ATM in one day. Then she stopped by the two places where she worked to let them know that she was quitting. She gave them Emma's address so that they could send her last check.

"If my husband comes by, you don't know where I am." Grace was crying and shaking because she was scared.

The restaurant manager hugged her and said, "Don't worry about it, I'll take care of everything."

She told the manager she felt that if she could work at this restaurant, she could do anything. She learned that she could adapt and do things outside of her comfort zone. She learned to work with all kinds of people.

Then Grace ordered burgers and tater tots and got an extra-large drink. She took it out to the kids waiting in the RV. She noticed there were tears in Ben's eyes when she got back in the RV. He was finally feeling safe enough to show his emotions. He was also smiling and asking a lot of questions.

Then they left town. It was six o'clock. Grace was worried that Perry would be in town looking for them. She had to come up with a plan of where to go. She needed to figure out which road she would take out of town, where she could go that Perry wouldn't find them. As they sat at a red light, the lady in the vehicle beside her reminded her that the RV had no tail lights. She had forgotten and knew she would have to stop driving soon.

The kids were excited to go to Ohio, but they were all scared of Perry finding them. They decided if he did discover them, they could always call 911 on the phone with no service because it can still allow emergency calls. If Perry called the police, they would serve him the order of protection. So, they felt better. They were all scared and excitedly talked about what they were going to do.

It was getting dark. Grace drove almost fifty miles in one hour. She stopped in a small town. Perry would hardly think to look for them there. They had driven through there a few times but never stopped. Around seven o'clock, she parked on a residential street and covered the windows. She put the windshield reflectors across the front windows and then climbed behind the curtain behind the driver's seat. They did not leave the RV. She hugged her kids and asked if they were okay. She was concerned that they might not understand why she was making the decision to leave and was worried they might resent her for it.

She asked, "How do you feel about me taking you away from your dad?"

Ben said, "I feel relieved.

Jimmy said, "You made the right decision. I'm glad you did it."

Emily said, "I feel safe."

Grace breathed a tremendous sigh of relief and felt confident she did the right thing. They laid on the bed and talked. She told the kids they could talk about anything they wanted. They could tell her anything they wanted. They were safe, and Perry could not hurt them anymore.

They were too nervous and excited and scared to sleep. Grace was scared that if they had stayed with Perry, he would eventually kill her. She was afraid if he found out they were leaving him, he might kill her. He had let her know several times that he could kill someone. They didn't go to sleep until after one o'clock. Grace slept fitfully for three or four hours.

Perry arrived back at the land at six o'clock. When he saw his family wasn't there, he panicked almost immediately. He was there for only short time, and then he drove into town looking for them, wondering where they were, wondering what happened to them. He thought they might have been in an accident or kidnapped. Perhaps they had gotten stuck somewhere and had no way to call him. It suddenly dawned on him they might have left because he had been so horrible to them.

His entire marriage flashed before his eyes. At that moment, he knew he had been doing everything wrong. He thought he was supposed to be the king of his home but realized that wasn't right. He knew he should have put Grace in charge of finances. He knew she should have been a stay at home mom, and he should have been working. He knew he was too harsh with the kids and he shouldn't have yelled at them. He understood why she left.

Forty-five minutes after Grace left Flagstaff, Emma received a text from Perry. He wanted to talk to her. He kept texting her and calling her. She did not want to talk to him because she was afraid he was going to want more money from her. She kept ignoring his calls and texts until she was in bed, ready to go to sleep. She remembered all the times she had talked to him on the phone when he was rude and dominating and disrespectful. She finally answered his call after ten o'clock that night to see what he wanted. He told her Grace, the kids, and the RV were missing, and he didn't know what to do. He was crying in desperation.

"Have you heard from Grace?"

"No, I haven't. Have you tried calling her?"

"I can't call her because we are down to one phone and I had the phone with me. I have no way to contact her."

"Well, why would you leave her with no phone? She can't call you if she wanted to. Have you called the police or the hospital?"

"No, I haven't, I was hoping you might know where she is, or that she might be coming to your house." He was hesitant to call the police. He was uninsured, and he had a fresh batch of marijuana with him. He hated cops.

"She never said that to me. Why would you think that?"

"Well, she's talked about missing her family and has mentioned that she wanted to go see you."

"She did? Really! I did not know that at all. Whenever I talked to her, she never said that. She always said everything was fine with you."

After their call, Emma went to sleep thinking she would pray and ask God to protect Grace and the kids. She cast all her cares on Christ and went to sleep.

Perry couldn't go to sleep. He was in anguish, but he did check if they were at the hospital. He sent more texts to Emma during the night, and his interchanges with her were kind and respectful.

The next day, Thursday, Perry decided to call a lawyer to get some advice.

"I can't talk to you because I talked to your wife yesterday."

Perry knew then that Grace was gone. He thought she must have filed for divorce. Perry continued texting and calling Emma asking if she had heard from Grace yet.

Emma reminded him to call the police and told him if he wouldn't call the police, she would. When he finally called the police, they told him they had some papers for him. He thought it was divorce papers.

Perry told Emma that Grace had wanted a divorce for years. He broke down crying. "God hates divorce. Grace wants to get divorced because she is selfish. I know what divorce will do to the kids. It will ruin their lives."

Emma defended Grace. "Don't you tell me that. I don't believe that Grace is selfish. If Grace left you, it would only be because she is trying to do the right thing. She loves her kids, and I know her mother heart is to take care of and protect her children."

"Well, I believe Grace is on her way to Ohio."

However, no one had heard from Grace.

Perry also talked to his father and brother Paul and told them Grace was missing. Scott told him to wait a while, and maybe Grace would show up again. Paul contacted Emma and told her he was supportive of Grace. He knew how awful Perry was since Perry had tortured Paul when they were children. When Patty heard Grace left Perry, she did a happy dance. Perry's Aunt Susan was cheering for Grace.

Emma decided to let her kids know that Grace and the kids were missing. She sent out texts letting them know what she knew so that they could pray. They started a long conversation revealing how they honestly felt about Perry. They did not trust or believe him. They were anxious that Perry might have done something to Grace. All they could do was pray and talk to each other.

Grace and the RV were on Highway 40 headed east. She was driving a wrecked RV with no driver's mirror. Because the left turn signal was out, she couldn't signal that she was turning left or moving into the left lane. When she merged into traffic, she really could not see the cars behind her, so she edged the left wheels over the line and hung there for a few seconds. She then slowly merged into the lane, unable to see what the traffic was doing behind her. If any cars were beside her, they would have time either to pass her, to brake and get back behind her or to change lanes. If there was a lot of traffic, she had to stay in the slow, right lane behind the slowest vehicles. It was always a risk pulling into the left lane. It took a long time to travel.

She did stop and fill up with propane gas so she could cook, and they could take showers. She hoped the engine was good and had enough oil. She didn't even know how to open the hood. They drove across the entire state of New Mexico on Thursday.

Grace headed to Texas. If Perry decided to follow her, she knew he would believe she had headed to Ohio. She needed to go to Texas because there were six boxes of things they had left in storage, things the kids had made and baby books and things that carried sentimental value. Grace did not know what was going to happen to her and Perry, but if they did get divorced or separated, she wanted those boxes. She knew Perry did not care about the boxes. She figured if Perry showed up in Ohio, she would not be there, so he would leave. She could arrive after he'd already gone.

Ben liked to sit in the front with Grace. He wanted to talk to her and ask her questions. He started singing and making up songs. She encouraged him to write down his songs. He did, and he sang them to her. She saw Ben changing right before her eyes into a bright and happy boy. His fear was leaving, and he was regaining his confidence.

The kids asked a lot of questions.

"Are you and Daddy getting divorced?"

She answered, "That's not what I want, but I don't know."

"Are we ever going to see Dad again?"

"Sure. It's just a matter of time. I don't know when, but we'll see him again."

"How long are we going to be at Grandma's?"

"I don't know. Maybe a month. It depends on Daddy. If he changes, then we can go back to him. Maybe it will take several months for him to change. Maybe we'll stay three or six months."

"How will we know if he's changed?"

"He'll have to be nicer to us. I'm going to get on Facebook and be friends with whomever I want. He'll have to let me be on Facebook. He'll have to accept that."

Ben agreed. "Yeah, it's good for you to be with your friends and family. You need to be around your family sometimes. I know you've been missing them for a long time."

Grace was happy to be going to her family, but she was struggling under an enormous load of guilt. She hadn't even left a note for Perry. She felt guilty that she had taken his clothes and even his home. She tried to leave his things at the lawyer's and the police station, but they both refused to let her do that. She had taken everything away from him.

She felt broken. Years of verbal and emotional abuse were holding her under, pressing on her like a thick, dark blanket. She was finally feeling the freedom of coming out from under that blanket, and she cried tears of happiness and relief. Ben often held her hand when she was crying. He comforted her and told her it was okay. He told her she was doing the right thing. Grace was struggling, but she was also happy.

Grace was thankful she did not have a phone. Perry would have been calling and texting nonstop. He would have been relentless. She was afraid if she had a phone, he would track her, and all she wanted to do was escape and hide.

Thursday evening, they reached Texas. They had found a rest area called 'Safety Rest Area.' Grace felt strangely comforted by the fact that they were in Texas at the 'Safety Rest Area.' She parked the RV alongside the big eighteen-wheeler trucks before it got dark. Grace and the kids got out and walked along the beautifully manicured lawns. And the kids played on a playground. They found a frog in the grass. Then they saw a snake. The snake tried to eat the frog. They weren't surprised; this was Texas. They were happy and free. They weren't as scared anymore. Grace cleaned up the RV and cooked them something to eat. They ate and washed up and went to bed. She slept a little better than the night before.

It was Friday. Nobody had heard from Grace. Nobody knew where she was. Perry had told the Chupps that Grace was probably heading out to them, but they began to doubt his story. They did not trust him. They began to worry he might have killed Grace or done something to her to get rid of her. The Chupps were all praying for her and the kids. They began to think he might still be in control of her and the kids, that he might have done something to them but be pretending they were missing so that the trail would go cold before anyone could start investigating.

Emma called the Flagstaff Police to let them know Grace and the kids were missing. They said they had not received a missing person report.

Susanna called the restaurant where Grace had worked and asked if Grace had worked there recently.

The manager said, "Yes, she worked here on Tuesday. I don't know where she is now. She hasn't called or shown up."

Susanna kept asking questions. "Did she say anything about making a change?'"

The manager said, "She said she's moving, but I'm not allowed to give out any more information." She was trying to protect Grace as she had promised Grace she would. Susanna was encouraged that they confirmed Grace had worked on Tuesday which meant she was alive on Tuesday.

"Did Grace leave an address with you?"

"Yes, but I'm not allowed to give you the address because it's confidential."

The only address she could think of was her mom's address. She asked, "If I guessed the right address, could you confirm it?"

The manager said she could.

Susanna rattled off Emma's address. The manager confirmed that was the address Grace had left on the note. Susanna burst into tears. She knew Grace was alive and was probably on her way to Ohio. Then Susanna called the Flagstaff police department and got an answering machine.

When somebody did call back, they confirmed that Grace was in on Wednesday filing a civil suit and it was an order of protection. Susanna knew then that Grace was alive after Wednesday afternoon. That was the last time anyone had seen her. When Susanna shared the news with the rest of the family, that Grace was perhaps alive and on her way to Ohio, they all cried tears of relief and joy and hope. After four long years, they began to hope they would finally reunite with their sister and daughter.

The police served the order of protection to Perry on Friday morning. His worst fears were confirmed. Not only was Grace alive, but she had left him intentionally.

Friday morning, at dawn, Grace headed to Arlington, Texas. She stopped at McDonald's for breakfast. It took all morning, about five or six hours of driving, to drive to Scott's house. Grace had lived in the Dallas-Fort Worth area before, so she knew the roads. She reached Scott's house by one o'clock in the afternoon. His parents were in the front yard when she parked her huge RV on the street in front of their home. They were so shocked and confused when they saw Grace and the kids jump out of the gigantic RV. The kids were excited to see them. It had been two years since they had seen them. The kids hugged their great-grandparents, even though Grandmother had Alzheimer's and had no idea who they were. Then Grandfather called Scott, who was at work. As they headed to the back porch, Grandfather pulled Grace aside.

"Alright, tell me what's really going on."

Grace told him honestly how Perry had been nasty and controlling, how he'd been beating the kids and keeping them away from their friends and family, and that he hadn't been working.

Grandfather put his arm around her and said, "I knew there had to be a reason."

When Scott arrived, he and Grace went to get the boxes out of storage. During the drive, Grace told Scott everything that had been going on. Scott agreed the way Perry had been treating them was not right. She wondered why she had tried to defend Perry's behavior in the past. She knew it was time for her to be honest and stop hiding the abuse. They put the six boxes into the loft of the RV. She gave Perry's clothes and shoes, and a few tools, to Scott so he could ship them to Perry.

Scott let Grace use his phone to call Perry because he knew how worried Perry was.

"Hello Perry, It's Grace."

She knew she had caught him off guard. "Grace, I can't believe you called me! What are you doing baby girl?"

"I'm leaving you."

"I get it, I know why you're leaving, Gracie. I'm so sorry I've been such a jerk to you and the kids lately. I understand why you left. Can we do family counseling? I think we should all get to say what we need to say and work it out."

Without thinking, Grace said, "Yes."

"We should all get in the same room and let the kids say whatever they want. We'll get professional counselors to help us work it out so I can be a better husband and father and we can live together again."

Grace thought it sounded like a good idea. He was very apologetic for the way he had acted.

"Grace, I'm sorry I didn't leave a phone with you. That was my fault. You know what's been good since you left? I've been talking to your mom. I feel like we have bonded, and we are friends again. You should call your mom because she's worried about you."

"Okay, I'll call her."

"Are you going to Ohio? I'm assuming you are."

She hesitated. "Yes, I am."

"You don't need to worry about me coming to Ohio. I will not go there. I have no desire to go to Ohio." Grace was relieved to hear that.

After her talk with Perry, she called Emma and told her she was coming to Ohio. Emma was excited.

"The whole family has been worried and praying for you when nobody had heard from you. What's happened?"

"I think I will arrive on Sunday. I will tell you everything then."

"I almost can't stand it that you don't have a phone. What if you were to have a breakdown or an accident?"

"I have been driving the speed limit. I'm a very cautious driver. That's why it's taking so long to get there. I can't drive at night because I don't have tail lights. If anything happens, we can always call 911 on the kids' phone if we have to."

While Grace was at Scott's, she filled the water tank and dumped the grey water. Scott took them out to eat, and they got some pizza. Then he gave her some directions so she could get to a road she could see on the atlas. As they were leaving, he handed her seventy dollars. She could feel his love and support as she drove away around four-thirty that afternoon.

The Dallas traffic was very thick, and it took her several hours to leave Texas. Grace drove up Interstate 75 to Oklahoma and found a truck stop to spend the night in Atoka, Oklahoma. They did not go outside the RV that night. It was warm, and they slept with the windows open. They did not have an air conditioner because they had left the generator on their land in Flagstaff.

The next day, Saturday, Grace started driving at the break of dawn. Once they were all awake, they stopped at a McDonalds for breakfast. They rode across Missouri and Illinois into Indiana. After dark, the kids played at the McDonald's play space. They went to bed that night, too excited to sleep.

The next day, Sunday, they were finally going to see Grace's family.

The kids were happy and were singing songs and asking questions. They felt free to talk about whatever they wanted, to listen to Christian music. Grace was struggling with guilt and wondered if this was the end of something that God had begun. She had made a promise to Perry in front of God and family and friends, and she worried about breaking that promise.

As they were listening to a song on the radio, some words came through clearly to Grace. *The world's not falling apart; it's falling into place.*

A voice inside her whispered, "It's okay. Everything's going to be all right. You're doing the right thing. Don't be afraid. You don't have to be afraid anymore."

Grace began crying again. She was confused and scared, but she was also happy to be free, at least for a while. Ben held her hand and offered her kind words. He was understanding. They had been through a lot of abuse together.

They had left Arizona four days earlier in a broken RV, traveling in the slow lane, unable to travel at night. Now they were almost to their final destination, where they would finally be with family members who loved them and welcomed them. Their emotions were jumbled.

That afternoon, they arrived at the Chupps' house. The kids were so happy to hug their grandma. Grace was ecstatic. It had been more than four years since she'd been home. Her entire family descended on her mother's house that day.

Kevin brought Grace flowers and a box of chocolates. Grace's brothers and sisters gathered around her, and they all hugged and cried and laughed. It was surreal to be back home and surrounded with love and kindness and people who cared.

Grace sat down and told her family everything and cried as she shared the struggles they had experienced. Her family finally knew what she had kept hidden all those years. She told them how badly Perry had been treating them. Ben told them how Perry had been beating him and Jimmy. The family was shocked, and they shook their heads in sadness. They saw the pain in Grace's eyes and the look of hopelessness on her face when she talked about Perry.

When someone asked Grace how long she was going to stay, she said she wasn't sure.

"Maybe a month or two."

Emma and Kevin shook their heads. Kevin said, "We're not going to let you go back, we want you to stay for years."

Grace appreciated their kindness and the welcome she received. When Grace shared how guilty she felt over leaving Perry with nothing and seemingly, breaking her promise to Perry in front of God and everybody, they assured her that Perry had hurt her long enough and he was the first to break his promise. The man she married, who was kind and sweet and fun and friendly, had left a long time ago. God did not want her to be oppressed.

Grace's family gathered around her and hugged her and wiped away her tears. She cried for joy, and because she felt guilty. She cried tears of regret, for all the things she missed. She cried because she was feeling hopeful again. She cried because she was feeling so loved. She laughed and cried at the same time. She was overwhelmed. That evening they had a great time and even went outside and played volleyball together. Before her family members returned to their own homes that night, they all gathered around and prayed for Grace.

The next day, Grace had a conversation with Perry. He was very apologetic. She told him it was good for her to be with her family. She wanted him to know she was going to be on Facebook. He agreed that it was good for her to connect with friends and family. He couldn't do anything to stop her.

"I expected you to be in another relationship by now," she said. He had often told her that if she left, he would be okay, and he would have a girl lined up to take her place so he wouldn't be alone. "Perry, you can find other relationships now since that is what you have wanted to do for half our marriage."

"No, I don't want anyone else. You're the love of my life. You're the most beautiful girl in the world. I would do anything for you," he whined.

"You have been pursuing other women for half of our marriage. Two weeks ago, you said you wanted more wives, so go ahead. I don't care. You can't hurt me anymore,"

"Grace, I'm sorry," Perry wailed, "I was wrong. That was juvenile." That was true. He seemed broken.

Perry was not providing for his family and saving money for his family and giving his protection and affection toward his family because his attention and affections were spread out to other women. If Grace and the kids had been his only priority, he would have been working and saving for them, protecting them and giving them his attention and affection.

Perry had mentioned many times that he wanted more girlfriends and other wives. Grace knew he was pursuing other women. They were not close because he focused on other women. She knew that he watched porn and texted women on his phone and had their pictures on his phone. It made her feel unimportant. She felt like she was competing with those women who held his attention. He tried to compensate by telling Grace how sexy and beautiful she was. He would caress her sometimes and tell her how turned on he was, but that never lasted very long, and then he'd be focused on somebody else again.

There was a time when they were in Flagstaff when Perry told Grace she needed to straighten up her attitude or God would take everything away from her until she learned her lesson. His prophecy had come true, but not for Grace. God had taken everything from him.

A few days later, Ben told Grace he wanted to talk to Perry. When Perry heard Ben's voice, he started crying. "I'm very sorry, Ben. Do you hate me?"

"No, I still love you."

"Ben, will I see you again?"

"You can see me when I'm eighteen."

Perry didn't like that, but there was nothing he could do about it. He asked Grace if she still loved him.

"There is a small corner of my heart that does, but I have tried to help you for so long that now I am giving up. I cannot go back to you."

"I can change. I am working on getting you back. I have been hurt so badly by you. You are causing a lot of damage to me and the kids by separating us. Think about what you are doing. Let's work together to build the relationship. I'm willing to work on it. I cry every day. I am having a tough time. I feel like you threw me away like a piece of trash. You don't care about me. Don't you love me anymore? Don't you want to get back together?"

"Perry, remember how much you have hurt us. I had many anxious nights, and I cried many, many times when I was with you. Now I'm finally happy. Now you get to feel some of the pain I felt being away from my family and friends."

It felt good to stand up to him and say what needed to be said. He didn't get to control them anymore. They were happy. They finally felt safe. Ben was feeling freedom for the first time in his life. He had suffered Perry's hatred for a long time, and he did not want to return to his abuser.

Grace asked Emma, "What just happened? Were the past twelve years just a big mistake? Was our entire marriage a giant waste of time? How do I deal with what is happening now?"

"Don't regret your life. It wasn't just a mistake. God blessed you with three beautiful children. They are a part of His plan. Don't be discouraged. See it as a chapter in your life that is closing. Now you are starting a new chapter. Your past does not have to be like your future. Your future is going to be better."

Grace thought those must be the wisest words ever spoken.

19

HEALING

Over the next month, Grace felt broken. She had to deal with the guilt and shame she felt. She felt ashamed because her marriage had failed. She was worried about the judgment she would receive. She heard Perry tell her that God hates divorce and that Satan was trying to destroy their family. Perry tried to convince her that he had changed, and she needed to return to him. She told him she would have to see changes before she went back to him so that they could feel safe with him.

"Perry, we are receiving counseling, and you should get counseling for yourself."

"I am going to counseling."

"Oh really, who is your counselor?"

"A friend." Grace's heart sank. She knew he was not seeing a professional counselor. He hated counselors. He had made it clear over the years he would never go to a counselor. She knew he was lying to her again, but she did not allow herself to become discouraged. If he did not get counseling, she was under no obligation to go back to him.

Grace struggled with the decision to leave Perry permanently. She kept thinking she would go back. She felt guilty because she had prayed and asked God to send her a husband and He had sent Perry. He was supposed to be the one. He was supposed to be her blessing. She felt like leaving Perry was rejecting God's blessings. How could God bless the decision of divorcing her husband when it was God who brought them together?

Throughout their marriage Grace repeatedly reminded herself she did not want to divorce Perry. She did not want to be a single parent. She did not want to raise the boys without their father. She wanted their father to be involved in their lives and to teach them things. She struggled with feeling guilty about that and wondered if she was making it worse than it was. Did Perry's treatment of her and the kids merit divorce? She felt like she had made promises that she was breaking. She had vowed to stay with Perry through hard times and good times. She was concerned that she was making the wrong decision.

Everyone told her it was the right decision. Perry had messed up his opportunity to be a father and a husband; even he admitted he messed up. He knew everything he did wrong as soon as she left. He knew it was healthy for her to be with her family. He knew he was too harsh with the kids and Grace. Perry shut her down and isolated them. He realized she needed to be in touch with her family.

Grace began to realize she could do a better job as a single parent than they could as a married couple. She recognized the kids did not need to be with Perry. They did not need abuse and oppression in their lives.

Perry had also abused Emma and other members of Grace's family. When they had phone conversations, he would interrupt them and yell at them. Perry accused them of things that were not true. If they fought him, he would not allow them to speak to Grace and the kids. He used to tell Emma she could not mention God or prayer or say anything regarding Christianity.

Now that Grace was no longer with Perry, Emma was able to stand up to him and say what she had always wanted to say. She told him to stay away and give Grace and the kids space. She threatened to call the police if he came to their house. Grace's siblings asked her what they did to make Perry so angry. She tried to assure them they didn't do anything. Perry was awful to her family, telling them they must respect him, but he was not respectful to them. She realized he was not respectful of her or their kids.

Emma wanted her to stay for a few years, for as long as they needed, to heal and make a good life. She even told Grace she hoped Grace would divorce Perry. Grace was shocked to hear her say that. She had always wanted to grow old with the love of her life, which was Perry. Grace believed God had brought him into her life. She had given him her heart. She had worked hard to make their marriage work. She was so in love with him in the beginning, but Perry made his decisions and messed up their lives. Grace was the one who had the hardest time accepting that her marriage was over. No one was more disappointed than she that it hadn't worked.

God helped Grace to see that she left at the right time. Things could have gotten much worse. She left before anyone committed suicide. She left before Perry punched her in the face, as he had threatened to do. She left knowing that she had given him every chance to fix their marriage, but it was too late. Perry had irretrievably broken their marriage. Perry was in a set pattern of behavior, and it was unlikely that he was going to change as long as she stayed with him.

Perry's relatives supported Grace. They were happy when they learned she had left Perry because that meant they could finally have a relationship with her. They saw how he treated her and knew he wouldn't accept responsibility for his behavior. They wanted to let her know they supported her.

Grace had to decide she wasn't going to be angry or bitter, or let hate fill her heart. She wanted happiness. She had been in a sad, dark place for a long time and she wanted to enjoy the beauty. Now that she was away from Perry, she saw the beauty in everything around her. She noticed how beautiful the flowers and trees were, how glorious the sunsets and fog, and the majesty of lakes and horses. She appreciated everything so much more. The world was bright and beautiful and colorful.

Grace found a new appreciation for everybody. She enjoyed seeing people she hadn't seen in years. She even enjoyed going to her uncle's funeral so she could touch base with relatives she hadn't seen in years. She was probably the happiest person at the funeral. She kept looking at everyone's faces, searching for familiarity in them, while they were looking sadly down at the floor. It was like a glorious reunion for her. She hugged everyone; she was just so excited to see them again. She kept reminding herself she was at a funeral and to stop smiling so much.

Grace had a dream that she was in a van in a forest. It was a very thick forest, so it was shadowy and dreary. She decided she was going to take a nap in the van. She looked behind her and saw she was on a driveway. She thought she would back up to the end of the driveway and take a nap there. As she backed up, she noticed she was going uphill. As she went on, she left the forest and darkness, and she emerged into the light. She looked up and saw the bright, blue, sunny skies and the beautiful flowers beside the driveway. She noticed how vibrant the colors were and realized it had been sunny the whole time, but she hadn't been able to see it because she was in a dark place. She was happy; she wanted to take pictures of the flowers.

The dream was an accurate depiction of how she came out of darkness into light. She had lived in darkness for so long, she had gotten used to the darkness. It seemed as though the world was brighter and more colorful. She noticed the beautiful flowers and the bright fluffy clouds, the love between a mare and foal, and the vibrant colors in the sunsets. She especially saw the kindness people showed toward her or each other. She especially loved to see a father show patience, kindness, and love to his child.

Grace had another dream that she was at a prison. She entered the prison with a suitcase. She set her case down near the entrance and began to walk across the prison. Somewhere in the middle of the prison, she sat down at a table with Perry, and they were talking. As they were talking, his face began to change. It changed into an ugly, grotesque, deformed face. She hardly recognized him. She knew it was still Perry. but he looked nothing like he used to.

She got up and left the prison. Somehow, she knew someone was letting her out, setting her free. The prison door that opened for her was a foot thick. She was excited to leave. She left the dimly lit prison and was free, but Perry was still a prisoner.

Leaving Perry had been like coming out of prison. She was happy to be out. She was delighted to see everyone and do fun things, but she also knew that Perry remained in his prison. She did not recognize him as the man she had married. He had changed right before her eyes.

She did not hate Perry. She pitied him. She wished he could find freedom and she hoped he would get the help he so desperately needed. He chose unhappiness and dysfunction. Grace knew she didn't have to stay with a toxic person. She did not have to be with a person who hurt her and others. The man she married left in their first year of marriage, and he breached the marriage contract first.

Grace decided to take a month-long break from talking to Perry. She told him she needed space and time to heal. It was an adjustment for her not to speak to him every once in a while. It was hard for the kids to go from seeing their father every day to not talking to him or seeing him. They struggled with missing him. They did ask to talk to him sometimes. Grace let them, but she did explain that he was not supposed to contact them since they had an order of protection.

Grace's mind began to heal. Perry had brainwashed her. She received prayer and was ministered to by women from a local church. She forgave Perry and named all the offenses, renounced strongholds in her life, and faced her fears and gave them to God. She also talked to the kids about forgiving Perry. They all named the things they forgave. They prayed together.

Grace also needed to forgive herself. She had beat herself up for not leaving sooner. She had to forgive herself for being so blind and not recognizing how truly awful it was. She had to forgive herself for hiding the abuse and not talking to anybody about it. She had to forgive herself for defending Perry for so long.

She found herself looking at couples and marriages and wondering if their marriage was okay. Were there wonderful husbands out there, taking care of their wives? Were they good fathers who were patient with their children? It was hard to imagine. She realized her father, Adam, wasn't perfect, but he was far better than Perry.

The best thing that Grace did for her children was to climb into her broken RV and drive away from the man who had abused them. She ended generations of abuse and sexual addictions at that moment. She showed her children that the example they saw in their father was not godly or healthy and it was not something they wanted to bring along into their lives. They did not want to bring any evil spirits or generational curses along into their beautiful new life. Their past was not going to define their future. They had a bright future ahead of them, one filled with hope and faith.

After a few months, Perry was still manipulative. He told the kids that Grace was the abuser and he was the innocent victim. He told them she was controlling. Perry tried to make himself look good by saying she was the one who was destroying the family. He cried and wanted them to feel sorry for him.

One night, on the phone, Perry was talking about getting back together. He asked, "Are you going to stay there? Are you happy?"

"Yes, we're happy here. We want to stay here. We don't want to go back to you. Why would we go back to our abuser?"

"I don't know if that's how the children feel. I want to ask them. They can tell me how they feel."

Grace handed the phone to Ben.

Perry asked him, "Do you want me in your life?"

"No, I do not want in my life. I am fed up with the abuse, and I do not want you in my life anymore. You treated me badly for a long time. I can't take it anymore. I don't want you to be a part of my life."

Then Perry asked to speak to Jimmy. "Do you want to see me again? Do you want me to be a part of your life?"

Jimmy said, "Yes, I want you in my life. I want to be able to talk to you sometimes, but I don't want to live with you."

"Thank you for saying that. That means a lot to me. I love you, Jimmy, You're a good boy. You have always been such a good boy. I can tell you are going to be something great when you grow up. You and I are going to have a tight relationship."

Then Perry asked to speak to Ben again.

"Jimmy respects me as his father. I'm going to have a relationship with him. We're going to be tight. You need to be more like Jimmy. You will be missing out on having a relationship with your father. You need to respect me and think about what you're doing. I can teach you things, but you're choosing to keep me out of your life. You need me in your life or else you're not going to do well in your life."

"I have been hurt enough by you. I don't want to talk to you anymore."

"I'm your father. You need your father in your life. I have some things to teach you." Perry talked and talked, hardly allowing Ben to get a word in edgewise. Ben was slumping over more and more. Grace could see that talking to Perry was bringing him down.

Finally, Grace grabbed the phone away from Ben and hung up. By this time, Ben felt sick to his stomach. He was visibly tired and worn out. It was hard for Grace to watch. No wonder Ben was done with him.

A few days later, Grace confronted Perry about how he had treated Ben. Again, he apologized and said he wouldn't do that again.

One December evening, Willie and Emma asked Grace why she was still talking to Perry.

"I don't particularly want to talk to him, but I'm afraid that if I don't, he'll come out here to see the kids, so I'm trying to hold him at bay by talking to him, which is certainly better than seeing him."

Her mother and brother suggested it would be wise to stop talking to him.

"You don't understand. Perry is a fighter. He's not going to simply go away. He's not just going to disappear out of our lives."

Christmas came, and it was magical. It was the first time Ben, Jimmy, and Emily had had Christmas with the Chupp family. There were many presents, much food, and lots of games. They were all together and had fun all day. The kids did not ask to talk to Perry. They did not even seem to think about him. In December, three months after they had left Arizona, they spoke with their father, and they did not talk to him again for nine months.

In January, Perry started texting Grace a lot. He wanted to talk to the kids.

Grace called the police. She had an order of protection, and she needed to enforce it so that they could move forward with a divorce. The police looked at all the texts Perry sent her.

"We can arrest him now, or we can call him and tell him he'll be arrested if he sends one more text."

Grace told them to call Perry. He got the message and stopped contacting her.

Once they stopped talking to Perry, their minds cleared. The kids realized his behavior was not normal. They had great examples of what a good man was by watching Adam, Willie, and their other uncles. They stopped asking to talk to Perry, and they weren't sad anymore.

One morning when Ben awoke, he realized there was an evil spirit with him in his room. He knew it had caused him to feel sad and depressed and to contemplate suicide. He told it to leave, and it did. That was a turning point for him where he stopped feeling bad. After the evil spirit departed, Ben changed. His emotions became balanced. He stopped thinking about suicide. Ben truly lived for God and boldly made his decision to follow Jesus.

Grace was slowly awakening to the fact that Perry had not changed, nor would he ever. He was a narcissist and would always be a narcissist. His entitled mindset of believing the world revolved around him and that nobody else's feelings mattered was ingrained in his personality. He would continue to be manipulative, deceitful and shallow until he died. However, Grace believed that if he turned his heart over to God, he could change with the Lord's help. Anything is possible with God.

He had not talked to a professional counselor, but that didn't matter because even if he did, Grace knew she would never allow him back into their lives. She began to understand that if Perry never changed, if he never got counseling, she could accept that, with hard boundaries. She realized he had caused tremendous damage. Even if he did get counseling and healing, and decided to try to win her back, there was no trust left. He would have to start over from the beginning where they were both single. He would have to prove that he had changed.

For Grace to know that he had changed, he would have to pay child support, which would prove he could provide for his family. He would have to keep the same job for a year, which would show he was stable. He would have to stop trying to manipulate them, which would prove that he understood what he had done and why it was toxic.

Before Grace left Perry, she had lost her faith. She was hardly praying. They weren't going to church. They were barely talking with other Christians. She certainly wasn't reading the Bible.

After Grace left Perry, she began to see God restore faith in her life as well as her kids' lives. Their faith in God started to grow. She was free to go to the church of her choice. She was delighted to be able to pray with her kids. They read the Bible together. They did devotions together and prayed for Perry, too. It was all new to the kids, and it was exciting and wonderful.

Grace began to realize the authority she had in Christ, given by God. She started to see the power of her words. The things she spoke in faith were beginning to happen. She saw God answering her prayers. She realized God had been with her the whole time she was in a state of depression and oppression. He saw everything they had gone through, and He had helped her get free. It was not God's desire for her to be depressed.

The whole time she was going through difficult times, Grace could have called out to God, but she was distracted by the words of her husband, who shut her down, held her back, belittled her, scolded her, and criticized her.

Now, she was free to move forward in her faith, unshackled from her husband, no longer held back from having faith in God. Perry no longer controlled her. His opinions and his words no longer held her down. It was like coming out of a prison of oppression and depression. She was experiencing freedom, and it felt great!

Grace and her children were free to have a relationship with Christ, talk about the Bible, read the Bible, pray about anything, and hear God speaking to them. Their faith in God was growing in leaps and bounds. Grace began to test God by praying for things or asking for things. He had always come through for her. She was seeing God answer her prayers. God became very real to her. She grew strong in her faith and began to speak things out into existence. She began to understand that God was a part of her and she was a part of Him. We are all connected.

I am the vine; you are the branches. If you remain in me and I in you, you will bear much fruit; apart from me you can do nothing. (John 15:5)

Grace prayed for the Lord to touch the hearts of her children so they would know that God was real and that He loved them. She prayed He would have an impact on their hearts. It was such a blessing to her heart when she saw them in church singing the songs, raising their hands, and dancing to the Lord. Grace saw God touching their hearts and working in their hearts. She saw God restore and heal them in their hearts and minds. She witnessed God restoring joy in them.

Ben, Jimmy, and Emily had gone through struggles and stress, but God began to bring laughter to their hearts. They were able to build relationships and make friends. They found things they enjoyed doing.

Grace prayed and gave her kids to the Lord. She trusted Him with her children. He knew what they needed. He knew how to help them. God loved them and cared about them.

God showed them that he loved them so much, he restored them. He healed their hearts and minds. He loved them so much He brought them out of captivity into freedom. He loved them so much He brought them out of darkness into light. He loved them so much He turned their depression into dancing and their tears into joy.

One Sunday at church, all three kids responded to an altar call, went to the front of the church, and publicly gave their hearts to the Lord. They all laughed, cried, and hugged each other. Grace's face was wet with tears, but this time they were tears of happiness.

Ben started praying about everyday decisions. He started reading the Bible and wanted to hear God talk to him. When Ben needed help to deal with painful emotions, he prayed and asked God to help him. When they lived with Perry, Ben held all his feelings inside, but now that he felt safe, he went to the other extreme and wore his heart on his sleeve. He struggled with showing his emotions at first, but he quickly learned how to turn to God and listen to God speak to Him.

When Grace was with Perry, she stopped doing many of the things she loved to do. At the time, she thought of it as a sacrifice, out of her love for Perry. She gave up playing guitar and singing. She gave up doing art and painting and making crafts. Perry hated the clutter of crafting and saw no value in it.

Grace gave up her dream of ever having a garden because they had lived in apartments and moved around frequently. She gave up going to church because it always caused a huge battle. She gave up many friendships; some of them were people that Perry had purposely cut off from her. He had not allowed her to be friends with certain people and unfriended some of her friends with whom he had arguments or who merely disagreed with him. Grace had stopped traveling and doing mission work before she got married, but since Perry was not financially frugal, it was out of the question to ever save up enough money to take a mission trip.

Lastly, Grace gave up her family because Perry had promised her they would enjoy greater intimacy and have a better marriage as a result. He had talked of having a great adventure out west and how she needed to disengage from her family so that they could move forward in what God wanted them to do.

When Grace left Perry, God restored all of those back to her. She began playing guitar again and singing with her family. They loved making beautiful music together. She and the kids started painting again; it was relaxing and fun. They filled the walls with their beautiful paintings. Grace finally had her first garden and was able to teach the kids about planting, weeding, watering, and picking vegetables. They enjoyed gathering produce out of the garden and celebrated making fresh foods.

They became involved in Grace's home church. They soon made friends and volunteered in several different areas of the church. Grace and the kids enjoyed having stability in their lives. Since the church made mission trips every year, taking mission trips again someday became a possibility.

Mostly, they enjoyed being with their family. The kids had lifelong friends in their cousins. Grace was having the time of her life being with friends and family. She appreciated everything so much more than she ever had before.

God restored bicycles into their lives. They received two bikes as birthday presents. A group of people donated and bought and presented a red minivan to Grace. It was a surprise that made her laugh and cry at the same time. Four years earlier, she had had a red minivan; it was what she had driven to Colorado when they first moved there.

God reminded her how He restores the things she had missed. *I will restore, repay, compensate the years the locusts have eaten.* (Joel 2:25)

Grace began to realize she needed to file for divorce. She had always wanted to be married with a family, but she began to see that she needed to cut Perry's toxicity out of her life so that she could move forward in her healing. She knew if she remained his wife, Perry would hold that obligation against her, demanding that she prove her love for him. It took a while for Grace to realize the healthiest thing she could do was to divorce Perry. They had had an ungodly, emotionally unhealthy, toxic relationship. For her and the kids to heal, she needed to shut his voice out of her head.

Grace filed for divorce. It seemed like a long journey. Perry got a lawyer. The hearing was postponed three times because Perry's lawyer kept asking for a continuance. It seemed he wanted to build a case against Grace.

Finally, it was just two days before the hearing on a Sunday morning. Grace found herself filled with fear and apprehension. She had not seen Perry since the day she left Arizona. She wondered what he would be like in court, whether he would lie and say she was the abuser, whether he would be angry or try to come to her parents' house. She was frightened he would try to kidnap the kids or bring a gun with him. She worried that he would kill her or one of her family members. The pain and anguish were almost too much to bear.

She went to her parents, unable to stop the tears.

Emma hugged her. "Gracie, what's wrong?"

"I don't know. I can't stop crying. Something's wrong."

"You're anxious about seeing Perry because you haven't had any practice seeing him or talking to him for a long time. It's natural."

Emma offered prayer and comforting words. Grace's friends and family rallied around her and prayed for her and comforted her. She went to church and cried through the entire service. Everything triggered tears. She felt as fragile as a butterfly in a windstorm.

The next day, she was relieved to hear the hearing was postponed again, this time for three weeks. She would not have to see Perry as soon as she had thought. She was glad to be able to rest and mentally prepare for the next hearing.

During the next three weeks, Grace felt weak, exhausted, and emotionally drained. She spent a lot of time reading the Bible and meditating on the scriptures. She wasn't sick, but she wasn't feeling one hundred percent herself. Each day she would learn something from the scriptures that God brought to her mind.

"The Lord is my shepherd; I shall not want. He makes me lay down in green pastures. He leads me beside still waters. He restores my soul." (Ps. 23:1–2)

"Trust in the Lord with all your heart and lean not on your own understanding. In all your ways submit to him, and he will make your paths straight." (Proverbs 3:5,6)

"I will say of the Lord, 'He is my refuge, and my fortress, my God, in whom I trust.' He will cover you with his feathers, and under his wings, you will find refuge. His faithfulness will be your shield and rampart. No harm will overtake you. No disaster will come near your tent." (Ps. 91:2, 4, 10)

"Do not fret because of those who are evil or be envious of those who do wrong. Trust in the Lord and do good. Dwell in the land and enjoy safe pasture. Take delight in the Lord, and he will give you the desires of your heart. Commit your way to the Lord; trust in him and he will do this: He will make your righteous reward shine like the dawn, your vindication like the noonday sun." (Ps. 37:1, 3-6)

"The Lord is with me. I will not be afraid. What can mere mortals do to me? The Lord is with me. He is my helper. I look in triumph over my enemies." (Ps. 118:6-7)

"The Lord is my rock, my fortress, and my deliverer; my God is my rock, in whom I take refuge, my shield and the horn of my salvation, my stronghold." (Ps. 18:2)

"Hear me, Lord, my plea is just; listen to my cry. Hear my prayer - it does not rise from deceitful lips. Let my vindication come from you; may your eyes see what is right." (Ps. 17:1-2)

"But in that coming day, no weapon turned against you will succeed. You will silence every voice raised up to accuse you. These benefits are enjoyed by the servants of the Lord; their vindication will come from me. I, the Lord, have spoken!" (Isaiah 54:17)

"Declare me innocent, O Lord, for I have acted with integrity. I have trusted in the Lord without wavering." (Ps. 26:1)

"Give all your worries and cares to God, for he cares about you." (1 Peter 5:7)

Even though she felt weak and tired, Grace felt the Lord was bringing her peace and building up her confidence. He was carrying her through this stressful time. She knew she was a child of God, so she had put her hope and trust in Him and trusted that He would handle her situation.

A week before the final hearing, Grace received a notice that Perry's lawyer had withdrawn from representing him. God was fighting for her. She didn't know what to think. Grace had never known Perry not to fight for something. She believed he would fight for his children, especially since he had told her so many times that he would take them, and she would never see them again.

Perry wasn't at the divorce hearing because he could not afford a lawyer. The court was in Grace's hometown, and Perry was in Texas. Perry had threatened to divorce her a month after she left. If he had, he could have fought for custody of the kids because they had been with him more during the preceding six months than with her. However, the fact that Perry could not afford a lawyer and was homeless, on top of the fact that Grace had gotten an order of protection, made it unlikely any court would grant him custody.

The day of the final hearing arrived. Grace arrived at the courthouse along with a few friends and family. Perry did not show up. The judge asked Grace some questions, and things went smoothly. It was over within fifteen minutes. It was a dream divorce—no drama and no accusations.

Grace finally felt free. The judge awarded her full physical and legal custody of the kids, while Perry's rights were revoked. They were no longer bound to him in any way. She knew God was with her and gave her favor in the divorce. She felt like God had carried her when she was weak. Grace trusted in the Lord. She meditated on the scriptures daily. When she was weak, he was strong. He did not let her down. She knew God did not condemn her for being divorced.

The Bible says, "There is therefore now no condemnation for those who are in Christ Jesus." (Romans 8:1)

If God did not condemn her, then it didn't matter if anyone else did. She put her life, her heart, and her kids into the hands of God and trusted Him to lead her and bring good people and good things into her life. She listened only to God for direction; there was no greater security for her.

When Grace was in a dark place, feeling hopeless and thinking about going to Ohio and visiting her family, she used to lay awake at night imagining she was in her parents' house with her children, playing, singing, eating, and having a wonderful time. Those thoughts created a seed of desire that grew until the it blossomed into reality. Imagination was first, desire next, and fulfillment came after. That is how her dreams were able to come true.

The message for all abused women is that you are beautiful, smart, funny, kind, and unique. You are loved. You are valuable. You are worthy of love and affection. Your worth is beyond anything on earth. You are worth being protected by the man you love. You deserve to be treated with respect, kindness, and love every day of your life. You are enough and never too much. You are precious, a rose, a diamond. You are the most stunning of all God's creation. You need to know that God has given you gifts, abilities. and talents that are inside that you have not used. There is a purpose to your life. No matter who you think you are, the reality is, you are powerful, strong, and capable. God needs you to use your talents and capabilities in the circle of influence that you have. Also, you need to be confident in who you are in Christ.

Any lie you hear that tells you otherwise is from Satan. You need to tell Satan, "No, Satan, not me. I'm awesome."

Your past does not have to define you. You can change and have a better future than your past. With God inside you, you can change. Everybody goes through struggles and pain. Pain is allowed in our lives to draw you closer to God. If nothing else, the pain will enable you to go deeper, to see and understand things more deeply. It causes you to be aware of a power outside of yourself. You turn to a higher power when you are experiencing pain or when you are seeking answers or relief. Pain causes you to think about things you would not think about if you were happy. It calls you to go higher, to seek a higher power.

The most important thing to remember is that there is never any excuse for abuse of any sort, regardless of someone's past or emotional issues or hurt. There is no justification or excuse for the way Perry treated Grace and their children.

20

RECOGNIZING ABUSE

Perry was abusive in several different ways, but the most damaging was the almost daily emotional abuse. Emotional abuse is detrimental because it happens in the heart and the mind. The reason it is damaging is that there is love for the abuser or from the abuser. Perry said he loved Grace. She loved him and tried to prove it and work on their relationship and fix the broken pieces, but then he said or did something that was very hurtful or manipulative. Grace was confused. She didn't understand why he was doing that if he loved her. She didn't feel respected or heard or valued.

At other times, Perry was a soft heart, loving, gentle and generous, the total opposite of what he had been the day before. She loved that side of him, sharing his struggles, his feelings of rejection or pain of the past as if he wanted to heal. She was there to comfort him and meet his needs and be what he needed. That is emotional abuse.

Perry drew her in when he was soft and sweet, so she opened her heart to him, and he used her vulnerability to hurt her. When she shared something with him, he used it against her later in a fight.

Grace was left feeling hurt and confused. Perry said he loved her more than anybody and said she was the most beautiful girl in the world. He said they were partners and he needed her, so how could he now be putting her down and trying to insult her and manipulate her?

Grace excused Perry's behavior and defended him. He was tired, or sick or just angry. He didn't mean it. She thought she knew how Perry felt about her. She knew she shouldn't take it personally, that he was doing it because he felt hurt. Women hurt him in the past, so she shouldn't hold his behavior against him. He was just a hurt little boy that needed healing.

We can examine an abuser's childhood and to figure out why he turned out to be abusive. His various excuses can include:

- *The women in my life have all hurt me;*

- *My parents neglected me;*

- *My family has a history of violence and abuse. I'm not as bad as they were. I don't beat you. I would never do that;*

- *You should know better than to anger me. If you choose that behavior, you should know I'm going to be triggered, and you're going to make me mad;*

- *Stop acting like a b**ch, and I'll stop calling you one;* and

- *If you respect me, I'll respect you.*

Regardless of someone's past, abuse is never justified. Many people get through hurt, but that is no excuse for them to hurt others; if anything, it should cause them to be sympathetic to the pain of others.

Abuse is not genetic. It is willful behavior. Somewhere in an abuser's mind, he has told himself his behavior is acceptable. With his words and actions, he shows himself and his victim that he is right, and she is wrong. Abusers are not just men. Women can be abusers, as well. Anything said here about abusive men is equally applicable to women who are abusers.

Emotional and psychological abusers are calculating. He may say terrible things, but he controls himself enough to stop before kicking her in the stomach.

He justifies calling his wife a b**ch because she challenges what he believes is his exclusive and God-given authority. He may demand respect from his victim, but he does not ever give respect back. Grace did not feel respected throughout the entirety of her marriage to Perry.

The abuser feels entitled, which is a dangerous place from which to operate. He expects his partner to take care of him. He feels he is entitled to special privileges. He believes that the rules don't apply to him—social or personal. When his partner does not meet his impossible expectations, he feels entitled to dole out harsh criticism and insults.

Abusers can become emotionally needy, seeking constant reassurance of his victim's love for him. An abuser will demand that his victim meet his needs, not only sexually, but also emotionally and physically. He will insist that she continually prove her love for him, but only by the methods he chooses. He wants to hear her say how much she needs him because he needs her to stroke his ego. Abuse victims will give until they are emotionally drained and empty.

Abusers believe they are entitled to demand sex whenever they want whether or not their partner derives any pleasure from it. An abuser will not accept rejection, yet he rejects his victims. He may even be offended if she does not have an orgasm because he wants to see himself as a great lover.

Perry let his opinions become the rule: once he had decided on a subject, anyone who disagreed with him was labeled stupid. He became angry if Grace dared to disagree with him, especially in public. Perry accused her of taking the leadership role away from him. If she was bold enough to express an opinion or desire, he disregarded it.

An abuser believes he is entitled to be free from any accountability. Perry had conflicts with anyone who was in a position of authority. Pastors, teachers, police officers, managers, bosses, counselors—they were all jerks in his eyes. He did not respect their positions of authority, and he either challenged or avoided them. He did not want to answer to anyone. He considered himself above correction or criticism.

An abuser believes he is entitled to strike his victim for any reason that he deems acceptable. He thinks he has the right to vent his anger, but if she dares to show a hint of displeasure or anger, he will become even angrier and show her that it is not safe to show her emotions or feelings. It is unrealistic to expect anyone to meet all the abuser's unfair demands and expectations, which he believes justifies him taking his anger out on her.

An abuser will twist things into their opposites. He may be violent toward his victim, but if she dares to defend herself, he cries that she's abusive to him. He thinks he is entitled to belittle her, and she should take it. If she fights him, he becomes angrier. He believes she must listen to him vent and she should not talk, even if he is name calling, criticizing, blaming, complaining or degrading her.

An abuser is disrespectful. He considers himself superior. He will call his victim the most reprehensible names he can come up with—b**ch, whore, retarded, fat, and stupid. In that way, he reduces her value and equates her to an object.

If an abuser sees his victim as an object, he ceases to see her as a valuable person. He does not need to care how she feels, or what she says or thinks.

He may say he loves her. He may say the reason he hurts her is that she means so much to him because they are so close, so when she angers him, he has a right to hurt her. He says he cares about her enough to control her, so she doesn't make bad decisions. When an abuser tells his victim he loves her, what he is saying is that he loves the way she makes him feel good. Love is the opposite of abuse.

Manipulation is one of the main tools of abusers. They will deny what they are feeling or doing. An abuser will blame his partner and deny his actions. He will verbally overwhelm his partner to try to convince his partner that only he knows what is best for her and that he is making decisions in her best interest, but in reality, he is making decisions based on his agenda. The behavior is selfishness masked as generosity.

An abuser will try to get his partner to feel sorry for him so that she will do what he wants. He will twist her words so that she becomes confused, and arguments will leave the partner feeling like she's going crazy. An abuser will lie to deceive his partner about his motives and actions. Repeated lying and deception are forms of psychological abuse.

Another form of manipulation often seen is being charming to her friends to gain their trust, then telling them bad things about his partner. Manipulation is subtle and can be hard to detect, especially if the abused has true feelings of love for her abuser.

Another form of abuse is isolation. The abuser separates his victim from her support systems because he wants power and control. He wants his victim to focus all her attention onto him. If she is devoting time to friends and family, then he believes she's not spending enough time with him. He isolates his victim from her friends and family because they can help her realize that he is controlling her and cause her to leave him.

An abuser will often accuse his victim of cheating on him or having an inappropriate relationship with another man. He believes the accusation gives him the right to isolate her. When an abuser accuses his victim of cheating, it is likely that he is guilty of the same behavior.

The abuser is demanding. He insists his partner needs to meet his sexual, emotional, and physical needs, yet he does not consider how he can fulfill her needs. It's all about him and what he believes she owes him.

If an abuser does act kindly or do something nice for his victim, he brings it up for years to come. Perry didn't often do kind deeds, but when he did, he wanted everyone to know. For example, he took pictures of the homeless man he gave food to and sent the images to Grace's mother, so she'd know what a good man he was. Perry would brag about himself when he fixed an issue with the SUV or RV. He boasted about how much money he saved, how many hours he worked, and what a genius he was.

If an abuse victim tells her abuser what she needs, he becomes angry and claims she is selfish, then again reminds her of what he does for her. He makes her feel guilty for expecting anything from him. He tells her how lucky she is to have him.

Abusers think they are right all the time. They do not value what their victim says or thinks. Abusers dominate conversations and attempt to convince their partners they are right. If a victim doesn't agree with her abuser, he may resort to name calling and degradation.

Perry treated Grace as if she was dumb and incapable of making decisions. His attitude toward her reflected in the way he talked about her to his friends. He was disrespectful and spoke about her family as if they were all dumb rednecks. Perry felt he had every right to control Grace and make all decisions for her just because she wasn't as experienced as he was when the truth was that she had a greater range of life experience than he did.

Once Grace left Perry, he realized she wasn't dumb, and he realized he couldn't treat her the way he had been. He gained respect for her because he saw her strength and wisdom. He never allowed her to use her God-given wisdom. His belief that she was dumb had locked him out of listening to and believing her.

An abuser can psychologically torture his partner by making her feel crazy. He tries to convince her and other people that she's the one with emotional issues. He uses a calm tone of voice, but he knows precisely what to say to hurt her.

An abuser can be physically violent and dangerous. Abusers control their victim's every move so that they know what she is doing all the time. He will text and call her all day to keep tabs on her. An abuser has specific ideas about everything—showers, dishes, cleaning, and even lovemaking. He will claim he loves her more than anyone does, yet he has no respect for her. Abuse victims live in fear of disobeying their abuser because they know his capacity for violence. A victim feels she has no choice but to submit to him to keep his rage in check.

On the other hand, an abuser can appear to be a complete gentleman. He may be sensitive and cry easily. He may be open to talking about his feelings. He may talk endlessly about how hurt he feels, but when his victim's feelings are hurt, he brushes it off and tells her to let it go. He bullies her into apologizing and blames her for everything that is wrong in his life. He hides his behavior so that nobody else sees. When an abuser feels hurt and his pain becomes the most important thing, and the entire family must stop what they are doing to focus on his hurt, the truth is the abuser is out of touch with his victim's feelings.

Abusers can psychoanalyze their victims as a way to control them. An abuser will spew psychobabble and try to convince his victim that all her 'problems' stem from her childhood. It appears he's sensitive and knows what he's talking about, intimidating her and making her believe she is flawed, making out that he knows more about her than she does. He tries to prove that he is not abusive when his control and manipulative mistreatment is abuse cloaked in the guise of sensitivity.

Abusers are usually sexually deviant. They may have multiple women with whom they have encounters. They are deceptive and lie about the affairs. Abusers often claim that women find him irresistible. He thinks he is an exceptionally skilled lover and God's gift to women.

Perry was a womanizer. He texted multiple women, displayed all the signs he was having affairs, yet when Grace confronted him, he denied it. He told Grace he had the green light from God to have multiple wives because he believed God wanted him to share his love, as love was his gift. Perry accused Grace of not meeting his sexual needs, so he threatened to turn to other women.

Abusers can also be intimidating and aggressive. They view compassion, softness, fear, femininity, and vulnerability as weaknesses. They can appear loving and kind at the beginning of a relationship, but they see women only as possessions or trophies. They are very often sociopaths or psychopaths.

An abuser may play the victim. He may claim women have wronged him, turned against him, or stabbed him in the back. If his victim claims he is abusive, he accuses her of being just like all the rest of the women in his life, mistreating him. He says she's a feminist or anti-male and out to ruin men's lives. He may claim that he's suffered so much abuse that he is no longer responsible for his behaviors.

An abuser can strike terror into the hearts of his wife and children. He is controlling and demanding. He seems to enjoy reminding his partner he could kill her and get away with it. He seems to get a thrill out of causing fear and pain. It is unlikely any amount of counseling will cause him to heal. The best thing a victim can do is safely get away from such a man. If she does leave, he will attempt to stalk her or try to control her. He will threaten to take her children as a way to keep her tethered to him. It is safest to get the police involved so that he can feel the consequences of his actions.

An abuser can often have a mental illness or addictions. It is highly unlikely that he will change without medication or therapy, but not every man who has a mental illness is abusive, nor is every abusive man mentally ill. The severity of an abuser's behaviors is determined by how deep his psychosis is.

An abuser with a narcissistic personality disorder focuses on himself. He thinks highly of himself and wants others to do so as well. If he can do something well, he may brag about his accomplishments or skills. He blames others for his mistakes, problems, and issues. A narcissist is self-centered in all situations, not just with his victim. Perry often drove recklessly and hogged the road, riding the middle line. When Grace would remind him he had to share the road with the other drivers, he would disagree. A narcissist cannot truly be helped by medication or therapy, because to change they would need to accept that something is wrong, and he would never do that.

Abusers with antisocial personality disorder lack a conscience. They have no regard for the emotions of others. They don't care if they hurt people or cause fear or embarrassment. They disrespect laws, they are often irresponsible, reckless and impulsive, and they show no remorse for their actions. They will do anything they can to get what they want, including lying, stealing, defrauding, and demanding. They tend to be cheaters. They can be physically violent and abusive to their wives and children. No medication will treat them, and they are resistant to therapy.

An abuser is often a combination of several different personality types. The more disorders he suffers from, the more dangerous he is. Abusers are deceitful. Sometimes, they are sweet, loving, open, affectionate, and caring, but eventually, the abuse always comes out again. Although there is never a truly safe time for a woman to leave her abuser, it is generally safer for a victim to go while her abuser is exhibiting loving behavior toward her, rather than in the middle of an explosive outburst. Leaving an abuser takes control away and losing control over their victims is most often what drives abusers to violence.

Often, an abuse victim does not realize she is a victim. She might think that it's normal for relationships to have troubles that need fixing. If she is not sure, she should examine whether she feels afraid of her partner.

For example:

- *Are her relationships with family and friends growing further apart?*

- *Does he cause friction in her relationships?*

- *Is her level of energy or her motivation getting lower?*

- *Does she feel as if she continually has to prove herself and try to be good enough for him?*

- *Is she always worried about fixing the relationship or afraid she's going to cause an outburst?*

- *Does she feel he is critical of her?*

- *Does he make her feel like everything is her fault or someone else's fault but hardly ever his fault?*

- *After a fight, is she left feeling confused and mentally messed up?*

- *Does she feel depressed, oppressed, or trapped?*

If the answer to any of these questions is yes, she needs to examine her situation. She is likely with an abuser and needs to plan to make a change.

What if an abuser apologizes? Should she forgive him? His apologies may sound genuine, and he may tell her she deserves better than him. He might blame his behavior on his childhood to explain why he acts the way he does. He may get her to feel sorry for him. She may end up apologizing to him for starting the fight or for triggering his behavior. She is the damaged party, but he expects her to forgive him and take him back. He has not learned a lesson, nor has he shown that he will change his behavior. All that has happened is that he has bought more time with her. As long as she stays with him, the abuse cycle continues, and she is enabling him.

An abuser will use several tactics in fights and arguments. He always has to win every battle. He either gets to make the final decision, or talks the most, or has the harshest put-downs. He sees his victim as wrong and her opinion as stupid and inaccurate, while he, on the other hand, is always right. He is a bully and uses several tactics to control her:

- *Sarcasm*
- *Ridicule*
- *Distorting what she says*
- *Misrepresenting earlier situations*
- *Sulking*
- *Accusing her of doing what he does (projection)*
- *Interrupting*
- *Refusal to respond*
- *Laughing at her*
- *Using what she said against her later*
- *Changing the subject toward what he wants to say*
- *Criticism*
- *Guilt*
- *Playing the victim*
- *Using facial expressions such as eye rolls and smirks to show contempt*
- *Yelling*
- *Cursing or swearing*

- *Insulting*

- *Leaving*

- *Standing over her*

- *Physical intimidation*

- *Blocking her from going*

- *Threatening to hurt her*

- *Threatening to take the kids.*

Another classic abuse behavior is the enforcing of double standards. An abuser will have rules for his partner to live by that do not apply to him. He wants his victim to be faithful to him, but he believes it's alright for him to cheat. If she yells or curses at him, she's dramatic, but if he does the same, he's standing up for himself. He may be abusive to the kids, but if she punishes one of the kids, he doesn't hesitate to call her a child abuser. He demands to know what she is doing all the time, but he doesn't tell her what he does. He believes he is entitled to special privileges.

An abuser can be sexually abusive to his partner. If he forces or manipulates her into having sex with him, that is abuse. She feels that each time they have sex, it's for him. He may see her as a sex object for his pleasure. He makes her believe she owes him sex. Abusers use sex as a way to have power and control. He views his victim as his property.

He may also use sex as a bargaining tool. He may withhold sex as punishment for challenging him in some way. He may not be attracted to her anymore because she doesn't measure up to his fantasies. If he watches porn, the unrealistic images may mislead him. If his partner stands up for herself and refuses to play the submissive role, he may not be turned on by her rebellion and independence. If he is dominating and he sees her as passive, that may turn him on sexually. If he is addicted to drugs or alcohol, it may diminish his sex drive.

It seems puzzling that he wants to have sex after he has abused her or after a fight, but to him, it's like a dog marking its territory. He gets to dominate her and own her, and she has no say in the matter. She does not feel loved. He may say he wants to have sex as a way to reconnect after a fight, but in his mind, he is winning the battle. She may end up feeling more broken and confused than ever.

Abusers and their victims may have great sex lives. The abuser wants to see himself as a great lover. It's not that he wants to make his victim happy or give her pleasure, he wants to brag about how women are crazy for him.

If a man is watching pornography, it's possible he is watching women being degraded and reduced to sexual objects for the pleasure of the man. Porn is unrealistic and sets up expectations and fantasies in the mind of a man that his partner is not able to fulfill. Porn often depicts violence against and degradation of women. If a man becomes addicted to the thrill and excitement of porn, he eventually becomes desensitized to it and believes his behavior justified.

The man who watches porn has generalized his affections and is not solely focused on his partner, and therefore, he is more critical, dissatisfied and less in love than someone who does not watch porn. Because of the thrill of porn, he may lose the ability to have erections and be less attracted and have more difficulty reaching orgasm with his real partner. Porn can lower a man's sex drive, not increase it. Porn makes real-life sex seem boring and his partner less stimulating. He's comparing the thrill of porn with real life.

Where does one draw the line of abuse? When does sex become abusive? If the wife feels uncomfortable, disrespected, humiliated, or forced, she knows something is not right. The abuser may push the blame onto her, telling her it's her problem, but his abusive behavior is working for him. He is getting what he wants, and so he sees no need to change anything. As long as his partner stays with him, the cycle of abuse will continue. Even if she tells him his behavior is unacceptable, as long as she remains with him, he will not change. He may show small signs of change here and there, but they are neither dramatic nor long-term changes.

An abuse victim should not be blinded or fooled if he says he will change. He will not change unless he submits himself to a higher power—whether it's a counselor, a group, a mentor, or God—and admits and takes responsibility for his problems. Only then is there hope for change. Many abusers will never change. If his issues are truly psychological, it is likely he is incapable of changing.

An abuser who victimizes his wife will most likely also abuse the children who live with him. The children will witness the abuse. They may not like it, they may know that it's wrong, but there is nothing they can do to stop it. They know that the abuser won't change, so they plead with their mother to give in to him, or they may even mirror his behavior towards her. They don't want to get on his bad side, so they side with him against their mother to gain his favor. He will use the children as a weapon against their mother.

Abusers are not mean and controlling all the time. Sometimes an abuser can joke and have fun with the kids, which will cause them to bond with him and to turn against their mother. They will start to believe what he says about her, that she is stupid and incompetent. In this way, he teaches them to be disrespectful to their mom. He controls everything, including their relationships with one another.

The children learn to blame their mother as they see their father accusing and blaming her. They understand how they can also manipulate and control others to get the results they want. Boys learn that they should be in leadership positions and girls learn that they should do follow orders. Children begin to see females as less valuable and stupid. The most damaging thing they learn is that they get to abuse those they love.

An abusive father may not be able to get all the children on his side so he may play favorites, thereby dividing the family. It will seem everyone is mad at each other instead of at him. They will be distracted from focusing on him and directing their anger toward him and will instead turn against each other.

It is next to impossible to get an abuser to change. No amount of pleading or reasoning will do it. The only thing a victim can do is no longer enable the abuser. If the victim removes herself and her children from the abuser, he can no longer abuse her. That is the only thing that will get his attention to recognize she will no longer take his abuse or put up with his mistreatment. As long as a victim stays with her abuser, the cycle of abuse will continue. No matter how many times he gets talked to, no matter how many promises he makes, he will not change. He can fake change for a while, but long-term change is next to impossible.

The only way an abuser will change is if he sees a need to change and he will only change if he wants to change. It is possible with God's help.

It is not easy to get away from an abuser. He may block his victim from leaving. She may feel trapped. He does not want her to leave, because her going takes away his power. She has to reach the point where she understands she has given him enough chances, and now it's time to take action and leave. She deserves to be respected. If he doesn't respect her, she doesn't have to be with him.

Abuse victims must form a plan to get away safely. It is wise to get away from him when the relationship is calm, and things are good. It is almost impossible to get away during a fight. She will need support. She should get the police involved. She should see if friends or family can help her. If she has neighbors, she can ask them for help, but it needs to be somebody she can trust. Most people will not know how to help a victim so the victim may need to form a plan and ask for help to carry out her plan to safely get away. It could be at a time when she is away from the abuser. She may be able to plan, but if she cannot, she should wait for the right opportunity to escape.

Once she is away from the abuser, she should cut off all contact with him. If she talks to him, he's going to want to know where she is. He will want to reason with her. He will want to apologize and manipulate her into coming back with lies and false promises of change. If she did go back, the abuse would likely be even worse. It would be very dangerous for her to go back to him. Abusers often kill women when they reconcile after a separation.

She should refuse to do any couples or family counseling with him. The less contact with him, the better. She knows if she meets him with a counselor, he will blame her and play the victim. It will be dangerous for her to try to go to counseling with him. He will try to convince the counselor that he was the abuse victim, or that she is overreacting or that his behavior is justified. He will try to control and manipulate the situation and her. She should insist on getting counseling for herself and let him go to counseling by himself.

It is doubtful that an abuser will go to a counselor by himself. But even if he does go, and he claims he has changed, there are some checkpoints she would need to see before she can believe he has changed.

He needs to admit that he abused her. He needs to name the abuse, whether sexual, physical, verbal, emotional, spiritual, or financial. He also needs to admit who else he abused—his children, grandparents, siblings, friends, strangers, neighbors or past partners. He needs to recognize his behavior was wrong without excuse. He has to accept it was his decision and not just something he did when he was angry or out of control.

He needs to recognize how damaging the abuse was. He needs to experience remorse or empathy for those he hurt. If he starts to talk about how hard it is for him, how hurt he is, then he's not taking responsibility for his actions. He needs to recognize his attitude of entitlement and recognize where those core beliefs started. If he is using respectful behavior to replace the disrespectful behavior, he should be listening without interruption, allowing the victim to make decisions, and he should be helping with child care and household chores.

His perception of his victim must change from thinking she was stupid or incompetent to now believing positive things about her and complimenting her strengths. He will affirmatively try to repair relationships he has damaged. He will start to realize he needs to put her needs first and put his own needs aside for a while. He needs to be willing to accept the consequences of his actions without blame or complaint. He needs to show his efforts not to repeat past behaviors, but to exhibit respectful behaviors and stick to that commitment.

He will give up his double standards and his cheating habits and his special privileges. If he is indeed going to change, it will be a long-term process, not something that will happen quickly He may even complain that he's apologized and made changes, but that his victim hasn't. She should not accept that unless she was also abusive to him.

The most significant step an abuser can take is to be accountable for his behavior. He needs to know he can't continue his past behaviors without accepting responsibility for them. He needs to accept criticism and help for his actions. It is not his partner's job to hold him accountable. He needs to be accountable to someone outside of his family. She can't be expected to be his counselor. He needs professional help. The best program for an abuser is an abuse program so that he can recognize what abuse is and how he can stop it.

If a victim decides she wants to get back together with the abuser, if he does one offensive action, she needs to separate right away again and not wait and give him one chance after another. It will just cause more damage. She will be giving him the message that his behavior is acceptable if she stays.

HEALING

It is essential for every woman and child to understand they deserve respect. They deserve to be treated with kindness and love every day. They should be able to state their own opinions, ideas, and values freely and without criticism and anger. Anyone who is receives anything less than kindness and respect from their partner should be able to stand up for themselves and defend themselves. Each person has a purpose. They are more valuable than diamonds and gold. They have something to say or something to share. They are unique; they can do something special. They each have a walk with God that is different from everyone else's. They all can listen to God. Each victim deserves to find happiness and to enjoy life. She should be surrounded by people who will be loving and supportive and make her heart glad.

Each victim will need to forgive their abuser for what he has done, not to set him free from his consequences, but to set herself free from anger, bitterness, and hatred. If she wants to move forward from her past, she will need to release herself from her abuser by forgiving him. Forgiveness will bring peace to her heart and will free her to move forward toward good things in her life.

It is crucial for each victim to talk about their experience. Telling their story will help them process and heal from their wounds. They should not be ashamed of their story. They should see their story as an inspiration and a help to somebody else. They do not have to tell the world (unless they want to), but they need to tell at least one person. Let the healing begin.

REFERENCES

Pg. 17, Strong, James. 1894. The Exhaustive Concordance of the Bible, Showing Every Word of the Text of the Common English Version of the Canonical Books. Hunt & Eaton. New York. Cranston & Curts. Cinncinati. Print.

Pg 17, John 8:32

Pg. 95 Proverbs 27:15

Pg. 229 Hutchinson, Ella, Dec. 21, 2016. Why is my husband so angry? It all Comes Down to Shame. Covenanteyes.com Web. http://www.covenanteyes.com/2016/12/21/why-is-my-husband-so-angry-it-all-comes-down-to-shame/?fbclid=IwAR1RlFNXWn8cIAkZ5MA_VXtdA5FQKqxGQltnxPWUrABkbGayUOXZIpNCl-s

Chapter 20. Bancroft, Lundy. Why Does He Do That? Inside the Minds of Angry and Controlling men. Berkley Books. Penguin Group. New York. 2003. Print.

Mailing Address
Madison Carter
P.O. Box 113
Lagrange, IN 46761

CPSIA information can be obtained
at www.ICGtesting.com
Printed in the USA
FSHW011620180419

9 781640 855274